Florence

DIRECTIONS

WRITTEN AND RESEARCHED BY

Jonathan Buckley

NEW YORK • LONDON • DELHI

www.roughguides.com

Contents

Introduction to Florence

◂ Riverside traffic

If one city could be said to encapsulate the essence of Italy it might well be Florence (Firenze in Italian), the first capital of the united country. The modern Italian language evolved from Tuscan dialect, a supremacy established by Dante, who wrote the *Divine Comedy* in the vernacular of his birthplace, but what makes this city pivotal to the culture not just of Italy but of all Europe is, of course, the Renaissance. The very name by which we refer to this extraordinary era was coined by a Tuscan, Giorgio Vasari, who wrote in the sixteenth century of the "rebirth" of the arts with the humanism of Giotto and his successors. Every eminent artistic figure from Giotto onwards – Masaccio, Brunelleschi, Alberti, Donatello, Botticelli, Leonardo da Vinci, Michelangelo – is represented here, in an unrivalled concentration of churches, galleries and museums.

When to visit

Midsummer in Florence can be a less than wholly pleasant experience: the heat is often stifling, and the inundation of tourists makes the major attractions a purgatorial experience. If you can only travel between Easter and September, make sure you have your accommodation reserved before you arrive, as it's not uncommon for every hotel in town to be fully booked. The worst month is August, when the majority of Italians take their holidays, with the result that many restaurants and bars are closed for the entire month. For the most enjoyable visit, arrive shortly before Easter or in October: the weather should be fine, and the balance between Florentines and outsiders restored to its rightful level. Winter is often quite rainy, but the absence of crowds makes this a good option for the big sights.

The imprint of the Renaissance is visible the moment you step out of the train station, with the pinnacle of Brunelleschi's stupendous dome visible over the rooftops. The Renaissance emphasis on harmony is exemplified in Brunelleschi's interiors at Santo Spirito, Santa Croce and San Lorenzo – where the genius of Michelangelo was also given free rein. Afternoons in the vast picture collections of the Uffizi and Palazzo Pitti will give you a grasp of the entire development of Renaissance painting, while the Bargello, the Museo dell'Opera del Duomo and the Accademia will do the same for the period's sculpture. Of course the achievements of the Renaissance were underpinned by the wealth and power accumulated in earlier decades, and in every quarter of the city centre you'll see churches and monuments that attest to the might of medieval Florence, ranging from the Duomo and Palazzo Vecchio to the great churches of Santa Croce and Santa Maria Novella, whose fabulously decorated chapels are the forerunners of such astonishing creations as Masaccio's frescoes at Santa Maria del Carmine.

▲ *Zanobini*, San Lorenzo district

▲ Piazza della Signoria

▲ *Le Volpi e L'Uva*, Central Oltrarno

Florence has been a magnet for tourists since the nineteenth century, and it has to be said that nowadays it can often seem that it's become too popular for its own good, with immense queues for the Uffizi and too many *menu turistico* restaurants. But if you time your visit carefully, don't rush around trying to see everything and make a point of eating and drinking in our recommended restaurants, cafés and bars, you'll have a visit you'll never forget.

◄ Retail therapy, Florence style

Florence
AT A GLANCE

The majority of the major sights in Florence are to be found on the north side of the River Arno, and most of these are within a fifteen-minute stroll of the Duomo, the hub of the whole city.

PIAZZA DEL DUOMO

All roads in Florence lead to Piazza del Duomo, site of the awe-inspiring cathedral and its attendant museum, with the elegant Baptistery and Campanile completing the magnificent ensemble.

▼ Piazza del Duomo

▲ Courtyard of the Bargello

THE BARGELLO

An unmatched collection of Renaissance sculpture, plus a fabulous array of applied art, is gathered inside the Bargello, midway between the Duomo and Signoria.

▲ Loggia della Signoria

PIAZZA DELLA SIGNORIA

The most important civic building in the city stands on Piazza della Signoria, next door to the Uffizi, the most important art gallery in the country.

SANTA MARIA NOVELLA

Right opposite the train station, a short way west of the city centre, stands Santa Maria Novella, a superb Renaissance building filled with stunning works of art.

▲ Santa Maria Novella

SAN LORENZO

The central market, the church of San Lorenzo (burial place of the Medici), the Accademia (home of Michelangelo's *David*) and the San Marco monastery-museum are the main attractions to the north of the Duomo.

▼ San Lorenzo

▲ *Dante* outside Santa Croce

SANTA CROCE

The sublime church of Santa Croce is the focus of the eastern side of the city centre, where there's a plethora of excellent restaurants and bars.

▼ Palazzo Pitti

PALAZZO PITTI

Over on the south bank of the river – the district known as Oltrarno – the gargantuan Palazzo Pitti is the dominant feature. Seminal Renaissance paintings can be seen in nearby Santa Maria del Carmine, and this area's good for eating and drinking too.

Ideas

The big six

You'd have a great time in Florence if you were simply to spend your days aimlessly wandering the streets. That said, there are some specific monuments and museums you really should make a point of visiting. Here are six of the city's premier attractions.

▲ Santa Croce

Glorious frescoes by Giotto and the serene Pazzi chapel are but two of the treasures of the mighty Santa Croce.

P.121 ▸ THE SANTA CROCE & SANT'AMBROGIO DISTRICTS

▼ San Lorenzo

Some of Florence's finest art and architecture are to be seen in the parish church and mausoleum of the Medici.

P.102 ▸ THE SAN LORENZO DISTRICT

▲ The Duomo

Brunelleschi's magnificent dome, crowning the Duomo, is the city's defining image.

P.51 ▸ PIAZZA DEL DUOMO

▶ The Uffizi

The Medici art collection is simply the finest gathering of Italian Renaissance art on the planet.

P.68 ▸ THE UFFIZI

▼ The Bargello

Michelangelo, Cellini and Donatello all feature prominently in this stupendous museum of sculpture and applied arts.

P.74 ▸ THE BARGELLO AND AROUND

▲ Santa Maria Novella

Alberti's innovative facade fronts yet another art-packed church, featuring some stunning frescoes by Uccello, Ghirlandaio, Masaccio and others.

P.94 ▸ THE SANTA MARIA NOVELLA DISTRICT

The museums

The Uffizi and Bargello are Florence's two essential museums, but there are many more remarkable collections to see, ranging from internationally famous galleries of painting and sculpture to a pair of very good science museums, including a truly startling array of medical waxworks.

MUSEO DI STORIA DELLA SCIENZA

▲ The Museo dell'Opera del Duomo

Ghiberti's "Gates of Paradise" plus masterpieces by Michelangelo and Donatello are on show in this superb museum.

P.57 ▸ PIAZZA DEL DUOMO

▲ The Accademia

The home of Michelangelo's *David* draws enormous crowds – if you're visiting in summer, buy your ticket in advance.

P.112 ▸ THE SAN MARCO AND ANNUNZIATA DISTRICTS

▶ The Museo di Storia della Scienza

Galileo and other Florentines have played a major role in the development of scientific knowledge; this well-presented museum fills in the story.

P.80 ▸ THE BARGELLO AND AROUND

▲ San Marco

In the cells that line the corridors of the Dominican monastery of San Marco you'll find wonderful frescoes by Fra' Angelico.

P.114 ▸ THE SAN MARCO AND ANNUNZIATA DISTRICTS

▼ La Specola

Fantastically detailed – and sometimes grisly – anatomical waxworks are the main attraction at this university museum.

P.138 ▸ CENTRAL OLTRARNO

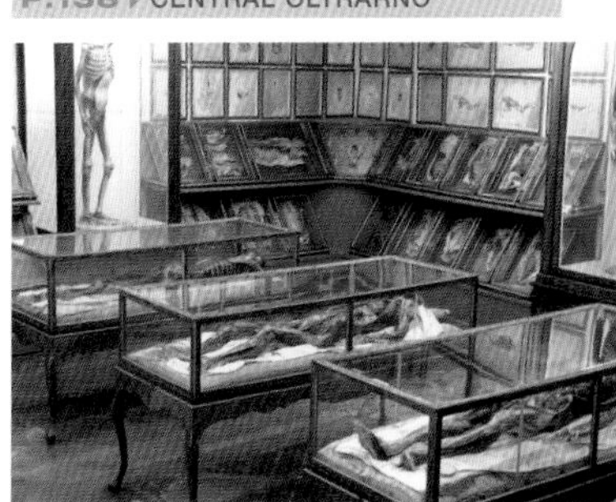

▼ Palazzo Pitti

The colossal Pitti palace contains a cluster of museums, one of them an amazing display of paintings.

P.135 ▸ CENTRAL OLTRARNO

Frescoes

From the early fourteenth century onwards, Tuscan painters excelled in the art of fresco, creating astonishingly durable works by painting directly onto plaster, usually before the plaster had dried. In Florence you can see some of the finest frescoes in the world: the great narrative cycles in the churches of Santa Maria Novella and Santa Croce are the most famous, but once you've seen those, be sure to check out some of the paintings below.

▲ Santa Maria Maddalena dei Pazzi

A luminous painting by Perugino, Raphael's master, covers a wall of the crypt of Santa Maria Maddalena dei Pazzi.

P.127 › THE SANTA CROCE & SANT'AMBROGIO DISTRICTS

▲ Santa Trìnita

Members of the Medici clan have walk-on roles in Ghirlandaio's scenes from the life of St Francis.

P.87 ▸ VIA DEI CALZAIUOLI AND WEST

▼ Santa Maria del Carmine

The startlingly original images created by Masaccio make the Carmine one of the most significant artistic monuments in Europe.

P.193 ▸ WESTERN OLTRARNO

▲ Santissima Annunziata

Frescoes by Andrea del Sarto and his contemporaries cover the walls of the atrium of Santissima Annunziata.

P.118 ▸ THE SAN MARCO AND ANNUNZIATA DISTRICTS

▼ The Cenacolo di Sant'Apollonia

Depictions of the Last Supper were something of a Florentine speciality, and none is a more arresting vision of the event than Andrea del Castagno's.

P.116 ▸ THE SAN MARCO AND ANNUNZIATA DISTRICTS

Power and politics

The Medici are the best known of Florence's political and financial dynasties, but they were just one of many families who played a crucial part in transforming the city into one of the major players in early modern Italy. Centuries later, Florence briefly became capital of the newly united Italy, an episode that has left a mark on the city's fabric.

▲ Cosimo il Vecchio

The great consolidator of the wealth and prestige of the Medici, Cosimo il Vecchio is buried in the most conspicuous spot in San Lorenzo.

P.102 ▸ THE SAN LORENZO DISTRICT

▲ The Palazzo Strozzi

Of all the rivals to the Medici, none was wealthier than the Strozzi, whose gargantuan palace is the biggest in the city centre.

P.88 ▸ VIA DEI CALZAIUOLI AND WEST

▲ Savonarola

For a few years at the end of the fifteenth century Florence was in thrall to the firebrand Dominican prior of San Marco, instigator of the original Bonfire of the Vanities.

P.115 ▸ THE SAN MARCO AND ANNUNZIATA DISTRICTS

▲ The Palazzo Medici-Riccardi

HQ of the family whose name is synonymous with that of their native city, the Palazzo Medici should be visited for its delightful frescoed chapel.

P.107 ▸ THE SAN LORENZO DISTRICT

▼ Piazza della Repubblica

In the middle of the nineteenth century blocks of inner-city slums were swept away to create the open space of Piazza della Repubblica.

P.83 ▸ VIA DEI CALZAIUOLI AND WEST

▼ The Palazzo Vecchio

The medieval hulk of the Palazzo Vecchio was the nerve centre of the Florentine republic.

P.64 ▸ PIAZZA DELLA SIGNORIA

Cafés and bars

The distinction between Florentine bars and cafés is tricky to the point of impossibility, as almost every café serves alcohol and almost every bar serves coffee – it's really just a question of degrees of emphasis. Here's a selection of the best of the spectrum, omitting the places that specialize in wine – you'll find them on pp.26–27.

▲ Procacci

You can't get a coffee at the famous *Procacci* café – it's the old-world ambience and the succulent truffle-butter brioche that bring in the customers.

P.92 ▸ VIA DEI CALZAIUOLI AND WEST

▼ Caffè Cibrèo

The classy *Cibrèo* café is one of the favoured haunts for cool Florentines and clued-up tourists.

P.128 ▸ THE SANTA CROCE & SANT'AMBROGIO DISTRICTS

▲ Nannini

If what you need is just a dash of top-quality coffee, *Nannini's* the place to go.

P.110 ▸ THE SAN LORENZO DISTRICT

▲ Caffè Italiano

One of the nicest café-bars in the centre of town, *Caffè Italiano* is good for light lunches as well as a quick shot of caffeine.

P.67 ▸ PIAZZA DELLA SIGNORIA

▲ Gilli

Why not while away an hour amid the bygone opulence of *Gilli*?

P.91 ▸ VIA DEI CALZAIUOLI AND WEST

▶ Ricchi

For a coffee-stop on the south side of the river, *Ricchi* is one of the best.

P.145 ▸ WESTERN OLTRARNO

Medieval Florence

It was during the fourteenth century that Florence rose to become the dominant power within Tuscany, and the city still preserves plentiful traces of the medieval era – including, of course, the Palazzo Vecchio, Bargello, Duomo and several of the other major churches. But this is far from a complete tally: almost every street in the centre bears witness to the prosperity of the pre-Renaissance period.

▲ Orsanmichele

Founded more than a thousand years ago, Orsanmichele is now an isolated outpost of piety on one of the busiest shopping streets.

P.82 ▸ VIA DEI CALZAIUOLI AND WEST

▲ The Palazzo Davanzati

When restoration is at last completed, the handsome Palazzo Davanzati will once again offer a fascinating glimpse of domestic life in the medieval city.

P.86 ▸ VIA DEI CALZAIUOLI AND WEST

▶ The Loggia del Bigallo

Formerly occupied by a charity devoted to the care of the sick and the orphaned, the Loggia del Bigallo now houses a minuscule museum.

P.57 ▸ PIAZZA DEL DUOMO

▼ The Torre della Castagna

The thirteenth-century Torre della Castagna is one of the few tower-houses left standing in the city centre.

P.79 ▸ THE BARGELLO AND AROUND

▼ The Porta San Niccolò

On your way to the church of San Miniato you'll pass the most imposing of the old city gates, the Porta San Niccolò.

P.150 ▸ EASTERN OLTRARNO

▼ The Ponte Vecchio

The shop-laden Ponte Vecchio has for centuries been the busiest pedestrian thoroughfare between the north and south banks of the Arno.

P.133 ▸ CENTRAL OLTRARNO

Renaissance architecture

The cityscape of Florence is dotted with buildings designed by some of the greatest names of early Renaissance architecture, most notably Filippo Brunelleschi and Leon Battista Alberti. In several instances they worked in collaboration with other artists and ceramicists, raising structures that are among the most beautiful of their time.

Cappella Rucellai

Alberti's diminutive building-within-a-building is one of Florence's hidden marvels.

P.89 ▸ VIA DEI CALZAIUOLI AND WEST

The Cappella del Cardinale del Portogallo

The work of no fewer than seven artists went into the creation of this exquisite chapel, in the church of San Miniato.

P.151 ▸ EASTERN OLTRARNO

▲ Santo Spirito

The spacious and airy interior of Santo Spirito is the culminating achievement of Brunelleschi's career.

P.141 ▸ WESTERN OLTRARNO

▲ The Cappella Pazzi

The Cappella Pazzi, adjoining the church of Santa Croce, is the epitome of Renaissance architectural harmony.

P.125 ▸ THE SANTA CROCE & SANT'AMBROGIO DISTRICTS

▶ The Palazzo Rucellai

The Palazzo Rucellai was designed by Alberti for one of Florence's most prominent plutocrats.

P.89 ▸ VIA DEI CALZAIUOLI AND WEST

▲ Spedale degli Innocenti

The former foundlings' hospital, designed by Brunelleschi and decorated by Della Robbia, occupies one side of the elegant Piazza Santissima Annunziata.

P.119 ▸ THE SAN MARCO AND ANNUNZIATA DISTRICTS

Michelangelo

The *David* is so famous it's become a sort of logo for the whole of Italy, but if you leave Florence having seen no more than this statue you'll barely have scratched the surface of Michelangelo's output. Painter, sculptor, architect, poet and tireless self-promoter, Michelangelo was a titanic figure of his age, and in Florence there's ample evidence of the unprecedented scope of his genius.

▲ The Biblioteca Medicea-Laurenziana

The bizarre vestibule and the well-ordered reading room of the Laurentian Library were both designed by Michelangelo.

P.105 ▸ THE SAN LORENZO DISTRICT

▼ Brutus

The redoubtable *Brutus* is in part a magnificent piece of political propaganda.

P.74 ▸ THE BARGELLO AND AROUND

▼ The Medici tombs

Commemorated by tombs carved by Michelangelo, set in a chapel designed by him, two of the Medici got a lot more than they deserved.

P.106 ▸ THE SAN LORENZO DISTRICT

▼ The Pietà

Michelangelo depicts himself in one of his last works, the Museo dell'Opera del Duomo's *Pietà*.

P.58 ▸ PIAZZA DEL DUOMO

▲ The Santo Spirito Crucifix

The Crucifix in the sacristy of Santo Spirito is generally agreed to be a youthful work by Michelangelo.

P.142 ▸ WESTERN OLTRARNO

▲ The Slaves

David is what sells the tickets for the Accademia, but the unfinished *Slaves* are equally stunning.

P.113 ▸ THE SAN MARCO AND ANNUNZIATA DISTRICTS

Wine bars

As you'd expect in a city that lies close to some of Italy's best vineyards, Florence has plenty of bars dedicated to the wines of Tuscan producers. At one end of the scale there are bars that consist of little more than a niche with a few shelves of workaday wines, plus a counter of snacks. At the opposite pole there are the *enoteche* (singular: *enoteca*), in effect restaurants devoted to wine: all have kitchens, but the wine menu will be far more extensive, often running to hundreds of vintages.

▲ All'Antico Vinaio

All'Antico Vinaio is more than one hundred years old and still going strong.

P.80 ▸ THE BARGELLO AND AROUND

▼ I Fratellini

Join the locals on the pavement for a *porchetta* roll and a glass of Chianti from the *Fratellini*.

P.92 ▸ VIA DEI CALZAIUOLI AND WEST

▶ Le Volpi e L'Uva

Fancy a reviving glass after an afternoon in the Pitti palace? Drop in at *Le Volpi e L'Uva*.

P.140 ▸ CENTRAL OLTRARNO

▲ Fuori Porta

Well stocked and nearly always busy, *Fuori Porta* has become something of an Oltrarno institution.

P.152 ▸ EASTERN OLTRARNO

◀ Zanobini

Simple snacks and more than decent wine are on offer at *Zanobini*, right by the central market.

P.110 ▸ THE SAN LORENZO DISTRICT

▼ Beccofino

High-grade wines and high-grade cooking are on the menu in *Beccofino*.

P.146 ▸ WESTERN OLTRARNO

Shops

If you're after high-quality clothes and accessories, paintings, prints and marbled paper, or any number of other luxury objects, then you'll find them in Florence – the main concentration of fashion outlets is around Via de' Tornabuoni, the city's premier shopping thoroughfare. Florence's best-known area of manufacturing expertise is leather goods, with top-quality shoes, bags and gloves sold across the city.

▲ Madova

Need a pair of leather gloves, small, in fuchsia? *Madova* will have them.

P.139 ▸ CENTRAL OLTRARNO

▼ Raspini

If your budget will bear it, get kitted out at *Raspini*, Florence's top multi-designer clothes shop.

P.90 ▸ VIA DEI CALZAIUOLI AND WEST

▶ Farmacia Santa Maria Novella

The ancient perfumery of Santa Maria Novella operates out of the city's most photogenic shop.

P.100 ▸ SANTA MARIA NOVELLA DISTRICT

▲ Alinari

Pick up a distinctive memento of Florence from Italy's biggest photo archive.

P.109 ▸ THE SAN LORENZO DISTRICT

▼ Alberti

Looking for a classic Eros Ramazzotti album? If *Alberti* doesn't have it, no one will.

P.109 ▸ THE SAN LORENZO DISTRICT

▼ Giulio Giannini e Figlio

Record your impressions of Florence in style, in a Giulio Giannini notebook.

P.139 ▸ CENTRAL OLTRARNO

Renaissance sculptors

As with painting, Florence looms large in the story of Renaissance sculpture: artists such as Donatello, Michelangelo (see p.24) and Benvenuto Cellini were dominant figures in their respective periods. Most of the works they carved or cast for outdoor display have now been replaced by high-quality copies, with the originals being removed to museums, notably the Bargello and the Museo dell'Opera del Duomo.

▲ The tomb of Carlo Marsuppini

Santa Croce has almost 300 funerary monuments, none more impressive than Carlo Marsuppini's, sculpted by Desiderio da Settignano.

P.124 ▸ THE SANTA CROCE & SANT'AMBROGIO DISTRICTS

▼ Giambologna

The *Rape of the Sabine*, demonstrates that nobody could match Giambologna's skill with hammer and chisel.

P.64 ▸ PIAZZA DELLA SIGNORIA

▼ Perseus

Cellini's bronze hero displays Medusa's severed head to the crowds on their way to the Uffizi.

P.64 ▸ PIAZZA DELLA SIGNORIA

▼ Luca della Robbia

Best known as a ceramicist, Luca della Robbia was also a brilliant sculptor in stone, as you'll see in the Museo dell'Opera.

P.58 ▸ PIAZZA DEL DUOMO

▲ Niccolò da Uzzano

The thrillingly immediate portrait bust of Niccolò da Uzzano is but one of many Donatello masterpieces in the Bargello.

P.76 ▸ THE BARGELLO AND AROUND

▲ The Gates of Paradise

Lorenzo Ghiberti devoted the best part of three decades to these amazing relief panels.

P.56 ▸ PIAZZA DEL DUOMO

Parks and walks

Florence is so intense an experience that even the most devoted student of culture might occasionally need an hour or two's escape from the streets and monuments. The city's not over-endowed with green spaces, but there are a few choice spots in which to unwind.

▲ The Cascine

Florence's only sizeable free public park lies on the western edge of the city centre.

P.154 ▸ THE CITY OUTSKIRTS

▼ Badia Fiesolana

For a change of air, spend an afternoon up in Fiesole, Florence's hill-town neighbour.

P.160 ▸ FIESOLE

▼ Giardino dei Semplici

The medicinal garden of Cosimo I provides a tranquil haven in the heart of the city.

P.117 ▸ THE SAN MARCO AND ANNUNZIATA DISTRICTS

▶ San Leonardo in Arcetri

A stroll out to San Leonardo gives you a taste of rural Tuscany on the city's doorstep.

P.152 ▸ EASTERN OLTRARNO

▲ The Giardino di Bóboli

The Palazzo Pitti boasts one of the most spectacular gardens in the country.

P.137 ▸ CENTRAL OLTRARNO

Ancient Florence

The Etruscans built a town on the site of modern Fiesole (and were to give their name to the province of Tuscany), and Florence began as a military camp for the Romans, the people who displaced the Etruscans. The intervening centuries have wiped away most remnants of these ancient cultures and their Christian successors – but not all.

▲ **Santa Reparata**

Beneath the Duomo lies an intriguing jumble of Roman and early Christian ruins.

P.53 ▸ PIAZZA DEL DUOMO

▼ **Museo di Firenze com'era**

The city's history is revealed at the "Museum of Florence As It Was".

P.59 ▸ PIAZZA DEL DUOMO

▲ Fiesole

Fiesole's open-air theatre is the best-preserved Roman structure in the vicinity of Florence.

P.159 ▸ FIESOLE

▲ Museo Archeologico

The lion-headed *Chimera* is but one of the Etruscan artworks on show in the archeological museum.

P.120 ▸ THE SAN MARCO AND ANNUNZIATA DISTRICTS

▶ The Baptistery

Florence's Roman ancestry is plain in the form and decoration of its oldest surviving building.

P.55 ▸ PIAZZA DEL DUOMO

▲ San Miniato al Monte

The ancient church of San Miniato looks down on the city from a hill once occupied by pagan temples.

P.150 ▸ EASTERN OLTRARNO

Restaurants

Florentine cuisine is characterized by modest raw materials and simple technique: beefsteak (*bistecca*), tripe (*trippa*) and liver (*fégato*) are typical ingredients, while grilling (*alla Fiorentina*) is a favoured method of preparation. In addition, white beans (*fagioli*) will feature on most menus. The cheapest places tend to be near the station and San Lorenzo market, while the main concentrations of mid-range and top-class restaurants are around Santa Croce and Sant'Ambrogio and over in Oltrarno.

▲ La Casalinga

This friendly, value-for-money Oltrarno trattoria has barely changed in decades.

P.147 ▸ WESTERN OLTRARNO

▼ Cento Poveri

It's not cheap, but the food at *Cento Poveri* is consistently good.

P.101 ▸ THE SANTA MARIA NOVELLA DISTRICT

▶ Zà-Zà

Outdoor tables make *Zà-Zà* perfect for summertime eating.

P.111 ▸ THE SAN LORENZO DISTRICT

▼ Cibrèo

Some say it's too popular for its own good, but nobody disputes the quality of the dishes at *Cibrèo*.

P.129 ▸ THE SANTA CROCE & SANT'AMBROGIO DISTRICTS

▲ Baldovino

Excellent pizzas and good-value Florentine dishes have made *Baldovino* a big hit.

P.129 ▸ THE SANTA CROCE & SANT'AMBROGIO DISTRICTS

◀ Quattro Leoni

The chic *Quattro Leoni* is one of the most fashionable restaurants on this side of the river.

P.140 ▸ CENTRAL OLTRARNO

Markets

Florence is not the most fertile territory for bargain-hunters, but the vast encampment of market stalls in the San Lorenzo area is the first place to go if you want to augment your wardrobe with a low-cost piece of Italian clothing. For a huge range of local edibles, the city has some superb food markets, while the Florence flea-market can offer some unusual souvenirs.

▲ Mercato Centrale

An amazing array of fresh produce is on sale in the covered Mercato Centrale, and you'll find thousands of shirts, jackets, bags and hats in the surrounding stalls.

P.108 ▸ THE SAN LORENZO DISTRICT

▲ San Lorenzo – clothes stalls

You can always find something decent amid the welter of pseudo-designer gear around San Lorenzo.

P.110 ▸ THE SAN LORENZO DISTRICT

◀ Cascine

On a Tuesday morning the Cascine is one of the busiest spots in town.

P.155 ▸ THE OUTSKIRTS

▼ Mercato di Sant'Ambrogio

Feeling peckish after a morning in Santa Croce? Put together a picnic at Sant'Ambrogio.

P.128 ▸ THE SANTA CROCE & SANT'AMBROGIO DISTRICTS

▲ Mercato Nuovo

For that bad-taste memento of the city of art, look no further than the Mercato Nuovo.

P.86 ▸ VIA CALZAIUOLI AND WEST

▼ Mercato delle Pulci

You might unearth a treasure under the Mercato delle Pulci's junk piles.

P.128 ▸ THE SANTA CROCE & SANT'AMBROGIO DISTRICTS

Nightlife

Florence has something of a reputation for catering primarily to the middle-aged and affluent, but like every university town it has its pockets of nightlife activity, not to mention the added nocturnal buzz generated by thousands of summer visitors. For up-to-the-minute information about what's on, call in at the tourist office in Via Cavour (see p.178) or at Box Office, Via Almanni 39.

▲ Capocaccia Noir

Recently renamed, and still the sexiest place in Florence – pack your best designer gear if you want to fit in at *Capocaccia Noir*.

P.92 ▸ VIA DEI CALZAIUOLI AND WEST

▲ Tabasco

The pioneering *Tabasco* – still out in front, after thirty years.

P.67 ▸ PIAZZA DELLA SIGNORIA

▲ Universale

Eat, drink and dance the night away at super-slick *Universale*.

P.147 ▸ WESTERN OLTRARNO

▲ Rex

Friendly, spacious and loud, *Rex* is one of the major nightspots on the east side of town.

P.131 ▸ THE SANTA CROCE & SANT'AMBROGIO DISTRICTS

◀ Tenax

It's a fair way out of the centre, but Tenax is well worth the taxi fare.

P.156 ▸ THE CITY OUTSKIRTS

▼ Space Electronic

The quintessential Eurodisco – but perennially popular nonetheless.

P.101 ▸ THE SANTA MARIA NOVELLA DISTRICT

Saints and sinners

To paraphrase Orson Welles, the price of great art in Renaissance Italy was murder and mayhem – and the history of Florence certainly has its share of bloody episodes. On the other hand, it has produced a fair number of spiritually elevated individuals too – though some were perhaps elevated to the brink of lunacy.

▲ St Giovanni Gualberto

Having been given a sign of approval by a miraculous Crucifix, Giovanni Gualberto went on to found the Vallombrosan order.

P.87 ▸ VIA DEI CALZAIUOLI AND WEST

▲ The Pazzi Conspiracy

The Pazzi family planned to murder Lorenzo de' Medici and his brother Giuliano; the plot half succeeded, but the retribution was terrible.

P.55 ▸ PIAZZA DEL DUOMO

▶ Alessandro de' Medici

The most disreputable of the Medici ended up being murdered by another Medici.

P.109 ▸ THE SAN LORENZO DISTRICT

▲ St Peter Martyr

The Dominican zealot had his skull split by an assassin's knife, but still managed to have the last word.

P.116 ▸ THE SANTA MARIA NOVELLA DISTRICT

▼ St Maria Maddalena dei Pazzi

Maria Maddalena dei Pazzi's wild religious visions earned her canonization and a church named after her.

P.127 ▸ THE SANTA CROCE & SANT'AMBROGIO DISTRICTS

Festivals

Florence maintains a good number of traditional folkloric events, ranging from festive religious processions to a spectacular free-for-all football competition between the historic quarters of the city. More sedately, this is also the venue for Italy's most celebrated music festival.

▲ **Festa dell'Unità**

The Communist party foots the bill for October's festival of the people.

P.182 ▸ FESTIVALS

▼ **Maggio Musicale Fiorentino**

May in Florence is all about classical music, opera and dance.

P.182 ▸ FESTIVALS

▲ The Scoppio del Carro

A fire-bearing dove sets off a spectacular explosion at midday on Easter Sunday.

P.181 ▸ FESTIVALS

▶ Festa delle Rificolone

Celebrations of the Virgin Mary's birthday focus on the lovely Piazza Santissima Annunziata.

P.182 ▸ FESTIVALS

▼ The Calcio Storico

Rules? What rules? The ball is not much more than an incidental detail in the Calcio Storico.

P.182 ▸ FESTIVALS

Florence viewpoints

Postcards simply aren't the same – you can't go home without taking a few panoramic shots of this most photogenic of cities. Here's the pick of Florence's vantage points, some of them slap bang in the centre, others at a slight remove.

▲ The Duomo

Snap a fabulous cityscape from the summit of Brunelleschi's dome.

P.51 ▸ PIAZZA DEL DUOMO

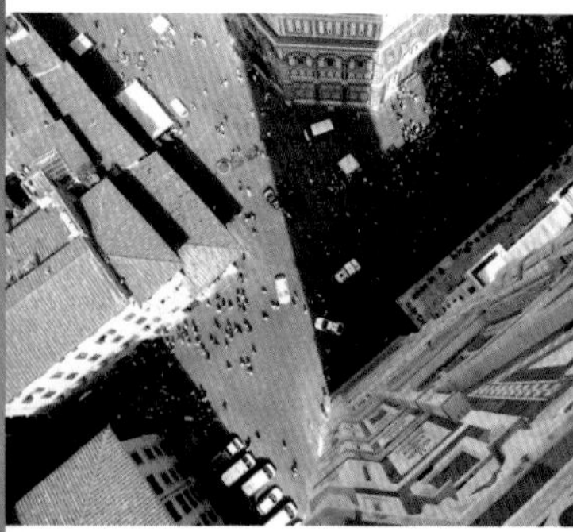

▲ The Campanile

Not for the faint-hearted: it's a sheer 85-metre drop from the top of the bell-tower.

P.54 ▸ PIAZZA DEL DUOMO

▶ Ponte Santa Trìnita

For the classic take on the Ponte Vecchio, walk downstream to Ponte Santa Trìnita.

P.88 ▸ CENTRAL OLTRARNO

▲ Forte di Belvedere

An alternative to Piazzale Michelangelo – without the traffic.

P.151 ▸ EASTERN OLTRARNO

▼ Fiesole

To get the whole of Florence in the frame, take the bus up to Fiesole.

P.158 ▸ FIESOLE

▼ Piazzale Michelangelo

Twenty minutes' walk from the river and you'll have the entire city centre laid out before you.

P.150 ▸ EASTERN OLTRARNO

Places

Piazza del Duomo

All first-time visitors gravitate towards Piazza del Duomo, beckoned by the pinnacle of Brunelleschi's dome, which lords it over the cityscape with an authority unmatched by any architectural creation in any other Italian city. Yet even though the magnitude of the Duomo is apparent from a distance, first sight of the cathedral and the adjacent Baptistery still comes as a jolt, their colourful patterned exteriors making a startling contrast with the dun-toned buildings around.

Once you've finished exploring the interiors of the cathedral and Baptistery, you could get an astounding view of the city and the hills beyond by climbing to the summit of the dome or the less busy **Campanile**, the Duomo's bell-tower. After that, the obvious next step is to visit the superb **Museo dell'Opera del Duomo**, a vast repository for works of art removed over the centuries from the Duomo, Baptistery and Campanile. Two of Florence's obscurer museums are close at hand as well: the **Museo di Firenze com'era**, which chronicles the changing face of the city, and the tiny **Museo del Bigallo**, formerly an orphanage.

The Duomo

Mon–Fri 10am–5pm, Thurs closes 3.30pm, Sat 10am–4.45pm, Sun 1.30–4.45pm; on 1st Sat of month closes 3.30pm. Free.

Some time in the seventh century the seat of the Bishop of Florence was transferred from San Lorenzo (see p.102) to Santa Reparata, a sixth-century church which stood on the site of the present-day Duomo, or Santa Maria del Fiore to give it its full name. Later generations modified this older church until 1294, when Florence's ruling priorate was stung into action by the magnificence of newly commissioned cathedrals in Pisa and Siena. A suitably immodest plan to remedy this shortcoming was ordered from Arnolfo di Cambio, who drafted a scheme to create the largest church in the Roman Catholic world. Progress on the project faltered after Arnolfo's death in 1302, but by 1418 only the dome – no small matter – remained unfinished.

Parts of the Duomo's **exterior** date back to Arnolfo's era, but most of the overblown main

▼ THE DUOMO

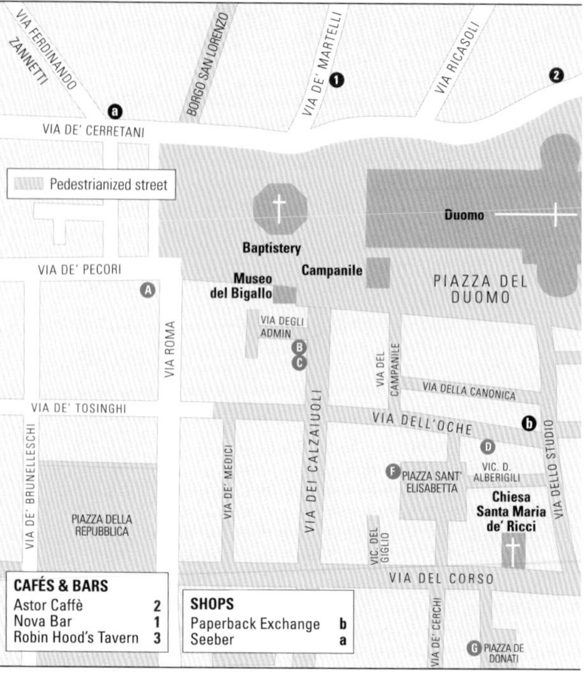

facade is a nineteenth-century simulacrum of a Gothic front. The cathedral's south side is the oldest part of the exterior but the most attractive adornment is the Porta della Mandorla, on the other side. This doorway takes its name from the almond-shaped frame (or *mandorla*) that contains *The Assumption of the Virgin* (1414–21), sculpted by Nanni di Banco.

▲ THE DUOMO INTERIOR

The Duomo's **interior** conversely is a vast, uncluttered enclosure of bare masonry. Judged by mere size, the major work of art is Vasari and Zuccari's uninspired fresco of *The Last Judgement*, which fills much of the interior of the dome. Far finer are a pair of frescoed memorials to *condottieri* (mercenary commanders) on the north side of the nave: Paolo Uccello's monument to Sir John Hawkwood, created in 1436, and Andrea del Castagno's monument to Niccolò da

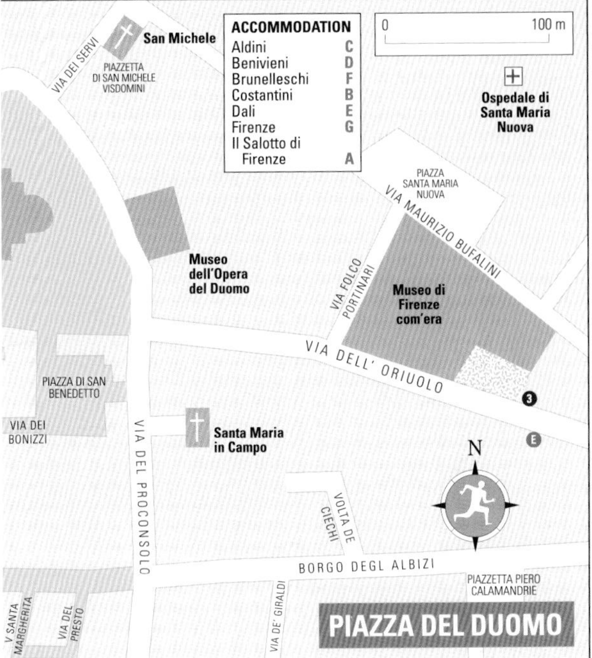

Tolentino, painted twenty years later, and clearly derived from Uccello's work, but with an aggressive edge that's typical of this artist. Just beyond the horsemen, Domenico di Michelino's 1465 *Dante Explaining the Divine Comedy* gives Brunelleschi's dome – then nearing completion – a place only marginally less prominent than the mountain of Purgatory.

Barriers often prevent visitors from going any further, but you might be able to take a look into the **Sagrestia Nuova**, where the lavish panelling is inlaid with beautiful intarsia work (1436–45) by Benedetto and Giuliano Maiano. The mighty sacristy door (1445–69), created in conjunction with Michelozzo, was Luca della Robbia's only work in bronze – he's most famous for terracotta pieces, such as the *Resurrection* above the entrance to the sacristy. It was in this sacristy that Lorenzo de' Medici took refuge in 1478 after his brother Giuliano had been mortally stabbed on the altar steps by the Pazzi conspirators (see box on p.55): the bulk of the recently installed doors protected him from his would-be assassins. Small portraits on the handles commemorate the brothers.

In the 1960s, remnants of the Duomo's predecessor, **Santa Reparata** (same hours as Duomo, except closed Sun; €3), were uncovered underneath the west end of the nave, where a flight of steps leads down into the excavation. Subsequent

Brunelleschi's dome

Since Arnolfo di Cambio's scale model of the Duomo collapsed some time in the fourteenth century, nobody has been sure quite how he intended to crown his achievement. In 1367 Neri di Fioraventi proposed the construction of a magnificent **cupola** that was to span nearly 43m, broader than the dome of Rome's Pantheon, which had remained the world's largest for 1300 years.

There was just one problem: nobody had worked out how to build such a thing. Medieval arches were usually built on wooden "centring", a network of timbers that held the stone in place until the mortar was set. In the case of the Duomo, the weight of the stone would have been too great for the timber. Eventually the project was thrown open to competition, and a goldsmith and clockmaker called **Filippo Brunelleschi** presented the winning scheme. The key to Brunelleschi's success lay in the construction of the dome as two masonry shells, each built as a stack of ever-diminishing rings. Secured with hidden stone beams and enormous iron chains, these concentric circles formed a lattice that was filled with lightweight bricks laid in a herringbone pattern that prevented the higher sections from falling inwards.

The dome's completion was marked by the **consecration** of the cathedral on March 25, 1436 – Annunciation Day, and the Florentine New Year – in a ceremony conducted by the pope. Even then, the topmost piece, the lantern, remained unfinished, with many people convinced the dome could support no further weight. But once again Brunelleschi won the day, beginning work on the dome's final stage in 1446, just a few months before his death. The whole thing was finally completed in the late 1460s, when the cross and gilded ball, both cast by Verrocchio, were hoisted into place. It is still the largest masonry dome in the world.

diggings have revealed a complicated jigsaw of Roman, Paleochristian and Romanesque remains, plus fragments of mosaic and fourteenth-century frescoes and Brunelleschi's tomb, a marble slab so unassuming that it had lain forgotten under the south aisle.

▲ THE CAMPANILE

Climbing the **dome** (Mon–Fri 8.30am–7pm, Sat 8.30am–5.40pm; 1st Sat of month closes 4pm; €6) is an amazing experience, both for the views from the top and for the insights it offers into Brunelleschi's engineering genius (see box above). Be prepared to queue, and be ready for the 463 lung-busting steps. Claustrophobics should note that the climb involves some very confined spaces.

The Campanile

Daily 8.30am–7.30pm. €6. The Campanile was begun in 1334 by Giotto during his period as official city architect and *capo maestro* (head of works) in charge of the Duomo. By the time of his death three years later, the base, the first of five eventual levels, had been completed. Andrea Pisano, fresh from creating the Baptistery's south doors (see p.56), continued construction of the second storey (1337–42), probably in accordance with Giotto's plans. Work was rounded off by Francesco Talenti, who rectified deficiencies in Giotto's original calculations in the process: the base's original walls teetered on the brink of collapse until he doubled their thickness.

A climb to the summit is one of the highlights of any Florentine trip: the parapet at the top of the tower is a less lofty but in many ways more satisfying viewpoint than the cathedral dome, if only because the view takes in the Duomo itself. George Eliot made the ascent in 1861, finding it "a very sublime getting upstairs indeed", her "muscles much astonished at the unusual exercise".

Most of the tower's decorative sculptures and reliefs are copies – you can get a closer look at the age-blackened originals in the Museo dell'Opera del Duomo.

The Baptistery

Mon–Sat noon–7pm, Sun 8.30am–2pm. €3. Generally thought to date from the sixth or seventh century, the Baptistery is the oldest building in Florence, and was first documented in 897, when it was the city's cathedral. Though its origins lie buried in the Dark Ages, no building better illustrates the special relationship between Florence and the Roman world.

The Florentines were always conscious of their Roman

The Pazzi Conspiracy

The Pazzi Conspiracy had its roots in the election in 1472 of Pope Sixtus IV, who promptly made six of his nephews cardinals. One of them, Girolamo Riario, received particularly preferential treatment, probably because he was in fact Sixtus's son. Sixtus's plan was that Riario should take over the town of Imola as a base for papal expansion, and accordingly he approached Lorenzo de' Medici for the necessary loan. When Lorenzo rebuffed him, and in addition refused to recognize Francesco Salviati as archbishop of Pisa, a furious Sixtus turned to the Pazzi, the Medici's leading Florentine rivals as bankers in Rome.

Three co-conspirators met in Rome in the early months of 1477: Riario, now in possession of Imola but eager for greater spoils; Salviati, incandescent at Lorenzo's veto; and Francesco de' Pazzi, head of the Pazzis' Rome operation and determined to usurp Medici power in Florence. After numerous false starts, it was decided to murder Lorenzo and Giuliano whilst they attended Mass in the cathedral. The date set was Sunday, April 26, 1478: Lorenzo's extermination was delegated to two embittered priests, Maffei and Bagnone, whereas Giuliano was to be dispatched by Francesco de' Pazzi and Bernardo Baroncelli, a Pazzi sidekick.

It all went horribly wrong. Giuliano was killed, but Lorenzo managed to escape, fleeing wounded to the Duomo's new sacristy. The conspirators were soon dealt with: Salviati and Francesco de' Pazzi were hanged from a window of the Palazzo della Signoria; Maffei and Bagnone were castrated and hanged; Baroncelli escaped to Constantinople but was extradited and executed; and Jacopo de' Pazzi, the godfather of the Pazzi clan, was tortured, hanged alongside the decomposing Salviati and finally hurled into the river.

▲ THE BAPTISTERY: MOSAIC CEILING

ancestry, and for centuries believed that the Baptistery was a converted Roman temple to Mars. This isn't the case, but its exterior marble cladding – applied in a Romanesque reworking between about 1059 and 1128 – is clearly classical in inspiration, while its most famous embellishments, the gilded **bronze doors**, mark the emergence of a more scholarly, self-conscious interest in the art of the ancient world.

The arrival of Andrea Pisano in Florence in 1330 offered the chance to outdo the celebrated bronze portals of arch-rival Pisa's cathedral. Within three months the Pisan sculptor had created wax models for what would become the Baptistery's **south doors**. Most of the doors' 28 panels, installed in 1339, form a narrative on the life of St John the Baptist, patron saint of Florence and the Baptistery's dedicatee.

Some sixty years of financial and political turmoil, and the ravages of the Black Death, prevented further work on the Baptistery's other entrances until 1401. That year a competition was held to design a new set of doors, each of the six main entrants being asked to create a panel showing the Sacrifice of Isaac. The judges found themselves equally impressed by the work of two young goldsmiths, Brunelleschi and Lorenzo Ghiberti (both winning entries are displayed in the Bargello). Unable to choose between the pair, the judges suggested that they work in tandem. Brunelleschi replied that if he couldn't do the job alone he wasn't interested – whereupon the contract was handed to Ghiberti.

His **north doors** (1403–24) show a new naturalism and classicized sense of composition, but they are as nothing to the gilded **east doors** (1425–52), which have long been known as the "Gates of Paradise", supposedly because Michelangelo once remarked that they were so beautiful they deserved to be the portals of heaven. (These are copies – the originals are in the Museo dell'Opera del Duomo.) Unprecedented in the subtlety of their casting, the Old Testament scenes – the Creation, the Ten Commandments, the Sacrifice of Isaac, and so on – are a primer of early Renaissance art, using rigorous perspective, gesture and sophisticated groupings to intensify the drama of each scene. The sculptor has also included an understandably self-satisfied self-portrait in the frame of the left-hand door: his is the fourth head from the top of the right-hand band – the bald chap with the smirk.

The Baptistery **interior**

is stunning, with its black and white marble cladding and miscellany of ancient columns below a blazing thirteenth-century mosaic ceiling, dominated by Christ in Judgement. The interior's semi-abstract mosaic floor also dates from the thirteenth century. The empty octagon at its centre marks the spot once occupied by the huge font in which every child born in the city during the previous twelve months would be baptized on March 25 (New Year's Day in the old Florentine calendar). To the right of the altar lies the tomb of Baldassare Cossa, the schismatic Pope John XXIII, who was deposed in 1415 and died in Florence in 1419.

The Museo del Bigallo

Tues–Sun 10am–1.30pm & 3–6.30pm. €3. The Loggia del Bigallo was built in the 1350s for the Compagnia della Misericordia, a charitable organization founded to give aid to the sick and to bury the dead. By the time the loggia was built, the Misericordia was also an orphanage – the building was commissioned as a place to display abandoned babies, in the hope that they might be recognized. For most of the fifteenth century the Misericordia was united with another orphanage, the Compagnia del Bigallo (from the village in which it began), hence the loggia's name. Nowadays it houses the Museo del Bigallo, a tiny collection of religious paintings commissioned by the two companies. The highlights are a remnant of a fresco painted on the outside of the loggia in 1386, showing the transfer of infants to their adoptive parents, and the *Madonna of the Misericordia*, painted in 1342 and featuring the oldest known panorama of Florence.

The Museo dell'Opera del Duomo

Mon–Sat 9am–7.30pm, Sun 9am–1.40pm. €6. In 1296 a body called the Opera del Duomo, literally the "Work of the Duomo", was created to oversee the maintenance of the Duomo. Since the early fifteenth century its home has been the building behind the east end of the cathedral at Piazza del Duomo 9, which now also houses the Museo dell'Opera del Duomo, a repository of the most precious and fragile works of art from the Duomo, Baptistery and Campanile.

Beyond the ticket office, rooms given over to Gothic sculpture from the Baptistery and the Duomo precede the museum's **courtyard**, now the home of all eight of Ghiberti's panels from the "Doors of Paradise", sharing the space with the graceful *Baptism of Christ* (1502–25), by Andrea Sansovino and assistants.

▼ DETAIL FROM THE GATES OF PARADISE, MUSEO DELL'OPERA DEL DUOMO

The largest room on this floor is devoted to the original sculptures of the cathedral's west front. Foremost among these are works by the cathedral's first architect, **Arnolfo di Cambio** (and his workshop), including an eerily glass-eyed *Madonna and Child*; and the vase-carrying figure of *St Reparata*, one of Florence's patron saints.

Up the stairs on the mezzanine level stands **Michelangelo**'s anguished **Pietà** (1550–53), moved from the cathedral in 1981 while restoration of the dome was in progress, but probably fated to stay here. This is one of the sculptor's last works, carved when he was almost 80, and was intended for his own tomb; Vasari records that the face of Nicodemus is a self-portrait. Dissatisfied with the quality of the marble, Michelangelo mutilated the group by hammering off the left leg and arm of Christ; his pupil Tiberio Calcagni restored the arm, then finished off the figure of Mary Magdalene.

Although he's represented on the lower floor, it's upstairs that **Donatello**, the greatest of Michelangelo's precursors, really comes to the fore. The first room at the top of the stairs features his magnificent **Cantoria**, or choir loft (1433–39), with its playground of boisterous *putti*. Facing it is another splendid *cantoria* (1431–38), the first-known major commission of the young **Luca della Robbia** (the originals are underneath, with casts replacing them in the *cantoria* itself).

Around the room are arrayed the life-size figures that Donatello carved for the Campanile, perhaps the most powerful of which is the prophet Habbakuk, the intensity of whose gaze is said to have prompted the sculptor to seize it and yell, "Speak, speak!" Keeping company with Donatello's work are four Prophets (1348–50) and two Sibyls (1342–48) attributed to Andrea Pisano, and *The Sacrifice of Isaac* (1421), a collaboration between Nanni di Bartolo and Donatello.

Donatello's later style is exemplified by the gaunt wooden figure of Mary Magdalene (1453–55), which confronts you on entering the room off the *cantorie* room. The *Magdalene* came from the Baptistery, as did the silver altar-front at the far end of the room, a dazzling summary of the life of St John the Baptist. Begun in 1366, the piece was completed in 1480, the culmination of a century of labour by, among others, Michelozzo (responsible for the central figure of *John the Baptist*), Antonio del Pollaiuolo (the *Birth of Jesus* on the left side) and Verrocchio (the *Decapitation* to the right).

On the other side of the *cantorie* room you'll find the bas-reliefs that once adorned the Campanile. Though many are darkened with age (they are currently being cleaned one by one), their allegorical panels remain both striking and intelligible, depicting the spiritual refinement of humanity through labour, the arts and, ultimately, the virtues and sacraments. The display reproduces the reliefs' original arrangement, the key panels being the hexagonal reliefs of the lower tier, all of which – save for the last five, by Luca della Robbia (1437–39) – were the work of Andrea Pisano and his son Nino (c.1348–50), probably to designs by Giotto.

A corridor leads from here past a display of some of the tools used to build the Duomo's dome. Brunelleschi's death mask, at the angle of the corridor, precedes a sequence of rooms showing various proposals for the completion of the balcony of the drum below the cupola and the Duomo's facade. The wooden model of the cathedral lantern is presumed to have been made by Brunelleschi as part of his winning proposal for the design of the lantern in 1436.

The Museo di Firenze com'era

Oct–May Mon–Wed 9am–2pm, Sat 9am–7pm; June–Sept Mon & Tues 9am–2pm, Sat 9am–7pm. €2.70. A short distance east of the Museo dell'Opera you'll find the Museo di Firenze com'era, the "Museum of Florence as it used to be". It begins the story of the city with a collection of models, plans and photographs of the excavation of the Piazza della Signoria that took place in the 1980s. A large, somewhat speculative model of the Roman city stands at the far end of the room, with coloured sections showing the buildings whose locations the archeologists are sure of. In the main gallery, maps, prints, photos and topographical paintings chart the growth of Florence from the fifteenth century to the present. One of the most impressive items comes right at the start: a meticulous 1887 reproduction of a colossal 1472 aerial view of Florence called the *Pianta della Catena* (Chain Map). It's the oldest accurate representation of the city's layout. Equally appealing are twelve pictures of the Medici villas (reproductions of which you'll see on postcards and posters across the city), and a wooden model of the Mercato Vecchio, the city's ancient heart, which was demolished to make space for the Piazza della Repubblica.

Shops

Paperback Exchange

Via delle Oche 4–6r ☎055.293.460. Mon–Fri 9am–7.30pm, Sat 10am–7.30pm. Located just a few metres south of the Duomo, this shop always has a good stock of English and American books, with the emphasis on Italian-related titles and secondhand stuff; also exchanges secondhand books and has informative and friendly staff.

Seeber

Via de' Cerretani 54r ☎055.215.697. Mon–Wed 9am–8pm, Thurs–Sat 9am–midnight, Sun 10am–8pm.

▼ OLD MAP OF FLORENCE, MUSEO DI FIRENZE COM'ERA

▲ PAPERBACK EXCHANGE

Displaced from its famous old HQ on Via de' Tornabuoni, the venerable Seeber now occupies a former cinema, and has been thoroughly modernized by its new owners. It's lost much of its soul in the process, but its stock of books is still impressive.

Cafés and bars

Astor Caffè

Piazza del Duomo 20r ⊕055.239.9000. Mon–Sat 10am–3am, Sun 5pm–3am. From its modest streetfront you wouldn't guess that this was the hottest spot on the piazza, with a glitzy and spacious interior spread over three floors. Food is served in the upstairs restaurant, in the basement you get DJs playing anything from hip-hop to Brazilian music most nights, and in the ground-floor bar you sip cocktails with the city's gilded youth.

Nova Bar

Via dei Martelli 14r ⊕055.289.880. Mon–Thurs 8am–2am, Fri & Sat 8am–3am, Sun 4pm–midnight. With a colour scheme of crimson, scarlet and fuchsia, this new designer bar is the brashest joint on the block – and the drinks list is maybe the quirkiest. Does anywhere else in Florence offer alcoholic tea cocktails to go with your focaccia?

Robin Hood's Tavern

Via dell'Oriuolo 58r ⊕055.240.224. Mon–Thurs 5pm–2am, Fri & Sat 5pm–3am, Sun 5pm–1am. One of the biggest and most successful of several places in Florence that try to affect the look of an English pub – probably because it's owned by a former biker from Birmingham.

Piazza della Signoria

Whereas the Piazza del Duomo provides the focus for the city's religious life, the Piazza della Signoria – site of the magnificent Palazzo Vecchio and forecourt to the Uffizi (see p.68) – has always been the centre of its secular existence. The piazza began its formal life in 1307, when a small area was laid out to provide a setting for the Palazzo Vecchio. Paved by 1385, the piazza was further altered during Cosimo I's reordering of the Uffizi around 1560, and more alterations followed in 1871, when the square attained its present-day dimensions.

The statues

Florence's political volatility is encapsulated by the Piazza della Signoria's array of statues. From left to right, the line-up starts with Giambologna's equestrian statue (1587–94) of Cosimo I; mimicking the famous Marcus Aurelius statue in Rome, it was designed to draw parallels between the power of medieval Florence (and thus Cosimo) and the glory of imperial Rome.

Next comes Ammannati's fatuous *Neptune* fountain (1565–75), a tribute to Cosimo's prowess as a naval commander. Neptune himself is a lumpen lout of a figure, who provoked Michelangelo to coin the rhyming put-down *Ammannato, Ammannato, che bel marmo hai rovinato* ("…what a fine piece of marble you've ruined"). After a copy of Donatello's *Marzocco* (1418–20), the original of which is in the Bargello, comes a replica of the same sculptor's *Judith and Holofernes* (1456–60), which freezes the action at the moment Judith's arm begins its scything stroke

▼ PIAZZA DELLA SIGNORIA

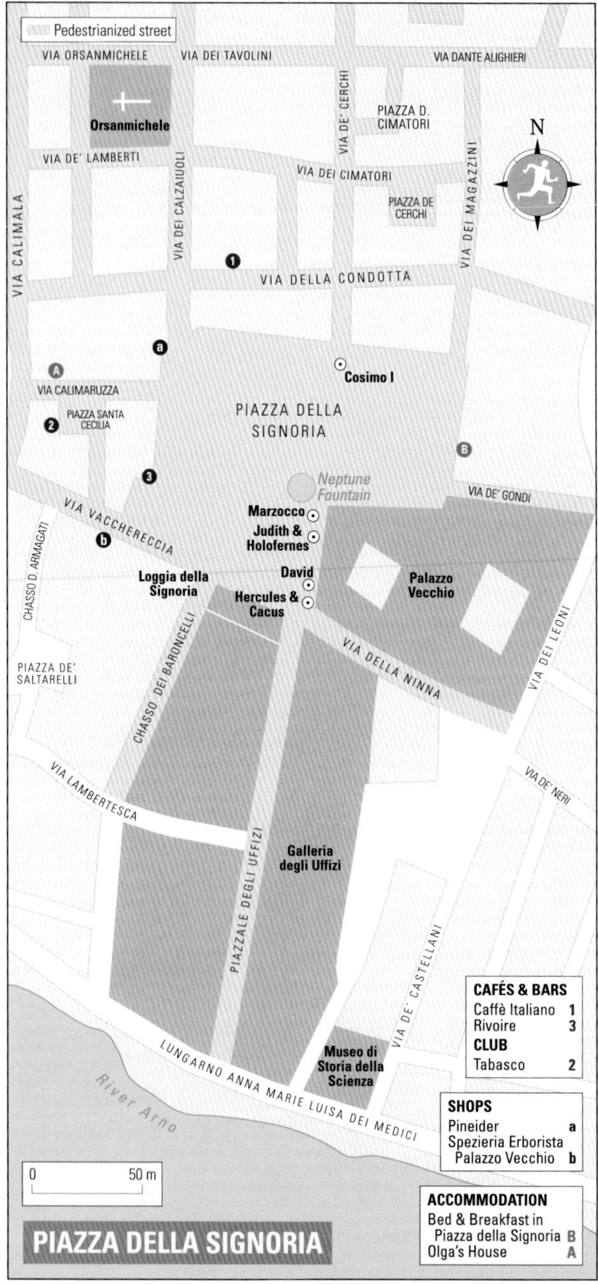

CAFÉS & BARS
Caffè Italiano 1
Rivoire 3

CLUB
Tabasco 2

SHOPS
Pineider a
Spezieria Erborista Palazzo Vecchio b

ACCOMMODATION
Bed & Breakfast in Piazza della Signoria B
Olga's House A

The Florentine Republic

Between 1293 and 1534 – bar the odd ruction – Florence maintained a republican constitution that was embodied in well-defined institutions. The rulers of the Republic were drawn exclusively from the ranks of guild members over the age of 30, and were chosen in a public ceremony held every two months, the short tenure being designed to prevent individuals assuming too much power. At this ceremony, the names of selected guild members were placed in eight leather bags (*borse*); the ones picked from the bags duly became the *Priori* (or *Signori*), forming a government called the *Signoria*. Once elected, the *Priori* moved into the Palazzo della Signoria, where they were expected to stay, virtually incommunicado, for their period of office.

Headed by the *Gonfaloniere* (the "Standard-Bearer"), the *Signoria* consulted two elected councils, or *Collegi*, as well as committees introduced to deal with specific crises. Permanent officials included the Chancellor (a post once held by Machiavelli) and the *Podestà*, a chief magistrate brought in from a neighbouring city as an independent arbitrator, and housed in the Bargello. In times of extreme crisis all male citizens over the age of 14 (apart from clerics) were summoned to a *Parlemento* in Piazza della Signoria. When a two-thirds quorum was reached, the people were asked to approve a *Balìa*, a committee to deal with the situation as it saw fit.

All this looked good on paper, but despite the *Signoria*'s apparently random selection process, political cliques had few problems ensuring that only the names of likely supporters found their way into the *borse*. If a rogue candidate slipped through the net, or things went awry, then a *Parlemento* was summoned, a *Balìa* formed and the offending person replaced by a more pliable candidate. It was by such means that the great mercantile dynasties – the Peruzzi, the Albizzi, the Strozzi and of course the Medici – retained their power even when not technically in office.

– a dramatic conception that no other sculptor of the period would have attempted. Commissioned by Cosimo de' Medici, this statue doubled as a fountain in the Palazzo Medici but was removed to the Piazza della Signoria after the expulsion of the family in 1495, to be displayed as an emblem of vanquished tyranny; the original is in the Palazzo Vecchio.

Michelangelo's *David*, at first intended for the Duomo, was also installed here in 1504 as a declaration of civic solidarity by the Florentine Republic; the original is now cooped up in the Accademia. Bandinelli's adjacent *Hercules and Cacus* (1534) was designed as a personal emblem of Cosimo I and a symbol of Florentine fortitude. Benvenuto Cellini described the musclebound figure of Hercules as looking like "a sackful of melons".

The Loggia della Signoria

The square's grace note, the Loggia della Signoria, was completed in 1382 and served

▲ THE *NEPTUNE* FOUNTAIN

▲ LOGGIA DELLA SIGNORIA

as a dais for city dignitaries, a forum for meeting foreign emissaries and a platform for the swearing-in of public officials. Its alternative name, the Loggia dei Lanzi, comes from Cosimo I's bodyguard of Swiss lancers, who were garrisoned nearby.

Although Donatello's *Judith and Holofernes* was placed here as early as 1506, it was only in the late eighteenth century that the loggia became exclusively a showcase for sculpture. In the corner nearest the Palazzo Vecchio stands a figure that has become one of the iconic images of the Renaissance, Benvenuto Cellini's *Perseus* (1554). Made for Cosimo I, the statue symbolizes the triumph of firm grand ducal rule over the monstrous indiscipline of all other forms of government. Equally attention-seeking is Giambologna's last work, to the right, *The Rape of the Sabine* (1583), the epitome of the Mannerist obsession with spiralling forms. The sculptor intended the piece merely as a study of old age, male strength and female beauty; the present name was coined after the event. The figures along the back wall are Roman works, traditionally believed to portray empresses, while of the three central statues only one – Giambologna's *Hercules Slaying the Centaur* (1599) – deserves such prominence.

The Palazzo Vecchio

Daily 9am–7pm, Thurs closes 2pm. €6. Florence's fortress-like town hall, the Palazzo Vecchio, was begun in the last year of the thirteenth century, as the home of the *Priori*, or *Signoria*, the highest tier of the city's republican government (see box, p.63). Changes in the Florentine constitution over the years entailed alterations to the layout of the palace, the most radical coming in 1540, when Cosimo I moved his retinue here from the Palazzo Medici and grafted a huge extension onto the

Percorsi Segreti

The Palazzo Vecchio's Percorsi Segreti ("Secret Passageways") allow guided-tour access (€9, includes admission to Palazzo Vecchio) to parts of the building that are normally off limits, such as the beautiful Studiolo di Francesco I, the Staircase of the Duke of Athens and the extraordinary space between the roof and ceiling of the Salone del Cinquecento. The tour lasts an hour and a quarter and is given at least four times a day, to groups of 12 maximum; the language used by the guide is determined by whoever books first – there's usually at least one tour in English every day. Places can be reserved at the ticket office or by calling ☎055.276.8224.

▲ SALONE DEL CINQUECENTO

rear. The Medici remained in residence for only nine years before moving to the Palazzo Pitti – largely, it seems, at the insistence of Cosimo's wife, Eleanor of Toledo. The "old" (*vecchio*) palace, which they left to their son, Francesco, then acquired its present name.

Work on the palace's beautiful inner **courtyard** was begun by Michelozzo in 1453; the overdone decoration was largely added by Vasari, court architect from 1555 until his death in 1574, on the occasion of Francesco de' Medici's marriage to Johanna of Austria in 1565. A rather more satisfying Vasari creation is the **monumental staircase**, which leads to the palace's first floor (visitors must sometimes take a different route upstairs).

Vasari was given full rein in the huge **Salone del Cinquecento** at the top of the stairs. The chamber might have had one of Italy's most remarkable decorative schemes: Leonardo da Vinci and Michelangelo were employed to paint frescoes on opposite sides of the room, but Leonardo's work, *The Battle of Anghiari,* was either abandoned or destroyed (work is under way to discover if any remnants survive behind the present walls), while Michelangelo's *The Battle of Cascina* had got no further than a fragmentary cartoon when he was summoned to Rome by Pope Julius II in 1506. Instead the hall received six drearily bombastic murals (1563–65) – painted by Vasari and his workshop – illustrating Florentine military triumphs. The **sculptural** highlight is Michelangelo's *Victory*, almost opposite the entrance door. Carved for the tomb of Pope Julius II, the statue was donated to the Medici by the artist's nephew, then installed here by Vasari in 1565 to celebrate Cosimo's defeat of the Sienese ten years earlier. Directly opposite, on the entrance wall, is the plaster model of a companion piece for the *Victory*, Giambologna's *Virtue Overcoming Vice*, another artistic metaphor for Florentine military might.

From the Salone del Cinquecento, a roped-off door allows a glimpse of the most bizarre room in the building, the **Studiolo di Francesco I**. Created by Vasari towards the end of his career and decorated by no fewer than thirty Mannerist artists (1570–74), this windowless cell was created as a retreat for the introverted son of Cosimo and Eleanor. Each of the miniature bronzes and nearly all the paintings reflect Francesco's interest in the sciences and alchemy.

Upstairs, in the six rooms of the Quartiere di Eleonora di Toledo, the star turn is the tiny and exquisite **Cappella di Eleonora**, vividly decorated in glassy Mannerist style by Bronzino in the 1540s. The **Sala dell'Udienza**, which was originally the audience chamber of the Republic, boasts a stunning gilt-coffered ceiling by Giuliano da Maiano and a vast fresco sequence (1545–48) by Cecchino Salviati, a cycle widely considered to be this artist's most accomplished work.

▼ STUDIOLO DI FRANCESCO I

Giuliano was also responsible, with his brother Benedetto, for the intarsia work on the doors and the lovely doorway that leads into the **Sala dei Gigli**, a room that takes its name from the lilies (*gigli*) that adorn most of its surfaces. The room has another splendid ceiling by the Maiano brothers, and a wall fresco by Domenico Ghirlandaio of *SS Zenobius, Stephen and Lorenzo* (1481–85), but the undoubted highlight here is Donatello's original *Judith and Holofernes* (1455–60).

Two small rooms are attached to the Sala dei Gigli: the **Cancelleria**, once Machiavelli's office and now containing a bust and portrait of the oft-maligned political thinker, and the impressive **Sala delle Carte**, decorated with 57 maps painted in 1563 by the court astronomer Fra' Ignazio Danti, depicting what was then the entire known world. A door (often locked) leads out from the second floor onto the broad balcony of the Palazzo Vecchio's **tower**. The views are superb, if not as good as those enjoyed from the prison cell in the body of the tower above, which was known ironically as the Alberghinetto (Little Hotel).

Shops

Pineider

Piazza della Signoria 13r & Via de' Tornabuoni 76r ⓣ055.284.655. Mon 3–7pm, Tues–Sat 10am–7pm.

Pineider sells briefcases, picture frames and other accessories for home and office, but its reputation rests on its colour-coordinated calling cards, handmade papers and envelopes – as used by Napoleon,

▲ *RIVOIRE* CAFÉ

Stendhal, Byron and Shelley, to name just a few past customers.

Spezieria Erborista Palazzo Vecchio

Via Vacchereccia 9r ⓣ055.239.6055. July & Aug Mon–Fri 9am–7.30pm, Sat 9am–5pm; Sept–June Mon–Sat 9.30am–7.30pm, plus 1st and last Sun of month 1.30–7pm. A celebrated old shop, selling its own range of unique perfumes, such as Acqua di Caterina de' Medici.

Cafés and bars

Caffè Italiano

Via della Condotta 56r ⓣ055.291.082. Mon–Sat 8am–8pm, Sun 11am–8pm; closed 2wks in Aug. Located one block north of the piazza, this is a combination of old-fashioned stand-up bar and smart café, with lots of dark wood, silver teapots and superb cakes, coffees and teas. Lunch is inexpensive and excellent, as you'd expect from a place owned by Umberto Montano, head of the outstanding Caffè Italiano restaurants (see p.131).

Rivoire

Piazza della Signoria 5r ⓣ055.221.4412. Tues–Sun 8am–midnight. If you want to people-watch on Florence's main square, this is the place to do so, and the outside tables are invariably packed. Founded in 1872, the café started life specializing in hot chocolate, and chocolate is still its main claim to fame. Ice creams are also good, but the sandwiches and snacks are grotesquely overpriced.

Club

Tabasco

Piazza Santa Cecilia 3r ⓣ055.213.000, ⓦwww.tabascogay.it. Tues–Sun 10pm–6am; DJs Thurs–Sun. One of the first gay clubs in Italy, now in operation for more than thirty years. The small dance floor gets busy at the weekend.

The Uffizi

The Galleria degli Uffizi, the finest picture gallery in Italy, is housed in what were once government offices (*uffizi*) built by Vasari for Cosimo I in 1560. After Vasari's death, work on the elongated U-shaped building was continued by Buontalenti, who was asked by Francesco I to glaze the upper storey so that it could house his art collection. Each of the succeeding Medici added to the family's trove of art treasures. The accumulated collection was preserved for public inspection by the last member of the family, Anna Maria Lodovica, whose will specified that it should be left to the people of Florence and never be allowed to leave the city. In the nineteenth century a large proportion of the statuary was transferred to the Bargello, while most of the antiquities went to the Museo Archeologico, leaving the Uffizi as essentially a gallery of paintings supplemented with some classical sculptures.

Pre-Renaissance and early Renaissance

On the ground floor, in rooms that once formed part of the church of San Pier Scheraggio, are shown **Andrea del Castagno**'s frescoes of celebrated Florentines; the imaginary portraits include Dante and Boccaccio, both of whom spoke in debates at the church. Upstairs, the beginnings of the stylistic evolution of the Renaissance can be traced in the altarpieces of the *Maestà* (Madonna Enthroned) by **Duccio**, **Cimabue** and **Giotto**. Dwarfing everything around them, these three paintings show the softening of the hieratic Byzantine style into a more tactile form of representation.

▼ *BATTLE OF SAN ROMANO* BY UCCELLO

▲ BOTTICELLI'S *PRIMAVERA*

Painters from fourteenth-century Siena come next, with **Simone Martini**'s glorious *Annunciation* taking pride of place; other trecento artists follow, among them Florence's first-rank Gothic painters, **Orcagna** and **Lorenzo Monaco**, whose majestic *Coronation of the Virgin* catches the eye first. The *Adoration of the Magi* by **Gentile da Fabriano** is the summit of the precious style known as International Gothic, spangled with gold that in places is so thick that the crowns of the kings, for instance, are like low-relief jewellery.

Gothic golds are left behind in Room 7, which reveals the huge diversity of early Renaissance painting. *The Madonna and Child with SS Francis, John the Baptist, Zenobius and Lucy* is one of only twelve extant paintings by **Domenico Veneziano**, whose greatest pupil, **Piero della Francesca**, is represented by the paired portraits of *Federico da Montefeltro and Battista Sforza*, the duke and duchess of Urbino, painted two years after Battista's death. Warfare is the ostensible subject of **Paolo Uccello**'s *The Battle of San Romano*, but this is just as much a compendium of perspectival effects – a horse and rider keeled onto their sides, the foreshortened legs of a kicking horse, a thicket of lances – creating a fight scene with little real sense of violence.

Lippi, the Pollaiuolos and Botticelli

Most space in Room 8 is given over to **Filippo Lippi**, whose *Madonna and Child with Two Angels* (c. 1465) supplies one of the gallery's most popular faces: the model was Lucrezia Buti, a convent novice with whom he produced a son, the aptly named **Filippino** "Little Philip" **Lippi** (whose lustrous *Madonna degli Otto* hangs nearby). Lippi's pupil, Botticelli, steals some of the thunder in the adjacent room, with two paintings relating to the story of Judith and Holofernes. The artists centre-stage, however, are **Piero** and **Antonio del Pollaiuolo** – their sinewy *SS Vincent, James and Eustace* (c. 1467), one of their best creations, is chiefly the work of Antonio.

Uffizi practicalities

The Uffizi is open Tues–Sun 8.15am–6.50pm; in high summer and at festive periods it sometimes stays open until 10pm. This is the busiest single building in the country, with over one and a half million visitors a year, so you should seriously consider paying the €3 surcharge for booking a ticket **in advance** – in summer you'd be mad not to. Tickets can be reserved at the Uffizi itself, or at the Firenze Musei ticket booth at Orsanmichele (Mon–Sat 10am–5.30pm; see p.82), or by calling ⓣ055.294.883 (see p.179 for more). Even if you have bought an advance ticket, get there half an hour before your allotted admission time, because the queues are often enormous. Full admission costs €6.50 but EU citizens aged 18–25 pay half price and entry is free to under-18s and over-65s; when special exhibitions are on, the price is a couple of euros higher. It's rare for the whole Uffizi to be open; a board by the entrance tells you which sections are closed. In 2004 it was announced that over the next few years the Uffizi would be doubling the number of rooms open to the public, in order to show works that have usually been kept in storage. This project has now at last begun, which means that some of the paintings might at some point be moved from the rooms in which they are currently hanging.

In the largest room in the Uffizi the greatest of **Botticelli**'s productions are gathered. The meaning of the *Primavera* (c. 1478) is contentious, but the consensus now seems to be that it shows the triumph of Venus, with the Graces as the physical embodiment of her beauty and Flora the symbol of her fruitfulness. The winsome *Birth of Venus* (c. 1482) probably takes as its source the myth that the goddess emerged from the sea after it had been impregnated by the castration of Uranus, an allegory for the creation of beauty through the mingling of the spirit (Uranus) and the physical world. A third allegory hangs close by: *Pallas and the Centaur*, perhaps symbolizing the triumph of reason over instinct. In later life, influenced by Savonarola's teaching, Botticelli confined himself to devotional pictures and moral fables, and his style became increasingly severe and didactic. The transformation is clear when comparing the easy grace of the *Madonna of the Magnificat* with the angular and agitated *Calumny of Apelles* (c. 1498).

Not quite every masterpiece in this room is by Botticelli. Set away from the walls is the *Adoration of the Shepherds* by his Flemish contemporary **Hugo van der Goes**. Brought to Florence in 1483, it provided the city's artists with their first large-scale demonstration of the realism of northern European oil painting, and had a great influence on the way the medium was exploited here.

Leonardo, Perugino and Piero di Cosimo

Works in Room 15 trace the formative years of **Leonardo da Vinci**, whose distinctive touch appears first in the *Baptism of Christ* (in Room 14) by his master Verrocchio: the wistful angel in profile and the misty landscape in the background were by the 18-year-old apprentice. A similar terrain of soft-focus mountains and water occupies the far distance in Leonardo's slightly later *Annunciation*, in which everything in the main scene is observed with a scientist's precision. In restless contrast to the poise of the *Annunciation*, the sketch of the *Adoration of the Magi* presents the infant Christ as the eye of a vortex of figures, all drawn into his presence by a force as irresistible as a whirlpool.

Most of the rest of the room is given over to Raphael's teacher, **Perugino**, who is represented by a typically contemplative *Madonna and Child with Saints* (1493) and a glassily meditative *Pietà* (1494–95). It also contains a bizarre *Incarnation* by **Piero di Cosimo**, and in his nightmarish *Perseus Freeing Andromeda* even the rocks and the sea seem to twist and boil monstrously.

Bronzino to Mantegna

The octagonal **Tribuna** houses the most important of the Medici's classical sculptures, chief among which is the *Medici Venus*, a first-century BC copy of the Praxitelean *Aphrodite of Cnidos*. Around the walls are hung some fascinating portraits by **Bronzino**, whose porcelain-like figures seem to inhabit a sunless world.

The last section of this wing throws together Renaissance paintings from outside Florence, with some notable Venetian and Flemish works. **Signorelli** and **Perugino** – with some photo-sharp portraits – are followed by a room largely devoted to **Cranach** and **Dürer**. Each has an *Adam and Eve* here, and Dürer's power as a portraitist is displayed in the *Portrait of the Artist's Father*, his earliest authenticated painting.

A taste of the Uffizi's remarkable collection of Venetian painting follows, with an impenetrable *Sacred Allegory* by **Giovanni Bellini** and some rare works by **Giorgione**. A clutch of northern European paintings, chiefly notable for some wonderful Memlings and **Holbein**'s *Portrait of Sir Richard Southwell* (1536), precedes a room in which you'll find some exquisite small paintings by **Mantegna**.

Michelangelo, Raphael, Titian and Mannerism

The main attraction in Room 25 is **Michelangelo**'s *Doni Tondo* (1505), the only easel painting he came close to completing. Room 26 contains **Andrea del Sarto**'s sultry *Madonna of the Harpies* and a number of compositions by **Raphael**, including the lovely *Madonna of the Goldfinch* and the

▼ STATUE OF MICHELANGELO

shifty *Pope Leo X with Cardinals Giulio de' Medici and Luigi de' Rossi* (1518). The Michelangelo tondo's contorted gestures, hermetic meaning and virulent colours were greatly influential on the Mannerist painters of the sixteenth century, as can be gauged from *Moses Defending the Daughters of Jethro* by **Rosso Fiorentino**, one of the seminal figures of the movement, whose paintings hang close to two major religious works by Bronzino and his adoptive father, Pontormo – one of the very few painters not seen at his best in the Uffizi.

Titian, with nine paintings on show, gets a room wholly to himself. His *Flora* and *A Knight of Malta* are stunning, but eyes tend to swivel first towards the *Urbino Venus* (1538), the most fleshy and provocative of all Renaissance nudes. A brief diversion through the painters of the sixteenth-century Emilian school follows, centred on **Parmigianino**, whose *Madonna of the Long Neck* (1534–40) is one of the pivotal Mannerist creations. Parmigianino was a febrile and introverted character who abandoned painting for alchemy towards the end of his short life, and many of his works are marked by a sort of morbid refinement, none more so than this one.

▼ *MADONNA OF THE LONG NECK* BY PARMIGIANINO

Venetian and later paintings

Artists from Venice and the Veneto dominate the following sequence of rooms, with outstanding paintings by **Moroni**, **Paolo Veronese** and **Tintoretto**. Sebastiano del Piombo's *Death of Adonis* was reduced to little more than postage-stamp tatters by the bomb that destroyed part of the Uffizi (and killed five people) in May 1993; the restoration is little short of miraculous.

After the Venetians come masterpieces by **Rubens** and **Van Dyck**, and Rubens's equally histrionic contemporary, **Caravaggio**, has a cluster of attention-grabbing pieces too. A fabulous array of **Rembrandt** portraits includes his sorrow-laden *Self-Portrait as an Old Man*, painted five years or so before his death – it makes a poignant contrast with the self-confident self-portrait of thirty years earlier. Although there are some good pieces from **Tiepolo**, portraits again command the attention in the following room of eighteenth-century works, especially the two of Maria Theresa painted by **Goya**, and **Chardin**'s demure children at play.

On the way back down to the lower floors, at the top of the stairs, you'll pass one of the city's talismans, the *Wild Boar*, a Roman copy of a third-century BC Hellenistic sculpture; it was the model for the *Porcellino* fountain in the Mercato Nuovo.

The Corridoio Vasariano

A door on the west corridor, between rooms 25 and 34, opens onto the Corridoio Vasariano, a passageway built by Vasari in 1565 to link the Palazzo Vecchio to the Palazzo Pitti through the Uffizi. Winding its way down to the river, over the Ponte Vecchio, through the church of Santa Felìcita and into the Giardino di Bóboli, it gives a fascinating series of clandestine views of the city. As if that weren't pleasure enough, the corridor is completely lined with paintings, the larger portion of which comprises a gallery of self-portraits that's littered with illustrious names: Andrea del Sarto, Bronzino, Bernini, Rubens, Rembrandt, Velázquez, David, Delacroix and Ingres. It's intended that these paintings will eventually be rehung on the first floor of the expanded Uffizi.

Because of staff shortages and strict limits on numbers allowed into the corridor (there is no fire escape), access is difficult. At the time of writing, **tours** were being conducted on some mornings, usually on Wednesday and Friday, but there is no definite schedule; for the latest situation you should ask at the gallery's ticket office.

The Bargello and around

The dense network of streets northeast of the Piazza della Signoria is dominated by the campanile of the Badìa Fiorentina, the most important of several buildings in the area that have the strongest associations with Florence's foremost poet, Dante Alighieri. Immediately opposite the church stands the forbidding bulk of the Bargello, once the city's prison, now home to a superb assemblage of sculpture and *objets d'art*: to get a full idea of the achievement of the Florentine Renaissance, a visit to the Bargello is as important as a day in the Uffizi. To the south of the Bargello, at the back of the Uffizi, lies the fascinating Museo di Storia della Scienza, a sight too often overlooked by art-obsessed visitors.

The Bargello

Tues–Sat 8.15am–2pm, with longer hours (and higher admission charge) for special exhibitions. €4. The Museo Nazionale del Bargello occupies the dour Palazzo del Bargello, which was built in 1255 and soon became the seat of the *Podestà*, the city's chief magistrate, and the site of the main law court. The building acquired its present name after 1574, when the Medici abolished the post of *Podestà* and the building became home to the chief of police – the *Bargello*.

▼ THE BARGELLO COURTYARD

You've no time to catch your breath in the Bargello: the room immediately behind the ticket office is crammed with treasures, chief of which are the work of **Michelangelo**, in whose shadow every Florentine sculptor laboured. The tipsy, soft-bellied figure of *Bacchus* (1496–97) was his first major sculpture, carved at the age of 22, a year or so before his great *Pietà* in Rome. Michelangelo's style later evolved into something less immediately striking, as is shown by the delicate *Tondo Pitti* of the Madonna and Child (1503–05). The square-jawed *Brutus* (1539–40) is the artist's sole work of this kind; a powerful

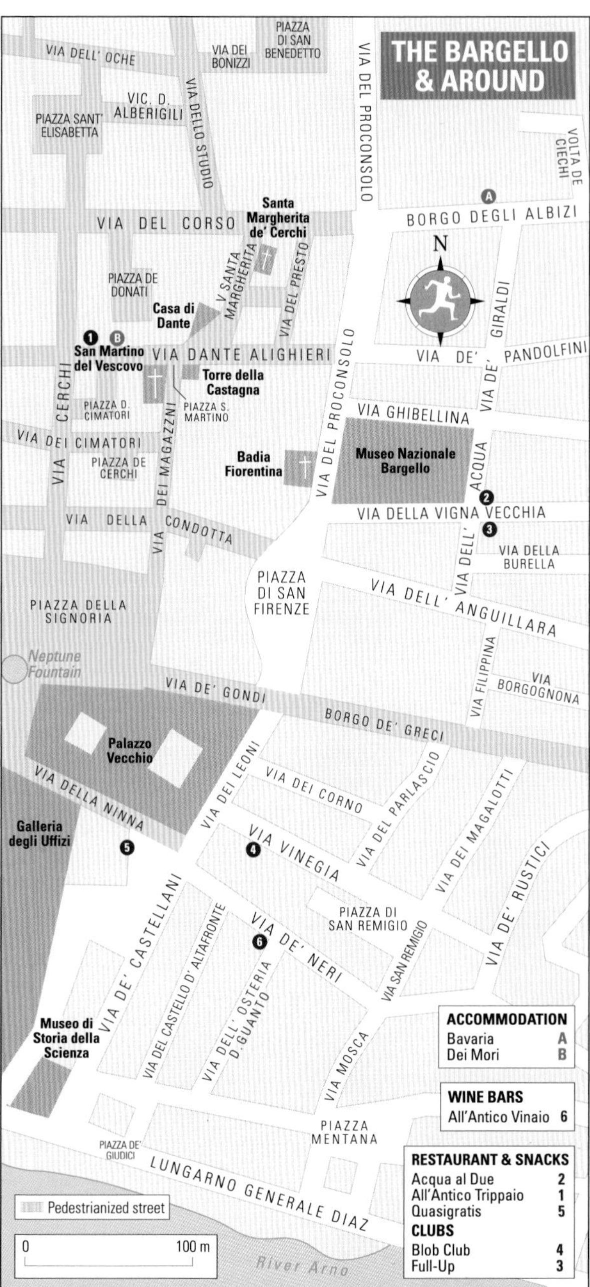
THE BARGELLO & AROUND
VIA DELL' OCHE
VIA DEI BONIZZI
PIAZZA DI SAN BENEDETTO
VIA DEL PROCONSOLO
VIC. D. ALBERIGILI
VIA DELLO STUDIO
PIAZZA SANT' ELISABETTA
VOLTA DE CIECHI
BORGO DEGLI ALBIZI
VIA DEL CORSO
Santa Margherita de' Cerchi
V. SANTA MARGHERITA
VIA DEL PRESTO
PIAZZA DE DONATI
Casa di Dante
N
VIA DE' GIRALDI
San Martino del Vescovo
VIA DANTE ALIGHIERI
Torre della Castagna
PIAZZA S. MARTINO
VIA DE' PANDOLFINI
VIA DEI CERCHI
PIAZZA D. CIMATORI
VIA GHIBELLINA
VIA DEI CIMATORI
PIAZZA DE CERCHI
VIA DEI MAGAZZINI
Badia Fiorentina
Museo Nazionale Bargello
VIA DELL' ACQUA
VIA DELLA VIGNA VECCHIA
VIA DELLA CONDOTTA
VIA DELLA BURELLA
PIAZZA DI SAN FIRENZE
VIA DELL' ANGUILLARA
PIAZZA DELLA SIGNORIA
Neptune Fountain
VIA FILIPPINA
VIA BORGOGNONA
VIA DE' GONDI
BORGO DE' GRECI
Palazzo Vecchio
VIA DEI LEONI
VIA DEI CORNO
VIA DEL PARLASCIO
VIA DEI MAGALOTTI
VIA DELLA NINNA
Galleria degli Uffizi
VIA VINEGIA
VIA DE' RUSTICI
PIAZZA DI SAN REMIGIO
VIA DE' CASTELLANI
VIA DEL CASTELLO D' ALTAFRONTE
VIA DE' NERI
VIA SAN REMIGIO
VIA DELL' OSTERIA D. GUANTO
Museo di Storia della Scienza
VIA MOSCA
PIAZZA MENTANA
PIAZZA DE' GIUDICI
LUNGARNO GENERALE DIAZ
River Arno
Pedestrianized street
0
100 m
ACCOMMODATION
Bavaria A
Dei Mori B
WINE BARS
All'Antico Vinaio 6
RESTAURANT & SNACKS
Acqua al Due 2
All'Antico Trippaio 1
Quasigratis 5
CLUBS
Blob Club 4
Full-Up 3

portrait sketch in stone, it's a coded celebration of anti-Medicean republicanism.

Works by Michelangelo's followers and contemporaries are ranged in the immediate vicinity. **Benvenuto Cellini**'s huge *Bust of Cosimo I* (1545–47), his first work in bronze, was a sort of technical trial for the casting of the *Perseus*, his most famous work. Alongside the two preparatory models for the *Perseus* in wax and bronze are displayed the original marble base and four statuettes that comprise the statue's pedestal; *Perseus* himself still stands in his intended spot, in the Loggia della Signoria. Close by, **Giambologna**'s voluptuous *Florence Defeating Pisa* (1575) takes up a lot of space, but is eclipsed by his best-known creation, the wonderfully nimble *Mercury* (1564).

There's more Giambologna at the top of the courtyard staircase, where the first-floor loggia has been turned into a menagerie for the bronze animals and birds he made for the Medici villa at Castello, just outside Florence. The doorway to the right opens into the Salone del Consiglio Generale, the museum's second key room, where the presiding genius is **Donatello**, the fountainhead of Renaissance sculpture. Vestiges of the sinuous Gothic manner are evident in the drapery of his marble *David* (1408), but there's nothing antiquated in the *St George* (1416), carved for the tabernacle of the armourers' guild at Orsanmichele. If any one sculpture could be said to embody the shift of sensibility that occurred in quattrocento Florence, this is it: whereas George had previously been little more than a symbol of valour, this alert, tensed figure represents not the act of heroism but the volition behind it. Also here is the sexually ambivalent bronze *David*, the first freestanding nude figure created since classical times (1430–40). Donatello was just as comfortable with portraiture, as his breathtakingly vivid terracotta *Bust of Niccolò da Uzzano* (c. 1430) demonstrates; it may be the earliest Renaissance portrait bust. When the occasion demanded, Donatello could also produce a straightforwardly monumental piece like the nearby *Marzocco* (1418–20), Florence's heraldic lion.

Donatello's master, **Ghiberti**, is represented by his relief of *Abraham's Sacrifice*, his entry in the competition to design the Baptistery doors in 1401 (see p.56), easily missed on the right-hand wall; the treatment of the theme submitted by Brunelleschi, effectively the

▼ GIAMBOLOGNA'S *MERCURY*

runner-up, is hung alongside. Set around the walls of the room, a sequence of glazed terracotta Madonnas embodies **Luca della Robbia**'s sweet-natured humanism.

The rest of this floor is occupied by a superb collection of European and Islamic applied art, with dazzling specimens of work in enamel, glass, silver, majolica and ivory: among the ivory pieces from Byzantium and medieval France you'll find combs, boxes, chess pieces, and devotional panels featuring scores of figures crammed into a space the size of a paperback.

▲ FRESCO DETAIL FROM THE CLOISTER OF THE ORANGES

Sculpture resumes upstairs, where you'll find rooms devoted to the della Robbia family and Italy's best assembly of small Renaissance bronzes in the Sala dei Bronzetti. Also on this floor there's an impressive display of bronze medals, and a room devoted mainly to some splendid **Renaissance portrait busts**, including Mino da Fiesole's busts of Giovanni de' Medici and Piero il Gottoso (the sons of Cosimo de' Medici).

The Badìa Fiorentina

Open to tourists Mon 4.30–6.30pm.

The Badìa Fiorentina is a place of reverence for admirers of Dante, for this was the parish church of Beatrice Portinari, for whom he conceived a lifelong love as he watched her at Mass here (see box, p.78). Furthermore, it was in the Badìa that Boccaccio delivered his celebrated lectures on Dante's theological epic. Tourist visits are allowed on Monday afternoons; at other times the church is open for prayer only, following the monastic rules of the Fraternity of Jerusalem, whose church this is.

Founded in 978 by Willa, widow of the Margrave of Tuscany, in honour of her husband, the Badìa was one of the focal buildings in medieval Florence: the city's sick were treated in a hospital founded here in 1031, while the main bell marked the divisions of the working day. The hospital owed much to Willa's son, Ugo, who further endowed his mother's foundation after a vision of the hellish torments that awaited him by "reason of his worldly life, unless he should repent". Inside the church you'll find the tomb monument to Ugo, sculpted by Mino da Fiesole between 1469 and 1481. The other outstanding work of art is Filippino Lippi's superb *Apparition of the Virgin to St Bernard* (c. 1485) in which Bernard is shown in the act of writing a homily aimed at those caught between the "rocks" of tribulation and the "chains" of sin; the presence of the four

Dante

Dante Alighieri was born in 1265 into a minor and impoverished noble family. He was educated at Bologna and later at Padua, where he studied philosophy and astronomy. The defining moment in his life came in 1274 when he met the eight-year-old Beatrice Portinari. Himself aged just nine at the time of the meeting, Dante later described his feeling following the encounter: "I saw in her such noble and praiseworthy deportment that truly of her might be said these words of the poet Homer: "She appeared to be born not of mortal man but of God." Unhappily, Beatrice's family had decided their daughter was to marry someone else – Simone de' Bardi. The ceremony took place when she was 17; seven years later she was dead.

His romantic hopes dashed, Dante settled down to a military and political career. In 1289 he fought for Florence against Arezzo and helped in a campaign against Pisa. Eleven years later he was dispatched to San Gimignano, where he was entrusted with the job of coaxing the town into an alliance against Pope Boniface VIII, who had designs on Tuscany. In June of the same year he sought to settle the widening breach between the Black (anti-imperial) and White (more conciliatory) factions of Florence's ruling Guelph party. The Black Guelphs eventually emerged triumphant, and Dante's White sympathies sealed his fate. In 1302, following trumped-up charges of corruption, he was sentenced with other Whites to two years' exile. While many of the deportees subsequently returned, Dante rejected his city of "self-made men and fast-got gain". He wandered instead between Forlì, Verona, Padua, Luni and Venice, writing much of *The Divine Comedy* as he went, before finally settling in Ravenna, where he died in 1321.

monks reinforces the message that redemption lies in the contemplative life.

A staircase leads from the choir – take the door immediately right of the high altar – to the upper storey of the Chiostro degli Aranci (Cloister of the Oranges), named after the fruit trees that used to be grown here. Two of its flanks are graced with an anonymous but highly distinctive fresco cycle (1436–39) on the life of St Benedict. A later panel (1526–28) – showing the saint throwing himself into bushes to resist temptation – is by the young Bronzino.

The Casa di Dante

Tues–Sat 10am–5pm, Sun 10am–1pm (1st Sun of month 10am–4pm; closed last Sun of month). €4 Somewhat fraudulently marketed as Dante's house, the Casa di Dante is actually a medieval pastiche dating from 1910. The modest museum is a homage to the poet rather than a shrine: it contains nothing directly related to his life, and in all likelihood Dante was born not on this site but somewhere in the street that bears his name. Numerous editions of the *Divina Commedia* are on show – including a poster printed with the whole text in minuscule type – along with copies of Botticelli's illustrations to the poem.

Santa Margherita de' Cerchi

Mon–Thurs & Sat 10am–noon & 3–5pm, Fri 10am–noon. As contentious as the Casa di Dante's claims is the story that Dante married his wife, Gemma Donati, in the nearby Santa Margherita de' Cerchi. Documented as early as 1032, the building does, however, contain several tombs belonging to the Portinari, Beatrice's family; the porch also features the Donati family crest, as this was also their local parish church. The church is worth a look chiefly for its altarpiece of the *Madonna and Four Saints* by Neri di Bicci.

San Martino del Vescovo

Mon–Thurs 10am–noon & 3–5pm, Fri 10am–noon. The tiny San Martino del Vescovo stands on the site of an oratory that served as the Alighieris' parish church. Rebuilt in 1479, it later became the headquarters of the Compagnia di Buonomini, a charitable body dedicated to aiding impoverished citizens for whom begging was too demeaning. The Buonomini commissioned from Ghirlandaio's workshop a sequence of frescoes showing various altruistic acts and scenes from the life of St Martin, and the result is as absorbing a record of daily life in Renaissance Florence as the Ghirlandaio frescoes in Santa Maria Novella (see p.95).

The Torre della Castagna

Opposite San Martino soars the thirteenth-century Torre della Castagna, meeting place of the city's *Priori* before they decamped to the Palazzo Vecchio. This is one of the most striking remnants of Florence's medieval townscape, when more than 150 such towers rose between the river and the Duomo, many of them over two hundred feet high. Allied clans would link their towers with wooden catwalks, creating a sort of upper-class promenade above the heads of the lowlier citizens.

▼ SAN MARTINO DEL VESCOVO

The Museo di Storia della Scienza

June–Sept Mon–Sat 9.30am–5pm; Oct–May Mon & Wed–Sat 9.30am–5pm, Tues 9.30am–1pm, plus 2nd Sun of month 10am–1pm. €6.50. Long after Florence had declined from its artistic apogee, the intellectual reputation of the city was maintained by its scientists, many of them encouraged by the ruling Medici-Lorraine dynasty. Two of the latter, Grand Duke Ferdinando II and his brother Leopoldo, both of whom studied with Galileo, founded a scientific academy in 1657. The instruments made and acquired by this academy are the core of the Museo di Storia della Scienza.

As you might expect, Galileo is a major presence: on the first floor you'll see the telescope with which he discovered the four moons of Jupiter, plus the museum's equivalent of a religious relic – the bones of one of the great scientist's fingers. On the floor above there are all kinds of wonderful scientific and mechanical pieces of equipment, including a perpetual motion machine and a huge lens made for Cosimo III, with which Faraday and Davy managed to ignite a diamond by focusing the rays of the sun. At the end you'll find a section of alarming surgical instruments and anatomical models for teaching obstetrics, and an old pharmacy displaying such unlikely cure-alls as Sangue del Drago (Dragon's Blood).

Wine bar

All'Antico Vinaio

Via dei Neri 65r. Tues–Sat 8am–8pm, Sun 8am–1pm; closed 3 weeks in late July & early Aug. Though recently revamped, this place – located between the Uffizi and Santa Croce – preserves much of the rough-and-ready atmosphere that's made it one of Florence's most popular wine bars for the last hundred years. Also serves coffee, rolls and plates of pasta.

Restaurants, bar and snacks

Acqua al Due

Via dell'Acqua 2r/Via della Vigna Vecchia 40r ☎055.284.170. Daily 7pm–1am. Always packed (often with foreigners but with Italians too), chiefly on account of its lively atmosphere and *assaggio di primi* – a succession of pasta dishes shared by everyone at the table. A three-course meal should cost around €35 per head.

All'Antico Trippaio

Piazza dei Cimatori. Mon–Fri 8.30am–8.30pm; closed last week of July and first 3 weeks of Aug. This stall specializes in a local delicacy called *lampredotto*: hot tripe served in a bun with a spicy sauce. Tripe salads are available in summer, while the less adventurous can go for cold cuts of *porchetta* (spit-roast pork).

Quasigratis

Piazza del Grano 10, corner of Via di Ninna. Daily 10am–11pm; closed Jan–Feb. Little more than a window in a wall at the back of the Uffizi, and it doesn't say *Quasigratis* ("Almost free") anywhere – just "Vini". Rolls, nibbles and wine – in tiny glasses called *rasini* – are consumed standing up.

▲ QUASIGRATIS

Clubs

Blob Club

Via Vinegia 21r ☎055.211.209. Daily 6pm–4am. A favourite with Florentine students, possibly on account of its free admission and the 6–9pm happy hour. Seating upstairs, bar and tiny dance floor downstairs, but don't expect to do much dancing – later on, especially on weekend nights, *Blob* gets packed full with a very happy and very drunken crowd. Quieter in the summer months.

Full-Up

Via della Vigna Vecchia 25r ☎055.293.006. Tues–Sat 11pm–4am; closed June–Sept. Situated close to the Bargello, *Full-Up* has been going so long it's become something of an institution. Music is usually fairly anodyne dance stuff with occasional hip-hop nights, the decor standard disco mirrors and flashing lights. Admission is usually free until around midnight and €10 after that (first drink included).

Via dei Calzaiuoli and west

The main catwalk of the Florentine *passeggiata* is Via dei Calzaiuoli, the broad pedestrianized avenue that links Piazza della Signoria with Piazza del Duomo. Shop-lined for most of its length, it boasts one stupendous monument, the church of Orsanmichele. Despite the urban improvement schemes of the nineteenth century and the bombings of World War II, several streets south of here retain their medieval character: an amble through Via Porta Rossa, Via delle Terme and Borgo Santi Apostoli will give you some idea of the feel of Florence in the Middle Ages, when every important house was an urban fortress. Best of these medieval redoubts is the Palazzo Davanzati, though it's been off-limits for a long time now, owing to a lengthy structural rescue job. Nearby, the fine church of Santa Trìnita is home to an outstanding fresco cycle by Domenico Ghirlandaio, while to the west of the glitzy Via de' Tornabuoni – Florence's prime shopping street – you'll find a marvellous chapel designed by Alberti and a museum devoted to the work of Marino Marini.

Orsanmichele

Tues–Sun 10am–5pm.

Resembling a truncated military tower more than a church, Orsanmichele is in itself a major monument, and is made even more impressive by the array of sculpture in the niches of its exterior, even if the statues are copies of the originals.

▲ VIA DEI CALZAIUOLI

The first building here was a small oratory secreted in the vegetable garden (*orto*) of a now-vanished Benedictine monastery. A larger church stood on the site from the ninth century: San Michele ad Hortum, later San Michele in Orte – hence the compacted form of Orsanmichele. This church was replaced by a grain market in the thirteenth century, and this in turn was replaced by a loggia designed to serve as a trade hall for the *Arti Maggiori*, the Great Guilds which governed the city. Between 1367 and 1380 the loggia was walled in, after which the site was again dedicated almost exclusively to religious functions, while leaving two upper storeys for use as emergency grain stores. It was the guilds who paid for the sculptures, which include Ghiberti's *John the Baptist* (the earliest life-size bronze statue of the Renaissance), Verrocchio's *The Incredulity of St Thomas*, Brunelleschi's *St Peter*, and Donatello's *St George* and *St Mark*.

Inside, the centrepiece is the pavilion-sized glass and marble tabernacle by Orcagna, the only significant sculptural work by the artist. Decorated with lapis lazuli and gold, it was completed in 1355 and frames a *Madonna* painted a few years earlier by Bernardo Daddi as a replacement for a miraculous image of the Virgin that was destroyed by fire in 1304. Upstairs, the vaulted halls of the granary house the **Museo di Orsanmichele**, which is entered via the footbridge from the Palazzo dell'Arte della Lana, the building opposite the church entrance. The hall itself is remarkable, and it houses the original versions of several of the most important exterior statues. However, unfortunately, the museum was closed at the time of writing, and will remain closed for an indefinite period.

Piazza della Repubblica

Halfway along Via dei Calzaiuoli, Via degli Speziali connects with the vacant expanse of Piazza della Repubblica. Impressive solely for its size, this square

▲ ORSANMICHELE

was planned in the late 1860s, when it was decided to demolish the central marketplace (Mercato Vecchio) and the tenements of the Jewish quarter in order to give Florence a public space befitting the capital of the recently formed Italian nation. However, the clearance of the Mercato Vecchio had not even begun when, in 1870, the capital was transferred to Rome, and it wasn't until 1885 that the marketplace and its disease-ridden slums were finally swept away. The free-standing column is the solitary trace of the piazza's history. Once surrounded by stalls, it used to be topped by Donatello's statue of Abundance, and a bell that was rung to signal the start and close of trading. Nowadays, Piazza della Repubblica is best known for the three large and expensive cafés that stand on the perimeter: the *Gilli* (see p.91), *Giubbe Rosse* and *Paszkowski*.

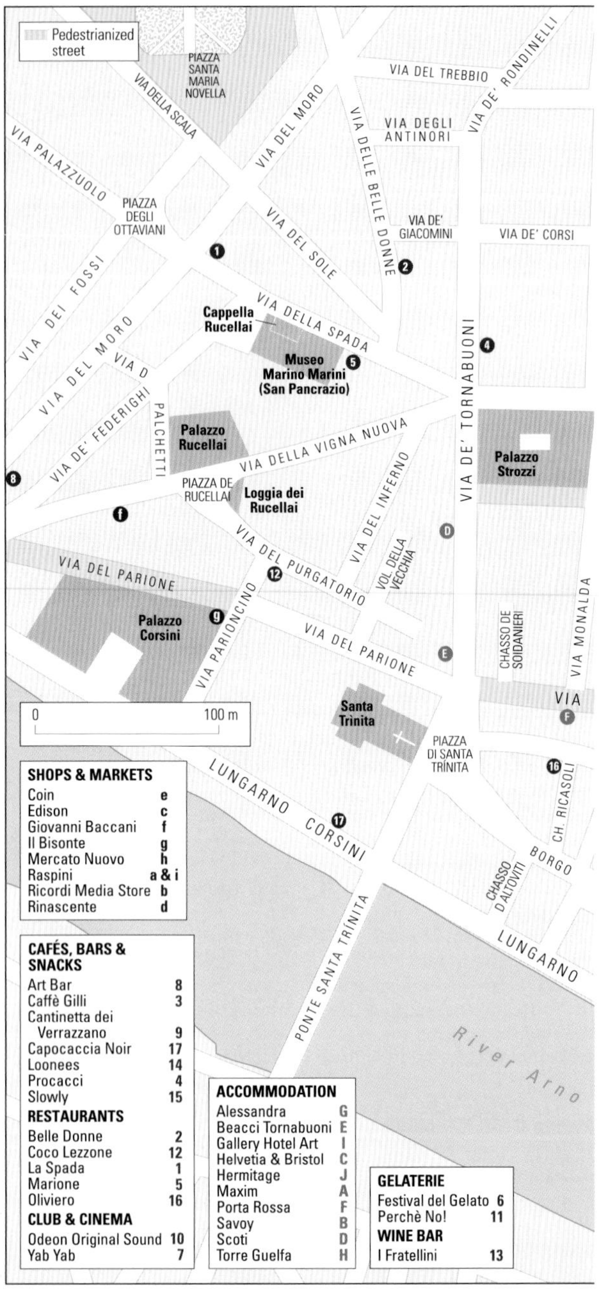

SHOPS & MARKETS

Coin	e
Edison	c
Giovanni Baccani	f
Il Bisonte	g
Mercato Nuovo	h
Raspini	a & i
Ricordi Media Store	b
Rinascente	d

CAFÉS, BARS & SNACKS

Art Bar	8
Caffè Gilli	3
Cantinetta dei Verrazzano	9
Capocaccia Noir	17
Loonees	14
Procacci	4
Slowly	15

RESTAURANTS

Belle Donne	2
Coco Lezzone	12
La Spada	1
Marione	5
Oliviero	16

CLUB & CINEMA

Odeon Original Sound	10
Yab Yab	7

ACCOMMODATION

Alessandra	G
Beacci Tornabuoni	E
Gallery Hotel Art	I
Helvetia & Bristol	C
Hermitage	J
Maxim	A
Porta Rossa	F
Savoy	B
Scoti	D
Torre Guelfa	H

GELATERIE

Festival del Gelato	6
Perchè No!	11

WINE BAR

I Fratellini	13

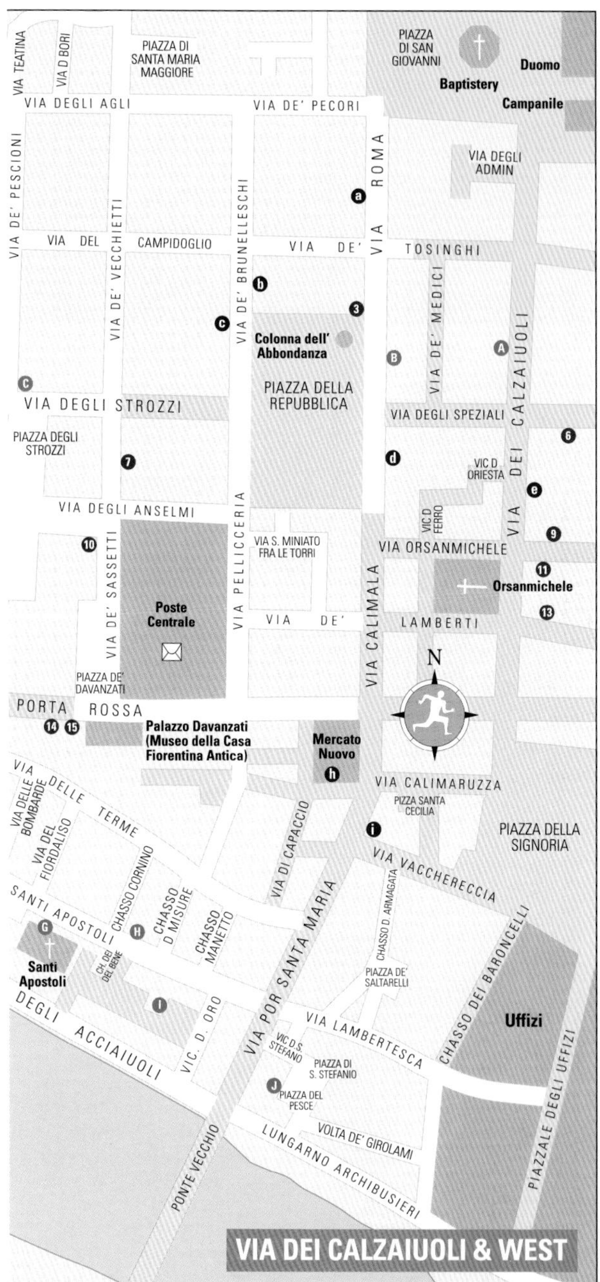
PIAZZA DI SANTA MARIA MAGGIORE
PIAZZA DI SAN GIOVANNI
Duomo
Baptistery
Campanile
VIA TEATINA
VIA D BORI
VIA DEGLI AGLI
VIA DE' PECORI
VIA ROMA
VIA DEGLI ADMIN
VIA DE' PESCIONI
VIA DE' VECCHIETTI
VIA DE' BRUNELLESCHI
VIA DEL CAMPIDOGLIO
VIA DE' TOSINGHI
VIA DE' MEDICI
VIA DEI CALZAIUOLI
Colonna dell' Abbondanza
PIAZZA DELLA REPUBBLICA
VIA DEGLI STROZZI
VIA DEGLI SPEZIALI
PIAZZA DEGLI STROZZI
VIC D ORIESTA
VIA DEGLI ANSELMI
VIC D FERRO
VIA PELLICCERIA
VIA S. MINIATO FRA LE TORRI
VIA ORSANMICHELE
Orsanmichele
VIA DE' SASSETTI
Poste Centrale
VIA DE' LAMBERTI
VIA CALIMALA
N
PIAZZA DE' DAVANZATI
PORTA ROSSA
Palazzo Davanzati (Museo della Casa Fiorentina Antica)
Mercato Nuovo
VIA CALIMARUZZA
PIZZA SANTA CECILIA
PIAZZA DELLA SIGNORIA
VIA DELLE TERME
VIA DELLE BOMBARDE
VIA DEL FIORDALISO
VIA DI CAPACCIO
VIA VACCHERECCIA
CHASSO CORNINO
CHASSO D MISURE
CHASSO MANETTO
CHASSO D. ARMAGATA
SANTI APOSTOLI
Santi Apostoli
CH. DEL DEL BENE
VIA POR SANTA MARIA
PIAZZA DE' SALTARELLI
CHASSO DEI BARONCELLI
Uffizi
DEGLI ACCIAIUOLI
VIC. D. ORO
VIA LAMBERTESCA
VIC D.S. STEFANO
PIAZZA DI S. STEFANO
PIAZZA DEL PESCE
VOLTA DE' GIROLAMI
LUNGARNO ARCHIBUSIERI
PIAZZALE DEGLI UFFIZI
PONTE VECCHIO
VIA DEI CALZAIUOLI & WEST

▲ PIAZZA DELLA REPUBBLICA

The Mercato Nuovo

Mid-Feb to mid-Nov daily 9am–7pm; mid-Nov to mid-Feb Tues–Sat 9am–5pm. The Mercato Nuovo, or Mercato del Porcellino, has been the site of a market since the eleventh century, though the present loggia dates from the sixteenth. Having forked out their euros at the souvenir stalls, most people join the small group that's invariably gathered round the bronze boar known as *Il Porcellino*: you're supposed to earn yourself some good luck by getting a coin to fall from the animal's mouth through the grille below his head. This superstition has a social function, as the coins go to an organization that runs homes for abandoned children.

▼ THE BRONZE BOAR IN THE MERCATO NUOVO

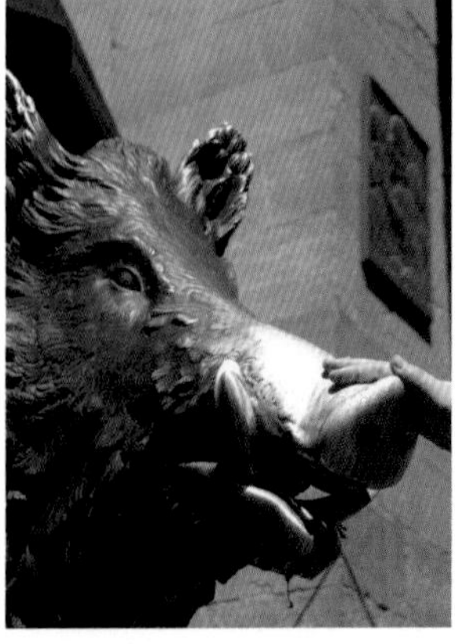

Palazzo Davanzati

Virtually every room of the fourteenth-century Palazzo Davanzati – now maintained as the **Museo della Casa Fiorentina Antica** – is furnished and decorated in medieval style, using genuine artefacts gathered from a variety of sources. However, the building was closed in 1995 for a major structural restoration, and only a small selection of the holdings of the museum has since been on display in the entrance hall (Tues–Sat 8.15am–1.50pm; 1st, 3rd & 5th Sun of month and 2nd & 4th Mon of month, same hours). The description that follows gives you an idea of the interior before closure, but as yet no full opening date has been fixed.

Merchants' houses in the fourteenth century would typically have had elaborately painted walls in the main rooms, and the Palazzo Davanzati preserves some fine examples of such decor – especially in the dining room. Before the development of systems of credit, wealth had to be sunk into tangible assets such as the tapestries, ceramics, sculpture and lacework that alleviate the austerity of many of these rooms; any surplus cash would have been locked away in a strongbox like the extraordinary example in the **Sala Piccola**, whose locking mechanism looks like the innards of a primitive clock. There's also a fine collection of *cassoni*, the painted chests in which the wife's dowry would be stored.

Plushest of the rooms is the first-floor bedroom, with a Sicilian linen bed-cover woven with scenes from the story of Tristan. But the spot where the occupants would have been likeliest to linger is the kitchen. Located on the top floor to minimize the damage that might be caused by the outbreak of a fire, it would have been the warmest room in the house. A load of ancient utensils are on show here, and set into one wall there is the most civilized of amenities, a service shaft connecting the kitchen to all floors of the building. The leaded glass was considered a marvel at a time when many windows were covered with turpentine-soaked rags stretched across frames to repel rainwater.

Santi Apostoli

Mon–Sat 10am–noon & 4–5.30pm, Sun 4–5.30pm. Legend has it that the church of Santi Apostoli was founded by Charlemagne, but it's not quite that ancient – the eleventh century seems the likeliest date of origin. Santi Apostoli possesses some peculiar relics, in the form of stone fragments allegedly brought from the Holy Sepulchre in Jerusalem by a crusading Florentine; on Holy Saturday sparks struck from these stones are used to light the flame that ignites the "dove" that in turn sets off the fireworks in front of the Duomo (see p.51).

▲ SANTA TRÌNITA

Santa Trìnita

Mon–Sat 8am–noon & 4–6pm, Sun 4–6pm. Santa Trìnita was founded in 1092 by a Florentine nobleman called **Giovanni Gualberto**, scenes from whose life are illustrated in the frescoes in the fourth chapel of the left aisle. One Good Friday, so the story goes, Gualberto set off intent on avenging the murder of his brother. On finding the murderer he decided to spare his life – it was Good Friday – and proceeded to San Miniato (see p.150), where a crucifix is said to have bowed its head to honour his act of mercy. Giovanni went on to become a Benedictine monk and founded the reforming Vallombrosan order and – notwithstanding the mayhem created on Florence's streets by his militant supporters – was eventually canonized.

The church was rebuilt between about 1300 and 1330, and piecemeal additions over the years have lent the church a pleasantly hybrid air: the largely

Gothic interior contrasts with the Mannerist facade, itself at odds with the Romanesque interior front wall. The fame of the building is due chiefly to Ghirlandaio's **frescoes** (1483–86) of scenes from the life of St Francis, in the Cappella Sassetti. Commissioned by Francesco Sassetti, a friend of Lorenzo the Magnificent, they place the narrative in the context of fifteenth-century Florence: St Francis is shown healing a sick child in Piazza Santa Trìnita, for example, while *St Francis Receiving the Rule* (in the lunette above the altar) is set in Piazza della Signoria and features (right foreground) a portrait of Sassetti between his son, Federigo, and Lorenzo the Magnificent.

Displayed in the neighbouring Cappella Doni is the miraculous crucifix that bowed its head to Gualberto. The third of the church's major works, a powerful composition by Luca della Robbia – the tomb of Benozzo Federighi, bishop of Fiesole – occupies the left wall of the Cappella Scali, the farthest chapel.

Ponte Santa Trìnita

The sleek Ponte Santa Trìnita was built on Cosimo I's orders after its predecessor was demolished in a flood. The roads on both banks were raised and widened to accentuate the dramatic potential of the new link between the city centre and the Oltrarno, but what makes this the classiest bridge in Florence is the sensuous curve of its arches, a curve so shallow that engineers have been baffled as to how the bridge bears up under the strain. Ostensibly the design was devised by Ammannati, one of the Medici's favourite artists, but the curves so closely resemble the arc of Michelangelo's Medici tombs that it's likely the credit belongs to him.

▼ PUCCI ON VIA DE' TORNABUONI

Via de' Tornabuoni

The shops of Via de' Tornabuoni are effectively out of bounds to those who don't travel first class. Versace, Ferragamo, Prada, Cavalli, Gucci and Armani have their outlets here: indeed, in recent years they have come to monopolize the street (and nearby Piazza Strozzi), to the dismay of many, who see further evidence of the loss of Florentine identity in the eviction of local institutions such as the Seeber bookshop, the Farmacia Inglese and the *Giacosa* café. Seeber has moved to new premises (see p.60), while *Giacosa* lives on in name only, as an adjunct to the huge Roberto Cavalli shop, with footage of Cavalli catwalk shows projected onto a big screen for the customers' entertainment.

The Palazzo Strozzi

Conspicuous wealth is nothing new on Via de' Tornabuoni. Looming above everything is the vast Palazzo Strozzi, the largest and most intimidating of all Florentine Renaissance palaces, with windows as big as gateways and embossed with lumps of stone the size of boulders. Designed by Giuliano da Sangallo, it was begun by the banker Filippo Strozzi, a figure so powerful that he was once described as "the first man of Italy", and whose family were ringleaders of the anti-Medici faction in Florence. He bought and demolished a dozen town houses to make space for this strongbox in stone, and the construction of it lasted from 1489 to 1536. The interior is open only for special exhibitions.

The Palazzo Rucellai

In the 1440s Giovanni Rucellai, one of the richest businessmen in Florence (and an esteemed scholar, too), commissioned a new house from Leon Battista Alberti, the brilliant architect, mathematician, linguist and theorist of the arts. The resultant Palazzo Rucellai was the first palace in Florence to follow the rules of classical architecture – its tiers of pilasters evoke the exterior wall of the Colosseum. In contrast to the feud between the Medici and the Strozzi, the Rucellai were on close terms with the city's first family: the **Loggia dei Rucellai**, on the opposite side of Via della Vigna Nuova (now a hi-fi shop), was probably built for the wedding of Giovanni's son to the granddaughter of Cosimo il Vecchio, and the frieze on the Palazzo Rucellai features the heraldic devices of the two families, the Medici emblem alongside the Rucellai sail.

▲ PALAZZO STROZZI

The Museo Marino Marini

Mon & Wed–Fri 10am–5pm; Oct–May also Sat 10am–5pm; closed Aug. €4. Round the corner from the Palazzo Rucellai stands the ex-church of San Pancrazio, deconsecrated by Napoleon, now the swish Museo Marino Marini. The museum holds around two hundred works left to the city in Marini's will (he died in 1980), with variations on the sculptor's trademark horse-and-rider theme – familiar from civic environments all over Europe – making up much of the show.

The Cappella Rucellai

June–Sept Mon–Fri 10am–5pm; Oct–May Mon–Sat 10am–noon & 5–5.30pm. Free. Once part of San Pancrazio but now entirely separate from the museum, the Cappella Rucellai, which was redesigned by Alberti, houses the **Cappella di San Sepolcro**, the most exquisite of his architectural creations. Designed as the funerary monument to Giovanni Rucellai, it takes the form of a diminutive reconstruction of Jerusalem's Church of the Holy Sepulchre. Access to the cappella is dependent upon voluntary staff, so it's prone to unscheduled periods of closure.

Shops and markets

Coin

Via dei Calzaiuoli 56r ⓣ055.280.531. Mon–Sat 10am–8pm, Sun 11am–8pm. A clothes-dominated chain store in an excellent central position. Quality is generally high, though styles are fairly conservative except for one or two youth-oriented franchises on the ground floor. Also a good place for linen and other household goods.

Edison

Piazza della Repubblica 27r ⓣ055.213.110. Mon–Sat 9am–midnight, Sun 10am–midnight. This US-style operation is Florence's newest bookstore; arranged on four floors (with English-language books on the top), it has a substantial stock and longer hours than any of its rivals.

▼ EDISON

Giovanni Baccani

Via della Vigna Nuova 75r ⓣ055.214.467. Mon 3.30–7.30pm, Tues–Sat 9am–1pm & 3.30–7.30pm; July closed Sat afternoon. You'll see prints and engravings in shops across Florence, but nowhere is the selection as mouthwatering as in Baccani, a beautiful old shop (established in 1903) that's crammed with all manner of prints, frames and paintings. Prices range from a few euros to the realms of credit-card madness.

Il Bisonte

Via del Parione 31–33r ⓣ055.215.722. Mon–Fri 9.30am–7pm, Sat 9am–2pm. Beautiful and robust bags, briefcases and accessories, many of them made from *vacchetta*, a soft cow-hide that ages very nicely.

Mercato Nuovo

Loggia del Mercato Nuovo. Mid-Feb to mid-Nov daily 9am–7pm; mid-Nov to mid-Feb Tues–Sat 9am–5pm. Also known as the Mercato del Porcellino, this is the main emporium for straw hats, plastic *Davids* and the like.

Raspini

Via Roma 25–29r ⓣ055.213.077 & Via Por Santa Maria 70r ⓣ055.213.901. Mon 3.30–7.30pm, Tues–Sat 10.30am–7.30pm, plus last Sun of month 10am–7pm. Florence's biggest multi-label clothes shop, with a good stock of diffusion lines. These are the two main branches; there's a third one at Via de' Martelli 5–7r (on the north side of the Baptistery). Leftovers from previous season are sold at big discounts at *Raspini Vintage*, Via Calimaruzza

17r, very close to the Via Por Santa Maria branch.

Ricordi Media Store

Via Brunelleschi 8–10r ☎055.214.104. Mon–Sat 9am–7.30pm; Sept–June also last Sun of month 3.30–7.30pm. The city's biggest general music and DVD store, just off Piazza della Repubblica.

Rinascente

Piazza della Repubblica 1 ☎055.239.8544. Mon–Sat 9am–9pm, Sun 10.30am–8pm. Like Coin, Rinascente is part of a countrywide chain, though this store, opened in 1996, is a touch more upmarket than its nearby rival. Sells clothing, linen, cosmetics, household goods and other staples. The rooftop café isn't one of the city's best, but it has perhaps the best location.

Gelaterie

Festival del Gelato

Via del Corso 75r. Tues–Sun 10am–midnight. Around seventy varieties of ice cream, with some very exotic combinations.

Perchè No!

Via de' Tavolini 19r. March–Oct Mon & Wed–Sat 11am–midnight, Tues noon–8pm; Dec–Feb Mon & Wed–Sat noon–7.30pm; closed Nov. A superb *gelateria*, in business since the 1930s; go for the *crema*, the chocolate or the gorgeous pistachio.

Cafés, bars and snacks

Art Bar

Via del Moro 4r ☎055.287.661. Mon–Sat 7pm–1am. A fine little bar near Piazza di Carlo

▲ TUBS OF ICE CREAM AT *PERCHÈ NO!*

Goldoni. The interior looks like an antique shop, while the club-like atmosphere attracts a rather smart crowd. Especially busy at happy hour (6.30–9pm), when the low-priced cocktails are in heavy demand. The after-hours ambience is also ideal for a laid-back nightcap.

Caffè Gilli

Piazza della Repubblica 36–39r ☎055.213.896. Mon & Wed–Sun 8am–1am. Founded in 1733, this most appealing of the square's expensive cafés moved to its present site in 1910. The staggering *belle époque* interior is a sight in itself (rumour has it that a modernization is imminent), but most people choose to sit on the big outdoor terrace. On a cold afternoon try the famous hot chocolate – it comes in five blended flavours: almond, orange, coffee, *gianduia* and cocoa.

Cantinetta dei Verrazzano

Via de' Tavolini 18–20r ☎055.268.590. July & Aug Mon–Sat 8am–4pm; Sept–June Mon–Sat 8am–9pm. Owned by Castello dei Verrazzano, a major Chianti vineyard, this wood-panelled place near Orsanmichele is part-bar, part-café and part-bakery, making its own excellent pizza, *focaccia* and cakes. A perfect spot for a light lunch or an early evening glass.

Capocaccia Noir

Lungarno Corsini 12–14r ☎055.210.751. Daily noon–3am. Recently revamped in moody nocturnal tones, the bar formerly known simply as *Capocaccia* has been voted the Florentines' favourite night-time rendezvous several times, and it remains out in front. It's roomy and has plenty of tables and stools; there's a DJ every night; and you'll be mixing almost entirely with fashionable locals, especially later on. If you have neither youth nor beauty on your side, however, you'd best stay away.

Loonees

Via Porta Rossa 15r ☎055.212.249. Tues–Sun 8pm–3am. Set up by a former biker from Birmingham, this bar is a favourite with the city's students. The music is loud right through the night, and live from Wednesday to Saturday.

Procacci

Via de' Tornabuoni 64r ☎055.211.656. Mon–Sat 10.30am–8pm; closed Aug. This famous little café doesn't serve coffee, just wine and cold drinks. Its reputation comes from the extraordinary and delicious *tartufati*, or truffle-butter brioche – from October to December, when truffles are in season, the wood-lined interior of *Procacci* is a swooningly aromatic environment.

▲ CAFFÈ GILLI

Slowly

Via Porta Rossa 63 ☎055.264.5354. Mon–Sat 7pm–2.30am; closed July & Aug. This extremely trendy bar attracts a showy, beautifully dressed young crowd, chatting over pricey cocktails and bar snacks. Time will tell whether its appearance in all the designer magazines will lead to style tourists edging out the Florentines.

Wine bar

I Fratellini

Via dei Cimatori 38r. Mid-June to Aug Mon–Fri 8am–5pm; Sept to mid-June daily 8am–8pm. This minuscule dirt-cheap wine bar is somehow clinging on in the immediate vicinity of the high-rent Via dei Calzaiuoli. Serves decent *panini* and local wines.

Restaurants

Belle Donne

Via delle Belle Donne 16r ☎055.238.2609. Daily noon–3pm & 8–11.30pm; closed Aug. A tiny, convivial, faux-rustic *trattoria*, where you sit elbow-to-elbow on bare benches and stools, under swags of foliage, drinking your wine from a tumbler. Not a place to linger over your meal, but it's honest food, cheerfully presented at honest prices. No reservations.

Coco Lezzone

Via del Parioncino 26r ☎055.287.178. Mon & Wed–Sat noon–2.30pm & 7–10pm, Tues noon–2.30pm; closed mid-July to mid-Aug. Stumble on this back-street place and you'd swear you'd found one of the great old-world Florentine *trattorie*. The food is sometimes good and sometimes not, the prices moderate (you'll pay around €35), but the service is frequently offhand – this place has been very fashionable for so long that the proprietors often seem to think they don't need to make an effort any more.

▲ MARIONE

La Spada

Via della Spada 62r ☎055.218.757. Daily noon–3pm & 6–10.30pm. This very congenial *rosticceria* specializes in roast meats, but also does some excellent pasta dishes. One of the best-value places to eat in the centre of the city.

Marione

Via della Spada 27r ☎055.214.756. Daily noon–3pm & 7–11.30pm; closed first two weeks of Aug. Simple, good-value Tuscan cooking, at prices that are a pleasant surprise for this location, a stone's throw from Via de' Tornabuoni.

Oliviero

Via delle Terme 52r ☎055.212.421. Mon–Sat 7pm–midnight; closed Aug. Currently enjoys a reputation for some of Florence's best food, but at a price. It has a welcoming and old-fashioned feel – rather like an Italian restaurant of the 1960s. The innovative food is predominantly Tuscan, but includes other Italian dishes. There's even fresh fish on the menu when available, something of a rarity in Florence. Expect to pay upwards of €50, without wine.

Club

Yab

Via de' Sassetti 5r ☎055.215.160. Mon & Wed–Sat 9pm–4am; closed June–Sept. This basement club-restaurant has been popular for years (formerly as *Yab Yum*) and is known throughout the country for Monday's Yabsmoove – Italy's longest-running hip-hop night. On other nights it doesn't have the most up-to-the-minute playlist in the world, but still offers the most relaxed and reliable night's clubbing in central Florence. Entry is free as long as you spend €15 on drinks.

Cinema

Odeon Original Sound

Via de' Sassetti 1 ☎055.214.068. Closed Aug. Mainstream films are screened in their original language at this air-conditioned cinema once a week, generally on Monday, for most of the year, plus Tuesday and Thursday in summer.

The Santa Maria Novella district

Right in front of you as you emerge from the train station rises the back wall of the church of Santa Maria Novella, one of Florence's major monuments. The square that it overlooks – Piazza Santa Maria Novella – was for many years a gathering place for drug dealers, winos and other undesirables, and had a smattering of low-budget tourist accommodation on its periphery, but in recent years a major redevelopment of the piazza has been underway, and the increase in the number of upmarket hotels here will doubtless be followed by more stringent policing of the area.

The train station

Most visitors barely spare a glance for Santa Maria Novella train station, but it's a superb building. Its principal architect, Giovanni Michelucci – who died in January 1991, just two days short of his hundredth birthday – was one of the leading figures of the Modernist movement, which in Mussolini's Italy was marginalized by the officially approved Neoclassical tendency. Accordingly, there was some astonishment when, in 1933, Michelucci and his colleagues won the competition to design the main rail terminal for one of the country's showpiece cities. It's a piece of impeccably rational planning, so perfectly designed that no major alterations were deemed necessary until very recently, when approval was given for the construction of a new terminal for the high-speed Milan–Rome rail line beneath the station. Designed by Foster Associates, it's due to open in 2011.

▼ TRAIN STATION TICKET HALL

Santa Maria Novella

Mon–Thurs 9am–5pm, Fri & Sun 1–5pm. €2.50. The graceful church of Santa Maria Novella was the Florentine base of the Dominican order, the vigilantes of thirteenth-century Catholicism. A more humble church, Santa Maria delle Vigne, which had existed here since the eleventh century, was handed to the Dominicans in 1221; they then set about altering the place to their taste. By 1360 the interior was finished, but only the Romanesque lower part of the **facade** had been completed. This state of affairs lasted until 1456, when Giovanni Rucellai paid for Alberti to design a classical upper storey

▲ SANTA MARIA NOVELLA

that would blend with the older section while improving the facade's proportions. The sponsor's name is picked out across the facade in Roman capitals, while the Rucellai family emblem, the billowing sail of Fortune, runs as a motif through the central frieze.

Santa Maria Novella's **interior**, which was designed to enable preachers to address their sermons to as large a congregation as possible, is adorned with a ground-breaking painting by Masaccio, a crucifix by Giotto and no fewer than three major fresco cycles. **Masaccio**'s extraordinary 1427 depiction of the **Trinity**, painted on the wall of the left aisle, was one of the earliest works in which the rules of perspective and classical proportion were rigorously employed, and Florentines queued to view the illusion on its unveiling, stunned by a painting which appeared to create three-dimensional space on a solid wall. **Giotto**'s *Crucifix*, a radically naturalistic and probably very early work (c.1288–90), now hangs in what is thought to be its intended position, poised dramatically over the centre of the nave.

The chapel to the right of the chancel is covered with a fabulous cycle of frescoes commissioned in 1489 from **Filippino Lippi** by the banker Filippo Strozzi. Illustrating the life of Strozzi's namesake, St Philip the Apostle, the paintings were commenced after Filippino had spent some time in Rome, and the work he carried out on his return displays an archeologist's obsession with ancient Roman culture. Behind the altar is Strozzi's tomb (1491–95), beautifully carved by Benedetto da Maiano.

As a chronicle of fifteenth-century life in Florence, no series of frescoes is more fascinating than **Domenico Ghirlandaio**'s pictures around the chancel and high altar. The artist's masterpiece, the pictures were commissioned by Giovanni Tornabuoni, a banker and uncle of Lorenzo

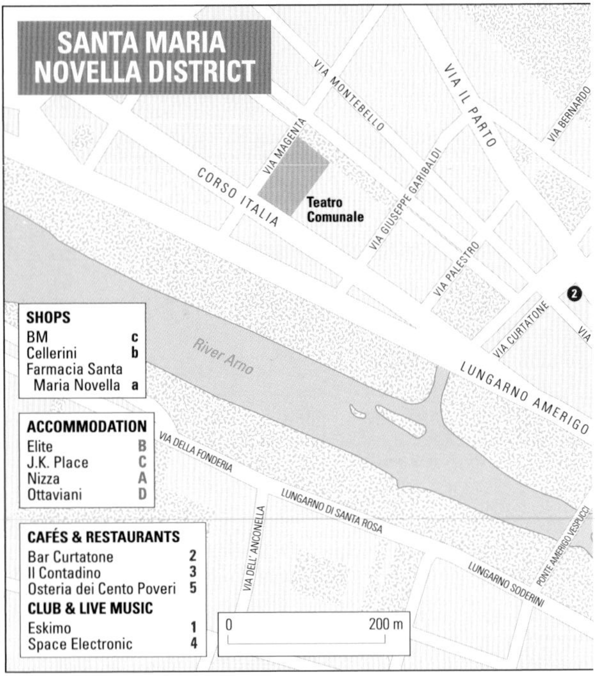

SANTA MARIA NOVELLA DISTRICT

Cascine

Via Montebello
Via il Parto
Via Bernardo
Via Magenta
Corso Italia
Teatro Comunale
Via Giuseppe Garibaldi
Via Palestro
Via Curtatone
Via
River Arno
Lungarno Amerigo
Via della Fonderia
Lungarno di Santa Rosa
Via dell' Anconella
Lungarno Soderini
Ponte Amerigo Vespucci

SHOPS
BM c
Cellerini b
Farmacia Santa Maria Novella a

ACCOMMODATION
Elite B
J.K. Place C
Nizza A
Ottaviani D

CAFÉS & RESTAURANTS
Bar Curtatone 2
Il Contadino 3
Osteria dei Cento Poveri 5

CLUB & LIVE MUSIC
Eskimo 1
Space Electronic 4

0 200 m

de' Medici (Lorenzo the Magnificent), which explains why certain illustrious ladies of the Tornabuoni family are present at the births of both John the Baptist and the Virgin. These frescoes are a proud celebration of Florence at its zenith – indeed, one of the frescoes includes a Latin inscription which reads: "The year 1490, when the most beautiful city renowned for abundance, victories, arts and noble buildings profoundly enjoyed salubrity and peace."

The church's third great fresco cycle is in the **Cappella Strozzi**, which lies above the level of the rest of the church at the end of the left transept. Commissioned in 1350 as an expiation of the sin of usury by Tommaso Strozzi, an ancestor of Filippo Strozzi, the pictures are the masterpiece of Nardo di Cione, brother of the better-

▲ THE CAPPELLA STROZZI

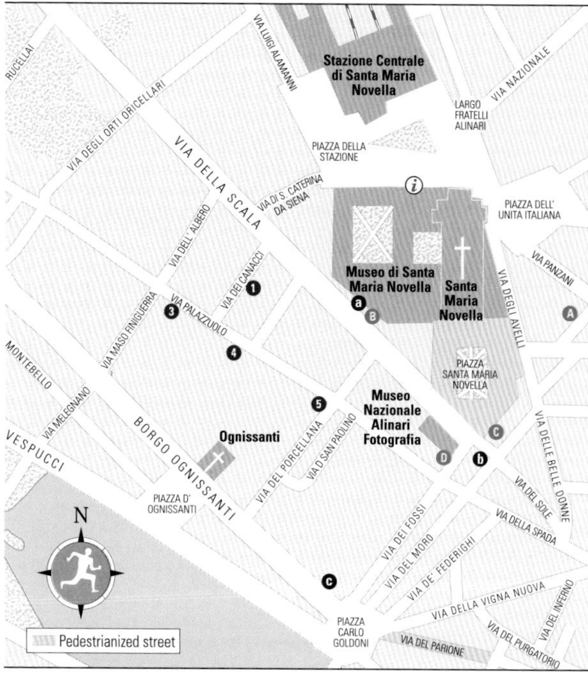

known Orcagna (Andrea di Cione), who painted the chapel's magnificent high altarpiece, *Christ Presenting the Keys to St Peter and the Book of Wisdom to Thomas Aquinas* (1357). Behind the altar, the central fresco depicts the *Last Judgement*, with Dante featured as one of the saved (in white, third from the left, second row from the top). So, too, are Tommaso Strozzi and his wife, shown being led by St Michael into paradise, with an angel helping the righteous up through a trapdoor; on the right of the altar, a devil forks the damned down into hell. The theme of judgement is continued in the fresco of Dante's *Inferno* on the right wall, faced by a thronged *Paradiso*.

The adjacent chapel, the Cappella Gondi, contains a crucifix carved by Brunelleschi, supposedly as a riposte to the uncouthness of Donatello's crucifix in Santa Croce.

The Museo di Santa Maria Novella

Mon–Thurs & Sat 9am–5pm. €2.70.
Further remarkable paintings are to be found in the spacious Romanesque conventual buildings to the left of the church of Santa Maria Novella, home to the Museo di Santa Maria Novella. The first set of cloisters beyond the entrance, the **Chiostro Verde**, dating from 1332–50, features frescoes of *Stories from Genesis* (1425–30) executed by Paolo Uccello

▲ *THE TRIUMPH OF THE CHURCH* FRESCO

and his workshop. The cloister takes its name from the green base *terra verde* pigment they used, and which now gives the paintings a spectral undertone. Best preserved of the frescoes is *The Flood*, a windswept scene rendered almost unintelligible by the telescoping perspective and the double appearance of the ark (before and after the flood), whose flanks form a receding corridor in the centre of the picture.

Off the cloister opens the **Cappellone degli Spagnoli**, or Spanish Chapel, which received its present name after Eleonora di Toledo, wife of Cosimo I, reserved it for the use of her Spanish entourage. Presumably she derived much inspiration from its majestic fresco cycle (1367–69) by Andrea di Firenze, an extended depiction of the triumph of the Catholic Church that was described by Ruskin as "the most noble piece of pictorial philosophy in Italy". Virtually every patch of the walls is covered with frescoes, whose theme is the role of the

The Paterenes and St Peter Martyr

In the twelfth century, Florence became the crucible of one of the reforming religious movements that periodically cropped up in medieval Italy. The **Paterenes** were convinced that everything worldly was touched by the Devil. Accordingly they despised the papacy for its claims to temporal power and spurned the adoration of all relics and images. Furthermore, they rejected all forms of prayer and all contracts – including marriage vows – and were staunch pacifists.

Inevitably their campaign against the financial and moral corruption of the Catholic Church brought them into conflict with Rome; the displeasure of the Vatican eventually found its means of expression in the equally zealous but decidedly non-pacific figure of the Dominican known as **St Peter Martyr**. Operating from the monastery of Santa Maria Novella, this papal inquisitor headed a couple of anti-Paterene fraternities, the Crocesegnati and the Compagnia della Fede, which were in effect his private army. In 1244 he led them into battle across the Piazza Santa Maria Novella, where they proceeded to massacre hundreds of the theological enemy. The epicentre of the carnage is marked by the Croce del Trebbio in Via delle Belle Donne, off the eastern side of the piazza.

After this, the Dominicans turned to less militant work, founding the charitable organization called the Misericordia, which is still in existence today. In 1252 Peter was knifed to death by a pair of assassins in the pay of a couple of Venetians whose property he'd confiscated, which is why he's usually depicted with a blade embedded in his skull. The official version, however, identifies the assassins as Paterene heretics, and relates that the dying man managed to write out the Credo with his own blood before expiring – an incident depicted in the frescoes in Santa Maria Novella's Cappellone degli Spagnoli. Within the year he'd been made a saint.

Dominicans in the battle against heresy and in the salvation of Christian souls. Most spectacular is the right wall, depicting *The Triumph of the Church*. The Dominicans are of course prominent among the ranks of figures representing religious orders: note St Dominic, the order's founder, unleashing the "hounds of the lord", or *Domini Canes*, a pun on the Dominicans' name. Heretics, the dogs' victims, are shown as wolves.

The contemporaneous decoration of the Chiostrino dei Morti, the oldest part of the complex, has not aged so robustly; it was closed for restoration at the time of writing. The Chiostro Grande, to the west, is also out of bounds, but for the more unusual reason that it is a practice parade ground for aspiring carabinieri, Italy's semi-military police force.

Museo Nazionale Alinari Fotografia

Mon, Tues, Thurs, Fri & Sun 9.30am–7.30pm, Sat 9.30am–11.30pm. €9.

The colonnaded building facing Santa Maria Novella across the piazza was formerly a hospital, which was founded back in the thirteenth century and rebuilt in the second half of the fifteenth, probably to a design by Michelozzo. Soon after its completion, Andrea della Robbia added the attractive terracotta medallions to the loggia. In the 1780s it became a crafts school for poor unmarried women, a function it retained until the twentieth century, when it was converted into a school for children. Now, having been handsomely restored, it's home to the Museo Nazionale Alinari Fotografia, which hosts top-quality photography exhibitions as well as housing a superb museum that draws on the colossal Alinari archive to cover the history of the art and its technology, from 1840s' daguerreotypes to the present.

Ognissanti

Daily 7.30am–12.30pm & 3.30–7.30pm.

In medieval times, one of the main areas of cloth production – the mainstay of the Florentine economy – was in the western part of the city. Ognissanti, or All Saints, the main church of this quarter, stands on a piazza that might be taken as a symbol of the state of the present-day Florentine economy, dominated as it is by the five-star *Grand* and *Excelsior* hotels.

Founded in 1256 by the Umiliati, a Benedictine order from Lombardy whose speciality was the weaving of woollen cloth, the church is notable for its paintings by **Ghirlandaio** and **Botticelli**. The young face squeezed between the Madonna and the dark-cloaked man in Ghirlandaio's *Madonna della Misericordia* (1473), the upper of two works over the second

▲ BOTTICELLI'S *ST AUGUSTINE*, OGNISSANTI

altar on the right, is said to be that of Amerigo Vespucci, an agent for the Medici in Seville, whose two voyages in 1499 and 1501 would lend his name to a continent. The altar was paid for by the Vespucci, a family of silk merchants from the surrounding district, which is why other members of the clan appear beneath the Madonna's cloak. Botticelli is buried in the church, beneath a round tomb slab in the south transept, and his fresco of *St Augustine's Vision of St Jerome* (1480) hangs on the same wall as the Madonna. Facing it is Ghirlandaio's more earthbound *St Jerome*, also painted in 1480. In the same year, Ghirlandaio painted the placid *Last Supper* that covers one wall of the **refectory** (Mon, Tues & Sat 9am–noon; free), reached through the cloister to the left of the church, entered at no. 42.

Shops

BM

Borgo Ognissanti 4r ⓣ055.294.575. Mon–Sat 9.30am–7.30pm; April–Dec also Sun 10.30am–1pm & 3.30–7pm. English-language bookshop with a wide selection of guidebooks and general titles, with particular emphasis on Italian literature in translation, as well as books on Italian art, cookery and travel in Italy.

▼ CELLERINI

Cellerini

Via del Sole 37r ⓣ055.282.533. Summer Mon–Fri 9am–1pm & 3–7pm, Sat 9am–1pm; winter Mon 3–7pm, Tues–Sat 9am–1pm & 3–7pm. Bags, bags and more bags. Everything here is made on the premises under the supervision of the firm's founders, the city's premier exponents of the craft; bags don't come more elegant, durable – or costly.

Farmacia Santa Maria Novella

Via della Scala 16 ⓣ055.216.276. Mon–Sat 9.30am–7.30pm; Sept–June also Sun 10.30am–6.30pm. Occupying the pharmacy of the Santa Maria Novella monastery, this sixteenth-century shop was founded by Dominican monks as an outlet for their potions, ointments and herbal remedies. Many of these are still available, including distillations of flowers and herbs, together with face-creams, shampoos and other more esoteric products. The shop's as famous for its wonderful interior as for its products, which are sold worldwide.

Café

Bar Curtatone

Borgo Ognissanti 167r ⓣ055.210.772. Mon, Wed–Fri & Sun 7am–1am, Sat 7am–2am; closed Aug. Despite the name, this slick establishment is more a café than a bar; a good place to recharge over an espresso and a slab of cake after exploring this district of Florence.

Restaurants

Il Contadino

Via Palazzuolo 71r ⓣ055.238.2673. Mon–Sat noon–3pm & 7pm–midnight. No-nonsense *trattoria* with stark black-and-white interior. Very popular with backpackers for its basic but good meals at fixed prices – around €10.

Osteria dei Cento Poveri

Via Palazzuolo 31r ⓣ055.218.846. May–Sept Tues–Sat 7pm–midnight, Sun 12.30am–2.30pm; Oct–April also open for lunch Tues–Sat. A small and popular restaurant (you won't be the only tourist here), offering more fish than is customary with meat-oriented Tuscan menus. The lobster gnocchi is an interesting novelty, and there's always a fish of the day. Fairly expensive, with main courses at around €20.

Club

Space Electronic

Via Palazzuolo 37 ⓣ055.293.082. Mon–Fri & Sun 10pm–2.30am, Sat 10pm–3am; winter closed Mon. You'll find all the disco clichés of a big Continental club here – glass dance floors and mirrored walls – and one or two less familiar features, such as the piranha tank in the downstairs bar, near the karaoke area. Cooler-than-thou clubbers might be sniffy about its popularity with youthful tourist coach parties and local lads on the pull, but it's fine if all you want to do is dance, and the music can be surprisingly good. Admission is around €15 which includes one free drink.

▲ OSTERIA DEI CENTO POVERI

Live music

Eskimo

Via dei Canacci 12r (no phone). Daily 6pm–4am; closed June–Sept. A small, well-established club close to Santa Maria Novella with live music every night. Its long-standing status as the prime lefty student bar is reflected in the music, which tends to be Italian solo singers or trios. The atmosphere is welcoming and you may catch the odd theatre and other cultural event. Members only, but you can get annual membership on the door, for around €7.

Theatre & classical music

Teatro Comunale

Corso Italia 16 ⓣ055.213.535. Florence's main municipal theatre, which hosts many of the city's major classical music, dance and theatre events. It has its own orchestra, chorus and dance company, attracting top-name international guest performers. The main season (concerts, opera and ballet) runs Jan–April and Sept–Dec, with concerts usually held on Friday, Saturday and Sunday evenings.

The San Lorenzo district

The San Lorenzo district is the city's main market area, with scores of clothing and accessories stalls encircling a vast and wonderful food hall. Racks of T-shirts, leather jackets and belts fill the road beside the church of San Lorenzo, a building of major importance that's often overlooked in the rush to the Duomo, Accademia and Uffizi. Attached to the church is another of the city's major draws, the Cappelle Medicee (Medici chapels). While various of the Medici's most important members are buried in the main part of San Lorenzo, dozens of lesser lights are interred in these chapels, with two of them being celebrated by some of Michelangelo's finest funerary sculpture. The Medici also account for the area's other major sight, the Palazzo Medici-Riccardi, with its exquisite fresco-covered chapel.

San Lorenzo

Mon–Sat 10am–5.30pm; March–Oct also Sun 1.30–5.30pm. €2.50.

Founded in 393, San Lorenzo has a claim to be the oldest church in Florence. For some three hundred years it was the city's cathedral, before renouncing its title to Santa Reparata, the precursor of the Duomo. By 1060 a sizeable Romanesque church had been built on the site, a building which in time became the Medicis' parish church. In 1419 Giovanni di Bicci de' Medici, founder of the Medici fortune, offered to finance a new church. **Brunelleschi** was commissioned to begin the project, but construction was hampered by financial problems, political upheavals and Brunelleschi's simultaneous work on the cathedral dome. Giovanni's son, Cosimo de' Medici, eventually saved the day, but his largesse was still not sufficient to provide the church with a facade. No less a figure than **Michelangelo** laboured to remedy the omission, one of many to devote time to a scheme to provide a suitable frontage. None of the efforts

▼ SAN LORENZO

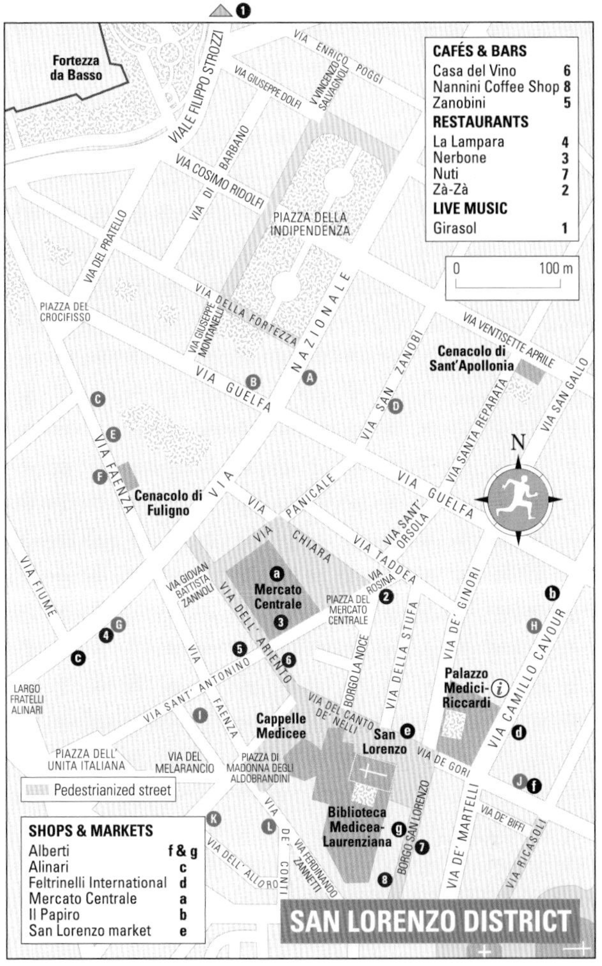

ACCOMMODATION					
Belletini	L	Locanda dei Poeti	B	Soggiorno Pezzati	D
Casci	H	Nella & Giovanna	F	Suore Oblate dello Spirito Santo (hostel)	G
Concordia	I	Ostello Archi Rossi (hostel)	C	Via Faenza 56	E
Kursaal Ausonia	A	Residenza Castiglioni	K		
		Residenza dei Pucci	J		

was to any avail: to this day the exterior's bare brick has never been clad.

What strikes you on stepping **inside the church** is the cool rationality of Brunelleschi's design, an instantly calming contrast to the hubbub outside. The first work of art to catch your attention, in the second chapel on the right, is Rosso Fiorentino's *Marriage of the Virgin* (1523), with its uniquely golden-haired and youthful

Michelangelo

One of the titanic figures of the Italian Renaissance, Michelangelo Buonarroti (1475–1564) was born in Caprese in eastern Tuscany. His family soon moved to Florence, where he became a pupil of Ghirlandaio, making his first stone reliefs for Lorenzo de' Medici. After the Medici were expelled from the city the young Michelangelo went to Rome in 1496. There, he secured a reputation as the most skilled sculptor of his day with the *Bacchus* (now in the Bargello) and the *Pietà* for St Peter's.

After his return to Florence in 1501, Michelangelo carved the *David* and the *St Matthew* (both in the Accademia). He was also employed to paint a fresco of the *Battle of Cascina* in the Palazzo Vecchio. Only the cartoon was finished, but this became the single most influential work of art in the city, its twisting nudes a recurrent motif in later Mannerist art. Work was suspended in 1505 when Michelangelo was called to Rome by Pope Julius II to create his tomb; the *Slaves* in the Accademia were intended for this grandiose project which, like many of Michelangelo's schemes, was never finished.

In 1508 Michelangelo began his other superhuman project, the decoration of the Sistine chapel ceiling in Rome. Back in Florence, he started work on the San Lorenzo complex in 1516, staying on in the city to supervise its defences when it was besieged by the Medici and Charles V in 1530. Four years later he left Florence for good, and spent his last thirty years in Rome, the period that produced the *Last Judgement* in the Sistine chapel. Florence has one work from this final phase of Michelangelo's long career, the *Pietà* he intended for his own tomb (now in the Museo dell'Opera del Duomo).

Joseph. There's another arresting painting at the top of the left aisle – Bronzino's enormous fresco of *The Martyrdom of St Lawrence* (1569) – but it seems a shallow piece of work alongside the nearby bronze pulpits by Donatello. Clad with reliefs depicting scenes preceding and following the Crucifixion, these are the artist's last works (begun c.1460), and were completed by his pupils as increasing paralysis limited their master's ability to model in wax. Jagged and discomforting, charged with more energy than the space can contain, these panels are more like virtuoso sketches in bronze than conventional reliefs. Donatello is buried in the nave of the church, next to his patron, Cosimo de' Medici, and commemorated by a memorial on the right wall of the chapel in the north transept, close to Filippo Lippi's 1440 altarpiece of the *Annunciation*. Cosimo's own tomb, in the centre of the church, bears the inscription "Pater Patriae" (Father of the Fatherland) – a title once borne by Roman emperors.

▼ ONE OF THE DONATELLO PULPITS, SAN LORENZO

Four other leading Medici lie buried in the **Sagrestia Vecchia**, an architectural masterpiece that is far more than simply a Medici mausoleum. It was one of Brunelleschi's earliest projects (1421–26), and the only one completed in his lifetime. The design – a cube and hemispherical dome – could hardly be more simple and yet more perfect. The space was commissioned by Giovanni Bicci de' Medici as a private chapel; on his death, Giovanni was buried beneath the massive marble slab at the centre of the chapel, with his wife, Piccarda. Another tomb, on the left as you enter, is the resting place of Giovanni's grandsons, Giovanni and Piero de' Medici.

More arresting than either of the tombs, however, is the chapel's ornamentation, which is largely the work of Donatello, carried out between 1434 and 1443. He created both the cherub-filled frieze and the eight extraordinary tondi above it, depicting the four Evangelists and a quartet of scenes from the life of St John. Donatello was also responsible for the two bronze doors, showing pairs of disputatious martyrs (the left door), and the Apostles and Fathers of the Church (the right). Lastly, the stellar fresco on the dome inevitably draws the eye: the painted stars might be intended to show the state of the heavens on July 16, 1416, the birthday of Piero de' Medici, or on July 6, 1439, the date on which the union of the Eastern and Western churches was celebrated at the Council of Florence.

The Biblioteca Medicea-Laurenziana

Mon–Sat 8.30am–1.30pm. €3.

A gateway to the left of San Lorenzo's facade leads through a pleasant cloister and through a doorway up to the Biblioteca Medicea-Laurenziana. Wishing to create a suitably grandiose home for the family's precious manuscripts, Pope Clement VII – Lorenzo's nephew – asked Michelangelo to design a new library in 1524. The Ricetto,

▲ BIBLIOTECA MEDICEA-LAURENZIANA: THE INTERIOR STAIRCASE

or vestibule, of the building he eventually came up with more than thirty years later is a showpiece of revolutionary Mannerist architecture, delighting in paradoxical display: brackets that support nothing, columns that sink into the walls rather than stand out from them, and a flight of steps so large that it almost fills the room, spilling down like a solidified lava flow.

From this eccentric space, you're sometimes allowed into the tranquil reading room; here, too, almost everything is the work of Michelangelo, even the inlaid desks. Exhibitions in the connecting rooms draw on the 15,000-piece Medici collection, which includes manuscripts as diverse as a fifth-century copy of Virgil – the collection's oldest item – and a treatise on architecture by Leonardo.

The Cappelle Medicee

Tues–Sat 8.15am–5pm, plus 1st, 3rd & 5th Sun of month and 2nd & 4th Mon of month same hours. €6.

Michelangelo's most celebrated contribution to the San Lorenzo complex forms part of the Cappelle Medicee, which are entered from Piazza Madonna degli Aldobrandini, at the back of the church.

After passing through the crypt, where almost fifty lesser Medici are buried, you climb up to the Cappella dei Principi (chapel of the Princes), an oppressively colourful stone-plated hall built as a mausoleum for Cosimo I and the grand dukes who succeeded him. Pass straight through for the Sagrestia Nuova, which was designed by Michelangelo as a tribute to Brunelleschi's Sagrestia Vecchia in the main body of San Lorenzo. Architectural experts go into raptures over the sophistication of the construction, notably the empty niches above the doors, which play complex games with the visual vocabulary of classical architecture, but the lay person will be drawn to the three fabulous **Medici tombs** (1520–34), two wholly and one partly by Michelangelo.

The tomb on the left, as you stand with your back to the entrance door, belongs to Lorenzo, Duke of Urbino, the grandson of Lorenzo the Magnificent. Michelangelo depicts him as a man of thought, and his sarcophagus bears figures of *Dawn* and *Dusk*, the times of day whose ambiguities appeal to the contemplative mind. Opposite stands the tomb of Lorenzo de' Medici's youngest son, Giuliano, Duke of Nemours; as a man of action, his character is symbolized by the clear antithesis of *Day* and *Night*. Both men are greatly flattered by Michelangelo's powerfully vivid portraits: in reality Giuliano was an easygoing but feckless individual, while Lorenzo combined ineffectuality with unbearable arrogance. Both

▼ MEDICI CHAPEL BY MICHELANGELO

▲ THE PALAZZO MEDICI-RICCARDI: THE GOZZOLI FRESCOES

died young and unlamented of tuberculosis, combined in Lorenzo's case with syphilis.

The two principal effigies were intended to face the equally grand tombs of Lorenzo de' Medici and his brother Giuliano, two Medici who had genuine claims to fame. The only part of the project completed by Michelangelo is the *Madonna and Child*, the last image of the Madonna he ever sculpted. The figures to either side are Cosmas and Damian, patron saints of doctors (*medici*) and the Medici. Although completed by others, they follow Michelangelo's original design.

The Palazzo Medici-Riccardi

Mon, Tues & Thurs–Sun 9am–7pm. €5. The Palazzo Medici-Riccardi was built for Cosimo de' Medici by Michelozzo between 1444 and 1462, possibly to a plan by Brunelleschi. The palace remained the family home and Medici business headquarters until Cosimo I moved to the Palazzo Vecchio in 1540. In Cosimo de Medici's prime, around fifty members of the Medici clan lived here; Donatello's statue *Judith and Holofernes* (now in the Palazzo Vecchio) adorned the walled garden, while the same artist's *David*, now in the Bargello, stood in the entrance courtyard.

The palace currently houses the offices of the provincial government, but you can visit parts of the building, notably the chapel and its **cycle of frescoes**, which a maximum of fifteen may view at any one time. To avoid the queues, book in advance at the ticket office, at Via Cavour 3, or call Ⓣ055.276.0340.

Painted around 1460, Benozzo Gozzoli's frescoes depict *The Journey of the Magi*, but probably portray the pageant of the Compagnia dei Magi, the most patrician of the city's religious confraternities, whose annual procession took place at Epiphany. Several of the Medici were prominent members, including Piero de' Medici (Piero il Gottoso – the Gouty), who may have commissioned the pictures. It's known that several of the Medici household are featured in the procession, but putting names to these prettified faces is a problem. The man leading the cavalcade on a white horse is almost certainly

▲ MERCATO CENTRALE

Piero. Lorenzo il Magnifico, 11 years old at the time the fresco was painted, is probably the young king in the foreground, riding the grey horse detached from the rest of the procession, while his brother, Giuliano, is most likely the one preceded by the black bowman. The artist himself is in the crowd on the far left, his red beret signed with the words "Opus Benotii" in gold.

Another set of stairs leads from the passageway beside the courtyard up to the **first floor**, where a display case in the lobby of the main gallery contains a *Madonna and Child* (late 1460s) by Filippo Lippi, one of Cosimo de' Medici's more troublesome protégés. Cosimo set up a workshop for him in the Medici palace, from which he often absented himself to go chasing women. On one occasion Cosimo actually locked the artist in the studio, but Filippo escaped down a rope of bed sheets. The ceiling of the grandiloquent **gallery** glows with Luca Giordano's enthusiastic fresco of *The Apotheosis of the Medici* (1683), from which one can only deduce that Giordano had no sense of shame. Accompanying Cosimo III on his flight into the ether is his son, the last male Medici, Gian Gastone, who grew to be a man so inert that he could rarely summon the energy to get out of bed in the morning.

The Mercato Centrale

See opposite for market opening times. The Mercato Centrale, Europe's largest covered food hall, was built in stone, iron and glass by Giuseppe Mengoni, architect of Milan's famous Galleria. Opened in 1874, it received a major overhaul a century later, reopening in 1980 with a new upper floor. Butchers, *alimentari*, tripe-sellers, greengrocers, pasta stalls – they're all gathered under the one roof, and all charging prices lower than you'll readily find elsewhere in the city.

Each day from 8am to 7pm the streets around the Mercato Centrale are thronged with stalls selling bags, belts, shoes, football shirts and leather jackets. The quality isn't the highest, of course, but if you fancy practising your haggling skills, this is the place to do it.

The Cenacolo di Fuligno

Tues, Thurs & Sat 9am–noon. Free. *Cenacoli* (Last Suppers) were something of a Florentine artistic speciality, and there's a beguiling example of the genre – the *Cenacolo di Fuligno* – in the former Franciscan convent in Via Faenza. Once thought to be by Raphael, then reassigned to Raphael's mentor Perugino – the orderliness and tranquility of the scene is typical of Perugino's style, and the Apostles' poses are drawn from a repertoire of gestures which the artist frequently deployed. It's now thought, however, that the fresco was designed by Perugino but painted mostly by a member of his workshop.

The Fortezza da Basso

The Fortezza da Basso was built to intimidate the people of Florence by the vile Alessandro de' Medici, who ordained himself duke of Florence after a ten-month siege by the army of Charles V and Pope Clement VII (possibly Alessandro's father) had forcibly restored the Medici. Within a few years the cruelties of Alessandro had become intolerable; a petition to Charles V spoke of the Fortezza da Basso as "a prison and a slaughterhouse for the unhappy citizens". Charles's response to Alessandro's atrocities was to marry his daughter to the tyrant. In the end, another Medici came to the rescue: in 1537 the distantly related Lorenzaccio de' Medici stabbed the duke to death as he waited for an amorous assignation in Lorenzaccio's house. Subsequently the Fortezza da Basso fell into dereliction. Since 1978 there's been a vast shed in the centre of the complex, used for trade fairs and shows such as the *Pitti Moda* fashion jamborees in January and July.

Shops and markets

Alberti

Borgo San Lorenzo 45–49r ☎055.294.271 & Via de' Pucci 16r ☎055.284.346. June–Sept Mon 3.30–7.30pm, Tues–Sat 9am–7.30pm; Oct–May Mon–Fri 9am–7.30pm, Sat 9am–1pm. This is the city's leading supplier of domestic hi-fi, videos, records and CDs. The Borgo San Lorenzo store is good for opera, classical and jazz, while the Via de' Pucci shop (a couple of blocks to the east) concentrates on contemporary music (dance, rock, etc).

Alinari

Largo Alinari 15 ☎055.239.51. Mon–Fri 9am–1pm & 2–6pm; closed 2wks in mid-Aug. Established in 1852, this is the world's oldest photographic business. Owners of the best archive of vintage photographs in Italy – 400,000 glass plates and 700,000 negatives – they will print any image you choose from their huge catalogue. They also publish books, calendars, posters and cards.

Feltrinelli International

Via Camillo Cavour 12r ☎055.219.524. Mon–Sat 9am–7.30pm. Bright and well staffed, this branch of Feltrinelli has plenty of English and other foreign-language books, as well as posters, cards and magazines. For titles in Italian, the main branch – a couple of minutes' walk west of the Duomo at Via de' Cerretani 30r – is better.

Il Papiro

Via Camillo Cavour 55r ☎055.215.262. Mon–Sat 9am–7.30pm, Sun 10am–6pm. Huge range of marbled paper and stationery-related gifts, with several other outlets around the city, including Via de' Tavolini 13r (near Orsanmichele) and Piazza del Duomo 24r.

Mercato Centrale

Piazza del Mercato Centrale. Mon–Sat 7am–2pm; winter also Sat 4–8pm. Europe's largest indoor food hall is situated at the heart of the stall-filled streets around San Lorenzo. It's great for picnic supplies, but well worth a sightseeing and people-watching visit whether you intend to buy anything or not.

San Lorenzo market

Piazza di San Lorenzo. Daily 9am–7pm. An open-air warehouse of cheap clothing, with fake brands accounting for a large percentage of turnover. San Lorenzo is as well organized as a shopping mall: huge waterproof awnings ensure that the weather can't stop the trading, and some of the stallholders accept credit cards.

Cafés and bars

Casa del Vino

Via dell'Ariento 16r ☎055.215.609. Mon–Fri 9.30am–7pm; Oct–April also Sat 10am–3.30pm; closed Aug. Located a few yards south of the Mercato Centrale, and passed by hordes of tourists daily – yet probably visited by only a handful. Patrons are mostly Florentines, who pitch up for a drink, a chat with owner Gianni Migliorini and an assault on various *panini* and *crostini*, as well as saltless Tuscan bread and salami.

Nannini Coffee Shop

Via Borgo San Lorenzo 7r ☎055.212.680. Daily 7.30am–8pm. The Florentine outpost of Siena's Nannini operation, famed for its superb coffee and tooth-wrecking *panforte*, an extremely dense and delicious cake.

▼ CASA DEL VINO

Zanobini

Via Sant'Antonino 47r ☎055.239.6850. Mon–Sat 8am–2pm & 3.30–8pm. Like the *Casa del Vino*, its rival just around the corner, this is an authentic Florentine place whose feel owes much to the presence of locals and traders from the nearby Mercato Centrale. Offers acceptable snacks, but most people are simply here for a chat over a glass of wine.

Restaurants

La Lampara

Via Nazionale 36r ☎055.215.164. Daily noon–midnight. Don't be put off by the multilingual menus: the food is very good, the prices moderate (you'll pay around €30 a head) and the waiters attentive. It's bigger than it appears from the street, but it's packed with locals at lunchtime and evening, so try to book a table.

Nerbone

Mercato Centrale. Mon–Sat 7am–2pm. This excellent *tavola calda* serves meatballs, pasta, stews, soups, salads and sandwiches – perfect for a hearty sit-down lunchtime snack, and you'll pay less than €10.

Nuti

Borgo San Lorenzo 39r ☎055.210.410. Summer daily 11.30am–1am; winter closed Sun. This massive place, arranged on both sides of the street, claims to be the oldest pizzeria in town; the menu isn't limited to pizzas, though, and prices are reasonable.

▲ NUTI

Zà-Zà

Piazza del Mercato Centrale 26r ☎055.215.411. Mon–Sat 11am–11pm; closed Aug. In business for thirty years, and perhaps the best of several *trattorie* close to the Mercato Centrale. In recent years it has raised its profile to the extent that booking is virtually obligatory in summer. The interior is dark, stone-walled and brick-arched, with a handful of tables – though in summer there are more tables on an outside terrace. There's usually a set-price menu for around €15, which offers a choice of three or four pastas and main courses; otherwise you'll pay around €30 per head.

Live music

Girasol

Via del Romito 1 ☎055.474.948. Tues–Sun 8pm–3am. Florence's liveliest Latin bar, located on a minor road due north of the Fortezza da Basso, is hugely popular. Rather than relying on salsa classes, cocktails and the usual vinyl suspects – although it does all these – the place draws in some surprisingly good live acts, with different countries' sounds each day of the week, from Brazilian bossa nova to Cuban son.

The San Marco and Annunziata districts

Halfway along busy Via Camillo Cavour, one of Florence's major north–south arteries, lies Piazza San Marco, home of the Museo di San Marco, a museum devoted chiefly to the paintings of Fra' Angelico. A couple of minutes from here stands the Accademia, famous above all for Michelangelo's *David*. A similar distance away is the graceful Piazza Santissima Annunziata, site of Brunelleschi's Spedale degli Innocenti and the superb church of Santissima Annunziata. East of Piazza Santissima Annunziata lie the Museo Archeologico and the church of Santa Maria Maddalena dei Pazzi, with its fine Perugino fresco.

The Accademia

Tues–Sun 8.15am–6.50pm. €6.50 – more during special exhibitions. The Galleria dell'Accademia has an extensive collection of paintings, but what draws the crowds is the sculpture of **Michelangelo**, in particular the *David*. So great is the public appetite for this one work in particular that you'd be well advised to book tickets in advance (see p.179).

Commissioned by the Opera del Duomo in 1501, the **David** was conceived to invoke parallels with Florence's recent liberation from Savonarola and the Medici. It's an incomparable show of technical bravura, all the more impressive given the difficulties posed by the marble from which it was carved. The four-metre block of stone – thin, shallow and riddled with cracks – had been quarried from Carrara forty years earlier. Several artists had already attempted to work with it, notably Leonardo da Vinci. Michelangelo succeeded where others had failed, completing the work in 1504 when he was still just 29. Displayed for almost four hundred years in the Piazza della Signoria, the *David* today occupies a specially built alcove, protected by a glass barrier that was built in 1991, after one of its toes was vandalized with a hammer. In 2004 he was given a thorough cleaning for the first time in decades, restoring the gangly youth to something like his original brilliance.

▼ QUEUE OUTSIDE THE ACCADEMIA

Michelangelo once described the process of carving as being

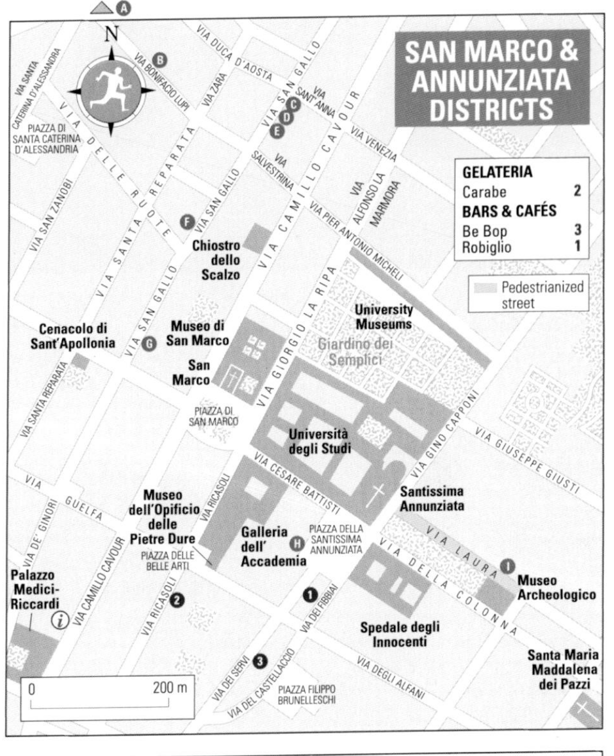

ACCOMMODATION

Accademia House	F	Loggiato dei Serviti	H	Residenza Johanna Due	A
Antica Dimora Firenze	E	Morandi alla Crocetta	I	Residenza Johanna Uno	B
Antica Dimora Johlea	C	Orto de' Medici	G	Residenza Johlea	D

the liberation of the form from within the stone, a notion that seems to be embodied by the unfinished **Slaves** (or Prisoners). His procedure, clearly demonstrated here, was to cut the figure as if it were a deep relief, and then to free the three-dimensional figure; often his assistants would perform the initial operation, so it's possible that Michelangelo's own chisel never actually touched these stones. Probably carved in the late 1520s, the statues were originally destined for the tomb of Julius II, a project that was eventually abandoned; four of the original six statues came to the Accademia in 1909, while two others found their way to the Louvre.

Close by is another unfinished work, *St Matthew* (1505–6), started soon after completion of the *David* as a commission from the Opera del Duomo; they actually requested a full series of the Apostles from Michelangelo, but this is the only one he ever began. As for the Accademia's pictures, they are generally unexciting, but seek out Pontormo's *Venus and Cupid*

▲ *DAVID* INSIDE THE ACCADEMIA

(1532), painted to a cartoon by Michelangelo, and a *Madonna of the Sea* (1470) attributed to Botticelli.

The Museo dell'Opificio delle Pietre Dure

Mon–Sat 8.15am–2pm (Thurs open till 7pm). €2.

Occupying a corner of the Accademia building, the Opificio delle Pietre Dure was founded in 1588 to train craftsmen in the distinctively Florentine art of creating pictures or patterns with highly polished inlaid semi-precious stones. The museum clearly elucidates the highly skilled processes involved in the creation of *pietre dure* work, and has some remarkable examples of the genre. If you want to see some more spectacular (and rather gross) specimens, you should visit the Cappelle Medicee or the Palazzo Pitti's Museo degli Argenti. While local workshops still maintain the traditions of this specialized art-form, the Opificio itself has evolved into one of the world's leading centres for the restoration of stonework.

▼ THE CLOISTER AT THE MUSEO DI SAN MARCO

The Museo di San Marco

Tues–Fri 8.15am–1.50pm, Sat 8.15am–6.50pm, plus 1st, 3rd & 5th Mon of month 8.15am–1.50pm, and 2nd & 4th Sun of month 8.15am–7pm. €4. Much of the north side of Piazza San Marco is taken up by the Dominican convent of San Marco, now the home of the Museo di San Marco. The Dominicans acquired the site in 1436, and the complex promptly became the recipient of Cosimo de' Medici's most lavish patronage. Ironically, the convent became the centre of resistance to the Medici later in the century: Girolamo Savonarola, leader of the government of Florence after the expulsion of the Medici in 1494, was the prior of San Marco (see box, p.116).

During the Medici-funded rebuilding, the convent was decorated by one of its friars and a future prior, Fra' Angelico, a Tuscan painter in whom a medieval simplicity of faith was uniquely allied to a Renaissance sophistication of manner. Twenty or so paintings by the artist are gathered in the ground-floor **Ospizio dei Pellegrini**, or Pilgrims' Hospice, including several of Angelico's most famous creations. Here you'll see a wonderful *Deposition* that originally hung in the church of Santa Trìnita, the *Madonna dei Linaiuoli* (1433), which was Angelico's first major public painting, and the so-called *Pala di San Marco* (1440), a painting that has been badly damaged by the passage of time and a disastrous restoration, but demonstrates Fra' Angelico's familiarity with the principle of a central vanishing point, as expounded in Alberti's *Della Pittura* (*On Painting*), published in Italian just two years before the picture was executed.

Elsewhere on ground level you'll find Fra' Bartolomeo's portrait of Savonarola, his unfinished *Pala della Signoria*, and – in the **Sala Capitolare**, or Chapter House – a powerful fresco of the *Crucifixion*, painted by Angelico and assistants. Before going upstairs, make sure you also see the **Refettorio Piccolo**, or Small Refectory, which has a lustrous *Last Supper* (1480) by Ghirlandaio.

At the top of the stairs you're confronted with one of the most sublime paintings in Italy: for the drama of its setting and the lucidity of its composition, nothing in San Marco matches

Savonarola

Girolamo Savonarola was born in 1452, the son of the physician to the Ferrara court. At the age of 23 he absconded to a Dominican monastery in Bologna, and within a few years the Dominicans had dispatched him to preach all over northern Italy. In 1489 he settled in the monastery of San Marco, where the intensity of his manner and his message attracted a committed following. Following the death of Lorenzo il Magnifico he became positively apocalyptic, telling the congregation: "Wait no longer, for there may be no more time for repentance."

When Charles VIII of France marched into Italy in September 1494 to press his claim to the throne of Naples, Savonarola presented him as the instrument of God's vengeance. The Medici soon fled, the French army and their king passed peacefully through Florence, and the political vacuum in Florence was filled by the declaration of a republican constitution which in effect left Savonarola as ruler of the city. Continual decrees were issued from San Marco: profane carnivals were to be outlawed, fasting was to be observed more frequently, luxuries of all types were condemned, a process that reached a crescendo with a colossal "Bonfire of the Vanities" on the Piazza della Signoria.

Meanwhile, Charles VIII was installed in Naples and a formidable alliance was assembled to overthrow him: the papacy, Milan, Venice, Ferdinand of Aragon and the emperor Maximilian. Savonarola declined to assist, and refused to attend when summoned to the Vatican to explain himself, thus setting off a chain of events that led to his excommunication in June 1497. When Pope Alexander threatened the whole city with excommunication if Savonarola weren't handed over, the people of Florence began to desert him. On Palm Sunday 1498 a siege of the monastery of San Marco ended with Savonarola's arrest.

Accused of heresy, he was tortured to the point of death, then burned at the stake in front of the Palazzo Vecchio, with two of his supporters.

▲ MUSEO DI SAN MARCO: FRA' ANGELICO'S *ANNUNCIATION*

Angelico's *Annunciation*. Angelico and his assistants also painted the simple and piously restrained pictures in each of the 44 **dormitory cells** on this floor, into which the friars would withdraw for solitary contemplation and sleep. Several of the scenes include one or both of a pair of monastic onlookers, serving as intermediaries between the occupant of the cell and the personages in the pictures: the one with the star above his head is St Dominic; the one with the split skull is St Peter Martyr.

The rooms once occupied by Savonarola now contain various relics questionably authenticated as worn by the man himself; the more luxuriously appointed cells 29 and 30 were the personal domain of Cosimo de' Medici – the fresco of the *Adoration of the Magi* may have been suggested by Cosimo himself, who liked to think of himself as a latter-day wise man and gift-giving king.

On the way to these VIP cells you'll pass the entrance to **Michelozzo's Library**, built in 1441–44 to a design that exudes an atmosphere of calm study. Cosimo's agents roamed as far as the Near East garnering precious manuscripts and books for him; in turn, Cosimo handed all the religious items over to the monastery, stipulating that they should be accessible to all, making this Europe's first public library. As the plaque by the doorway tells you, it was on this spot that Savonarola was arrested in 1498.

San Marco church

Mon–Sat 9.30am–noon & 4–5.30pm. The church of San Marco is worth a quick visit for two works on the second and third altars on the right: a *Madonna and Saints* painted in 1509 by Fra' Bartolomeo, and an eighth-century mosaic of *The Madonna in Prayer* (surrounded by later additions), brought here from Rome. This had to be cut in half in transit, and you can still see the break across the Virgin's midriff.

The Cenacolo di Sant'Apollonia

Daily 8.15am–1.50pm; closed 1st, 3rd & 5th Sun of month, and 2nd & 4th Mon. Free. Most of the former Benedictine convent of Sant'Apollonia has now been turned into apartments, but the lower part of an entire wall of the former refectory is taken up with Andrea del Castagno's disturbing *Last Supper* (c. 1447). Blood-red is the dominant tone, and the most commanding figure is the diabolic, black-bearded Judas, who sits on the near side of the table. The seething patterns in the marbled panels behind the Apostles seem to mimic the turmoil in the mind of each as he hears Christ's announcement of the betrayal. Castagno also painted the *Crucifixion*,

Deposition and *Resurrection* above the illusionistic space in which the Last Supper takes place, and the *Crucifixion* and *Pietà* on the adjacent walls.

The Chiostro dello Scalzo

Mon, Thurs & Sat 8.15am–1.50pm. Free. Lo Scalzo was the home of the Brotherhood of St John, whose vows of poverty entailed walking around barefoot (*scalzo*). The order was suppressed in 1785 and their monastery sold off, except for the cloister, which was the training ground for Andrea del Sarto; his monochrome paintings of the *Cardinal Virtues* and *Scenes from the Life of the Baptist* occupied him off and on for a decade from 1511. A couple of the sixteen scenes – *John in the Wilderness* and *John meeting Christ* – were executed by his pupil Franciabigio in 1518, when del Sarto was away in Paris.

The Giardino dei Semplici

April–Oct Mon & Fri 9am–noon & 2.30–5pm, Wed–Fri 9am–noon. €3. The Giardino dei Semplici or Orto Botanico, was set up in 1545 for Cosimo I as a medicinal garden, following the examples of Padua and Pisa, and now covers five acres, most of the area being taken up by the original flowerbeds and avenues. It's the nearest equivalent to the Bóboli garden on the north side of the city, but unfortunately it closes at exactly the time you could use it for a midday break.

The university museums

The entrance to the Giardino dei Semplici at Via Micheli 3 also gives access to a number of museums administered by the university. The Museo Botanico is open only to scholars and the Museo di Minerologia e Litologia is too recondite for most tastes, but the **Museo di Geologia e Paleontologia** (Mon, Tues, Thurs, Fri & Sun 9am–1pm, Sat 9am–5pm; €4) is one of Italy's biggest fossil shows, featuring such delights as prehistoric elephant skeletons from the upper Valdarno and a skeleton from Grosseto once touted as the missing link between monkeys and *Homo sapiens*.

Piazza Santissima Annunziata

Nineteenth-century urban renewal schemes left many of Florence's squares rather grim places, which makes the pedestrianized Piazza Santissima Annunziata, with its distinctive arcades, all the more attractive a public space. It has a special importance for the city, too. Until the end of the eighteenth century the Florentine year used to begin on March 25, the Festival of the Annunciation – hence the Florentine predilection for paintings of the Annunciation, and the fashionableness of the Annunziata church, which has long been the place for society weddings. The festival is still

▼ THE CHIOSTRO DELLO SCALZO

▲ PIAZZA SANTISSIMA ANNUNZIATA: EQUESTRIAN STATUE OF FERDINANDO I

marked by a huge fair in the piazza and the streets leading off it; later in the year, on the first weekend in September, the square is used for Tuscany's largest crafts fair.

Brunelleschi began the piazza in the 1420s, with additions made later by Ammannati and Antonio da Sangallo. The equestrian statue of Grand Duke Ferdinando I (1608) at its centre was Giambologna's final work, and was cast by his pupil Pietro Tacca, who was also the creator of the bizarre fountains.

Santissima Annunziata

Daily 7.30am–12.30pm & 4–6.30pm.

Santissima Annunziata is the mother church of the **Servites**, or Servi di Maria (Servants of Mary), a religious order founded by Filippo Benizzi and six Florentine aristocrats in 1234. From humble beginnings, the order blossomed after 1252, when a painting of the Virgin begun by one of the monks but abandoned in despair because of his inability to create a truly beautiful image was supposedly completed by an angel while he slept. So many people came to venerate the image that by 1444 a new church, financed by the Medici, was commissioned from Michelozzo (who happened to be the brother of the Servites' head prior). The project, completed by Leon Battista Alberti in 1481, involved laying out the present-day Via dei Servi, designed to link Santissima Annunziata and the cathedral, thus uniting the city's two most important churches dedicated to the Madonna.

As the number of pilgrims to the church increased, so it became a custom to leave wax votive offerings (*voti*) in honour of its miraculous Madonna. These became so numerous that in 1447 a special atrium, the **Chiostrino dei Voti**, was built onto the church, and in 1516 a major fresco cycle was commissioned, on the occasion of the canonization of Filippo Benizzi. Three leading artists of the day, Andrea del Sarto, Jacopo Pontormo and Rosso Fiorentino, were involved, together with several lesser painters. Some of the panels are in a poor state – all were removed from the walls and restored after the 1966 flood (see box, p.124) – but their overall effect is superb.

Just inside the church itself, on the left, stands the ornate tabernacle (1448–61) designed by Michelozzo to house the miraculous image of the Madonna. The nearby **Cappella Feroni** features a fresco by Andrea del Castagno of *Christ and St Julian* (1455–56); a more striking fresco by the same artist, the *Holy Trinity and St Jerome* (1454), can be seen in the adjacent chapel. Now restored, both frescoes were obliterated after Vasari spread the rumour that Castagno had poisoned his erstwhile friend, Domenico Veneziano, motivated by envy of the other's skill with oil paint. Castagno was saddled with this crime until the nineteenth century, when an archivist discovered that the alleged murderer in fact predeceased his victim by four years. The church's other notable painting is Andrea del Sarto's intimate *Madonna del Sacco* (1525) in the spacious **Chiostro dei Morti**, over the door that opens from the north transept (you may need to find the sacristan to open it); the picture – more formally known as the *Rest during the Flight into Egypt* – takes its curious name from the sack on which St Joseph is leaning.

The Spedale degli Innocenti

Mon–Sat 8.30am–7pm, Sun 8.30am–2pm. €4. Piazza Santissima Annunziata's most elegant building is the Spedale degli Innocenti, or Ospedale. Commissioned in 1419 by the Arte della Seta, the silk-weavers' guild, it opened in 1445 as the first foundlings' hospital in Europe, and is still an orphanage today. It was largely designed by Brunelleschi, and his nine-arched loggia was one of Europe's earliest examples of the new classically influenced style. Andrea della Robbia's blue-backed ceramic tondi of well-swaddled babies advertise the building's function, but their gaiety belies the misery associated with it. Slavery was part of the Florentine economy as late as the fifteenth century, and many of the infants given over to the care of the Innocenti were born to domestic slaves.

The building within centres on two beautiful **cloisters**, Brunelleschi's central Chiostro degli Uomini (Men's Cloister) and the narrow, graceful Chiostro delle Donne (Women's Cloister) to the right. (These can be visited throughout the day, free of charge.) Stairs from the left-hand corner of the former lead up to the museum, a miscellany of mostly minor Florentine Renaissance

▼ SANTISSIMA ANNUNZIATA

▲ THE SPEDALE DEGLI INNOCENTI

art that includes one of Luca della Robbia's most beguiling Madonnas and an *Adoration of the Magi* (1488) by Domenico Ghirlandaio.

The Museo Archeologico

Mon 2–7pm, Tues & Thurs 8.30am–7pm, Wed & Fri–Sun 8.30am–2pm. €4. The special strength of the Museo Archeologico is its Etruscan finds, many of them part of a Medici bequest. On the ground floor there's a comprehensive display of Etruscan funerary figures, but even more arresting than these is the *François Vase*, an Attic *krater* (bowl) from the sixth century BC, discovered in an Etruscan tomb at Chiusi. Pride of place in the first-floor Egyptian collection, where the rooms are handsomely decorated in mock-Egyptian funerary style, goes to a Hittite chariot made of bone and wood and dating from the fourteenth century BC. The rest of this floor and much of the floor above are given over to the Etruscan, Greek and Roman collections, arranged with variable clarity. Of the Roman pieces the outstanding item is the *Idolino*, probably a copy of a fifth-century BC Greek original. Nearby is a massive Hellenistic horse's head, which once adorned the garden of the Palazzo Medici, where it was studied by Donatello and Verrocchio. In the long gallery you'll find the best of the Etruscan pieces: the *Arringatore* (Orator), the only known Etruscan large bronze from the Hellenistic period; and the *Chimera*, a triple-headed monster dating from the fifth century BC.

Gelateria

Carabe

Via Ricasoli 60r. May–Oct daily 10am–midnight; Nov, March & April daily noon–7.30pm; first half of Dec & last half of Jan Tues–Sun noon–7.30pm; closed mid-Dec to mid-Jan. Wonderful Sicilian ice cream made with Sicilian ingredients as only they know how. Also serves a variety of cakes.

Bars and cafés

Be Bop

Via dei Servi 76r ☎055.490.397. Daily 5pm–2am. A nice and rather classy rock, jazz and blues bar with bow-tied bar staff and faux Art Nouveau decor. It's located close to the university district, and often full of students as a result. There's no dance floor as such; this is more a place to sit and chill out to the music.

Robiglio

Via dei Servi 112r ☎055.214.501. Mon–Sat 7.30am–7.30pm. Famed for its pastries, *Robiglio* also specializes in a hot chocolate that's so thick it's barely a liquid.

The Santa Croce and Sant'Ambrogio districts

The vast Franciscan church of Santa Croce is one of the most compelling sights in Florence, and forms the centrepiece of an area which, prior to the 1966 flood, was one of the city's more densely populated districts. When the Arno burst its banks, this low-lying quarter, packed with tenements and small workshops, was virtually wrecked, and many of its residents moved out permanently in the following years. Now, however, the district is enjoying a big revival. The more traditional shops, bars and restaurants that survived the flood have been joined by a growing number of new and often extremely good bars and restaurants, a transformation that's particularly noticeable around the Sant'Ambrogio market. In addition to the great church and its museum, the district's cultural attractions are the Museo Horne, a modest but pleasing collection of art treasures, and the Casa Buonarroti, a less satisfying homage to Michelangelo.

Santa Croce

Mon–Sat 9.30am–5.30pm, Sun 1–5.30pm. €5. The church of Santa Croce is the Franciscans' principal church in Florence – a rival to the Dominicans' Santa Maria Novella – and is said to have been founded by St Francis himself. In truth it was probably begun seventy or so years after Francis's death, in 1294, possibly by the architect of the Duomo, Arnolfo di Cambio. Ironically, it was the city's richest families who funded the construction of the church, to atone for the sin of usury on which their fortunes were based. Plutocrats such as the Bardi, Peruzzi and Baroncelli sponsored the extraordinary **fresco cycles** that were lavished on the chapels over the years, particularly during the fourteenth century, when artists of the stature of Giotto and the Gaddi family worked here. In further

▼ CAPPELLA PAZZI, SANTA CROCE

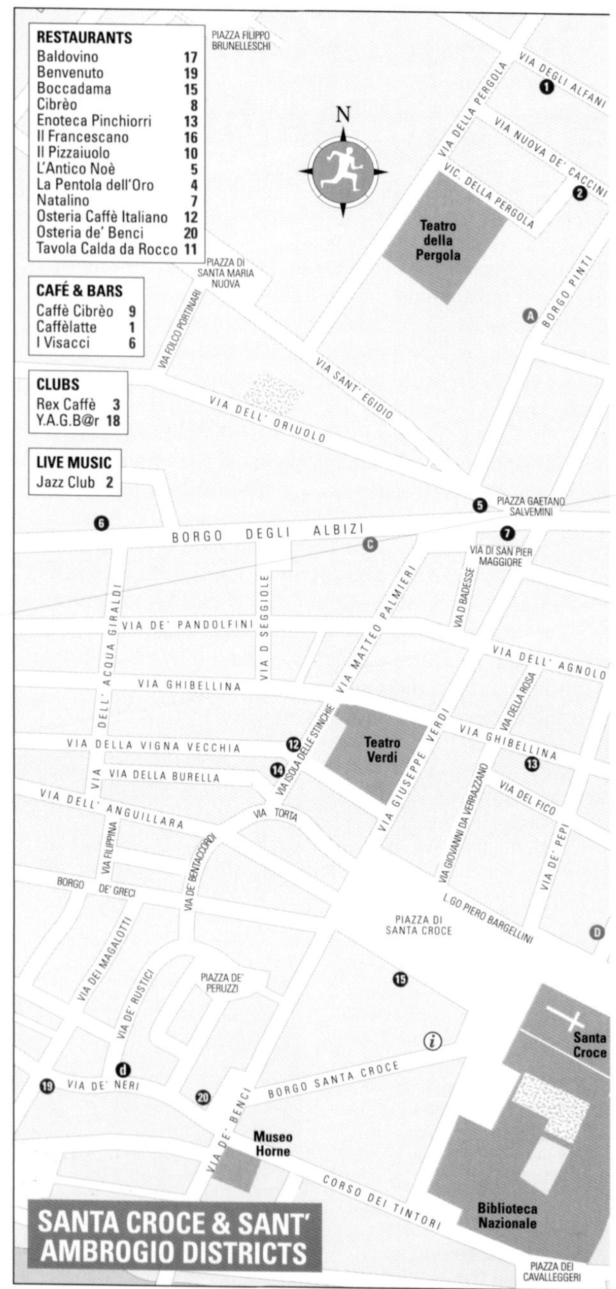
RESTAURANTS
Baldovino 17
Benvenuto 19
Boccadama 15
Cibrèo 8
Enoteca Pinchiorri 13
Il Francescano 16
Il Pizzaiuolo 10
L'Antico Noè 5
La Pentola dell'Oro 4
Natalino 7
Osteria Caffè Italiano 12
Osteria de' Benci 20
Tavola Calda da Rocco 11
CAFÉ & BARS
Caffè Cibrèo 9
Caffèlatte 1
I Visacci 6
CLUBS
Rex Caffè 3
Y.A.G.B@r 18
LIVE MUSIC
Jazz Club 2
N
PIAZZA FILIPPO BRUNELLESCHI
VIA DEGLI ALFANI
VIA DELLA PERGOLA
VIA NUOVA DE' CACCINI
VIC. DELLA PERGOLA
Teatro della Pergola
BORGO PINTI
PIAZZA DI SANTA MARIA NUOVA
VIA FOLCO PORTINARI
VIA SANT' EGIDIO
VIA DELL' ORIUOLO
PIAZZA GAETANO SALVEMINI
BORGO DEGLI ALBIZI
VIA DI SAN PIER MAGGIORE
VIA D BADESSE
VIA MATTEO PALMIERI
VIA DE' PANDOLFINI
VIA D SEGGIOLE
VIA DELL' ACQUA GIRALDI
VIA GHIBELLINA
VIA DELL' AGNOLO
VIA DELLA ROSA
VIA DELLA VIGNA VECCHIA
VIA ISOLA DELLE STINCHIE
Teatro Verdi
VIA GIUSEPPE VERDI
VIA DELLA BURELLA
VIA DEL FICO
VIA GIOVANNI DA VERRAZZANO
VIA DELL' ANGUILLARA
VIA TORTA
VIA FILIPPINA
VIA DE' BENTACCORDI
VIA DE' PEPI
BORGO DE' GRECI
L.GO PIERO BARGELLINI
PIAZZA DI SANTA CROCE
VIA DEI MAGALOTTI
VIA DE' RUSTICI
PIAZZA DE' PERUZZI
Santa Croce
VIA DE' NERI
BORGO SANTA CROCE
VIA DE' BENCI
Museo Horne
CORSO DEI TINTORI
Biblioteca Nazionale
PIAZZA DEI CAVALLEGGERI
SANTA CROCE & SANT' AMBROGIO DISTRICTS

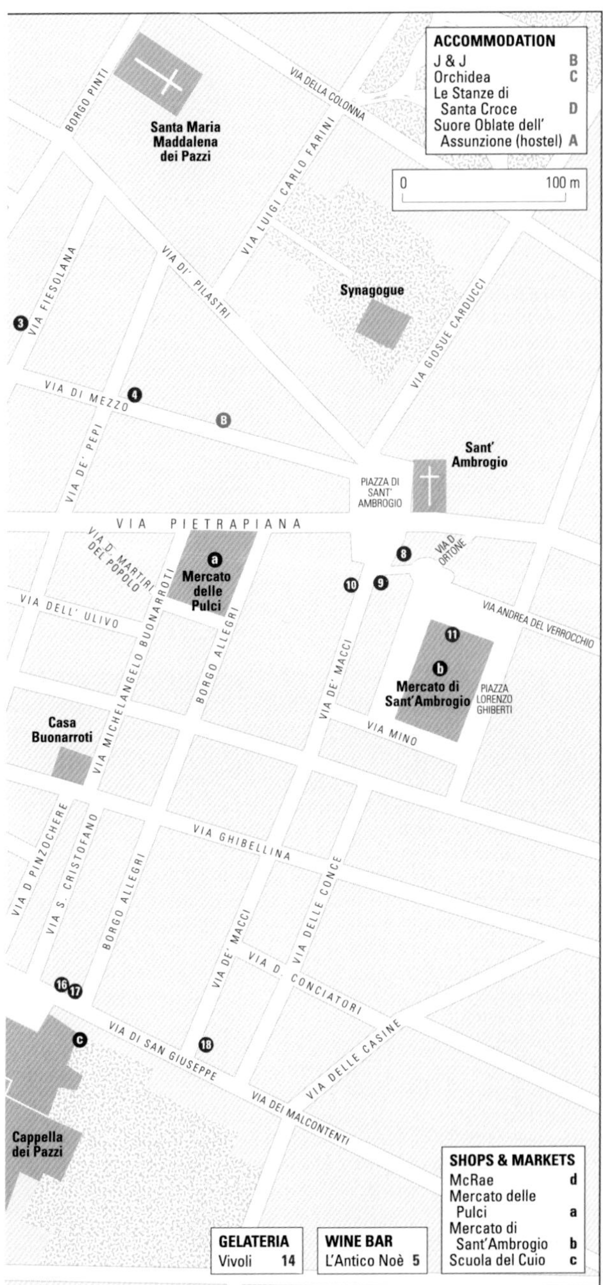
ACCOMMODATION
J & J B
Orchidea C
Le Stanze di Santa Croce D
Suore Oblate dell' Assunzione (hostel) A
0 100 m
Santa Maria Maddalena dei Pazzi
Synagogue
Sant' Ambrogio
PIAZZA DI SANT' AMBROGIO
Mercato delle Pulci
Mercato di Sant'Ambrogio
PIAZZA LORENZO GHIBERTI
Casa Buonarroti
Cappella dei Pazzi
VIA DELLA COLONNA
BORGO PINTI
VIA LUIGI CARLO FARINI
VIA DI' PILASTRI
VIA FIESOLANA
VIA GIOSUE CARDUCCI
VIA DI MEZZO
VIA DE' PEPI
VIA PIETRAPIANA
VIA D. MARTIRI DEL POPOLO
VIA MICHELANGELO BUONARROTI
VIA DELL' ULIVO
BORGO ALLEGRI
VIA DE' MACCI
VIA D ORTONE
VIA ANDREA DEL VERROCCHIO
VIA MINO
VIA GHIBELLINA
VIA D PINZOCHERE
VIA S. CRISTOFANO
VIA DELLE CONCE
VIA D. CONCIATORI
VIA DI SAN GIUSEPPE
VIA DELLE CASINE
VIA DEI MALCONTENTI
SHOPS & MARKETS
McRae d
Mercato delle Pulci a
Mercato di Sant'Ambrogio b
Scuola del Cuio c
GELATERIA
Vivoli 14
WINE BAR
L'Antico Noè 5

contradiction of the Franciscan ideal of humility, Santa Croce has long served as the national pantheon: the walls and nave floor are lined with the monuments to more than 270 illustrious Italians, many of them Tuscan, including Michelangelo, Galileo, Machiavelli, Alberti and Dante (though the last is not buried here).

On your way to the frescoed chapels be sure to take a look at Donatello's gilded stone relief of the *Annunciation*, and – beyond the door – Bernardo Rossellino's much-imitated tomb of Leonardo Bruni, chancellor of the Republic, humanist scholar and author of the first history of the city. The inscription on Bruni's tomb – "After Leonardo departed life, history is in mourning and eloquence is dumb" – was penned by his successor as chancellor, Carlo Marsuppini, who is commemorated by a splendid tomb in the opposite aisle, carved by Desiderio da Settignano. The **Cappella Castellani**, at the end of the south aisle, is strikingly, if patchily, covered in frescoes by Agnolo Gaddi and his pupils, while the adjoining **Cappella Baroncelli** was decorated by Agnolo's father, Taddeo, a long-time assistant to Giotto. Both the **Cappella Peruzzi** and the **Cappella Bardi** – the two chapels on the right of the chancel – are entirely covered with frescoes by Giotto, with some assistance in the latter. Their deterioration was partly caused by Giotto's having painted some of the pictures onto dry plaster, rather than the wet plaster employed in true fresco technique, but the vandalism of later generations

The 1966 flood

It rained continuously in Florence for forty days prior to November 4, 1966. When the water pressure in an upstream reservoir threatened to break the dam, it was decided to open the sluices. The only people to be warned about the rapidly rising level of the river were the jewellers of the Ponte Vecchio, whose private nightwatchman phoned them in the small hours of the morning with news that the bridge was starting to shake. Police watching the shopkeepers clearing their displays were asked why they weren't spreading the alarm. They replied, "We have received no orders." When the banks of the Arno finally broke down, a flash flood dumped around 500,000 tonnes of water and mud on the streets, moving with such speed that people were drowned in the underpass of Santa Maria Novella train station. In all, 35 Florentines were killed, over 15,000 cars wrecked and thousands of works of art damaged, many of them ruined by heating oil flushed out of basements.

Within hours an impromptu army of rescue workers had been formed to haul pictures out of slime-filled churches and gather fragments of paint in plastic bags. Donations came in from all over the world, but the task was so immense that the restoration of many pieces is still unaccomplished. In total around two-thirds of the 3000 paintings damaged in the flood are now on view again, and two massive laboratories – one for paintings and one for stonework – are operating full time in Florence, developing restoration techniques that are often taken up by galleries around the world. Today, all over the city, you can see small marble plaques with a red line showing the level the floodwaters reached on that dreadful day in 1966.

was far more destructive. In the eighteenth century they were covered in whitewash, then they were heavily retouched in the nineteenth; restoration in the 1950s returned them to as close to their original state as was possible.

Scenes from the lives of St John the Evangelist and St John the Baptist cover the Peruzzi chapel, while a better-preserved cycle of the life of St Francis fills the Bardi. Despite the areas of paint destroyed when a tomb was attached to the wall, the *Funeral of St Francis* is still a composition of extraordinary impact, the grief-stricken mourners suggesting an affinity with the lamentation over the body of Christ – one of them even probes the wound in Francis's side, echoing the gesture of Doubting Thomas. On the wall above the chapel's entrance arch is the most powerful scene of all, *St Francis Receiving the Stigmata*, in which the power of Christ's apparition seems to force the chosen one to his knees.

On the other side of the church there's a second **Cappella Bardi**, which houses a wooden crucifix by Donatello, supposedly criticized by Brunelleschi as resembling a "peasant on the Cross". According to Vasari, Brunelleschi went off and created his own crucifix for Santa Maria Novella to show Donatello how it should be done (see p.97). The door in the right aisle leads through into the church's Primo Chiostro (First Cloister), site of Brunelleschi's **Cappella Pazzi**, the epitome of the learned, harmonious spirit of early Renaissance architecture.

▲ SECOND CLOISTER, SANTA CROCE

Geometrically perfect without seeming pedantic, the chapel is exemplary in its proportion and in the way its decorative detail harmonizes with the design. The polychrome lining of the portico's shallow cupola is by Luca della Robbia, as is the garland of fruit which surrounds the Pazzi family crest, and – inside – the twelve blue and white tondi of the Apostles. The four vividly coloured tondi of the Evangelists in the upper roundels were produced in the della Robbia workshop, possibly to designs by Donatello and Brunelleschi.

Flanking the cloister, the **Museo dell'Opera di Santa Croce** houses a sizeable miscellany of works of art, foremost of these being Cimabue's famous *Crucifixion*, very badly damaged in 1966 and now the emblem of the havoc caused by the flood. The farthest part of the Santa Croce complex is the spacious **Inner Cloister**, another project by Brunelleschi, and the most peaceful spot in the centre of Florence.

The Casa Buonarroti

Mon & Wed–Sun 9.30am–2pm. €6.50. The enticing name of the Casa Buonarroti is somewhat misleading. Michelangelo Buonarroti certainly owned three houses here in 1508, and probably lived on the site intermittently between 1516 and 1525, but little trace of the earlier houses remains. Today the house contains a smart but low-key museum, nicely decorated in period style and adorned with beautiful furniture, *objets d'art*, frescoed ceilings and the like, but only a handful of the works of art on display are by Michelangelo. The *Madonna della Scala* (c.1490–92) is Michelangelo's earliest known work, a delicate relief carved when he was no older than 16. The similarly unfinished *Battle of the Centaurs* was created shortly afterwards, when the boy was living in the Medici household. In the adjacent room you'll find the artist's wooden model (1517) for the facade of San Lorenzo, close to the largest of all the sculptural models on display, the torso of a *River God* (1524), a work probably intended for the Medici chapel in San Lorenzo. Other rooms contain small and fragmentary pieces, possibly by the master, possibly copies of works by him.

▼ SANT'AMBROGIO CHURCH

Mercato delle Pulci

See p.128 for market hours. Piazza dei Ciompi is the venue for the Mercato delle Pulci, or Flea Market. Much of the junk maintains the city's reputation for inflated prices, though you can find a few interesting items at modest cost – old postcards, posters and so on. Vasari's Loggia del Pesce (1567) gives the square a touch of style; built for the fishmongers of the Mercato Vecchio in what is now Piazza della Repubblica, it was dismantled when that square was laid out, and rebuilt here in 1951.

Sant'Ambrogio church

Daily 8am–12.30pm & 4–7pm. Sant'Ambrogio is one of Florence's oldest churches, having been documented in 988, though rebuilding over the centuries means that it is now somewhat bland in appearance. Inside you'll find a *Madonna Enthroned with SS John the Baptist and Bartholomew* (second altar on the right), attributed to Orcagna (or the school of Orcagna), and a recently restored triptych in the chapel to the right of the main altar, attributed to Lorenzo di Bicci or Bicci di Lorenzo. More compelling than either painting, though, is the Cappella del Miracolo, the chapel to the left of the high altar, and its tabernacle (1481–83) by Mino da Fiesole, an accomplished sculptor whose name crops up time and again across Tuscany. Cosimo Rosselli's narrative fresco (1486) alongside Mino's tabernacle alludes to the miracle that gave the Cappella del Miracolo its name: it describes the discovery of a chalice full of blood which the Florentines believed later saved them from, among other things, a plague outbreak of 1340. The painting is full of portraits of Rosselli's contemporaries, making it another of Florence's vivid pieces of Renaissance social reportage: Rosselli himself is the figure in the black beret at the extreme left of the picture.

The synagogue

A short distance north of Sant'Ambrogio rises Florence's enormous synagogue; the ghetto established in this district by Cosimo I was not demolished until the mid-nineteenth century, which is when the present Moorish-style synagogue was built. It contains a small **museum** that charts the history of Florence's Jewish population (Nov–March Sun–Thurs 10am–3pm, Fri 10am–2pm; April–Oct Sun–Thurs 10am–5/6pm, Fri 10am–2pm; €4).

Santa Maria Maddalena dei Pazzi

The church of Santa Maria Maddalena dei Pazzi is named after a Florentine nun who was famed for her religious visions: when Maria de' Medici went off to marry Henry IV of France, Maria Maddalena transmitted the news that the Virgin expected her to re-admit the Jesuits to France and exterminate the Huguenots, which she duly did. Founded

▲ SANTA MARIA MADDALENA DEI PAZZI

in the thirteenth century but kitted out in Baroque style, the church is not itself much of an attraction, but its **chapterhouse** – reached by a subterranean passageway that's accessed from the top of the right aisle – is decorated with a radiant Perugino fresco of the *Crucifixion* (Mon–Sat 9–11.50am & 5–5.20pm & 6.10–6.50pm, Sun 9–10.45am & 5–6.50pm; €1).

The Museo Horne

Mon–Sat 9am–1pm. €5. The Museo della Fondazione Horne, one of Florence's more obscure museums, was left to the state by the English art historian Herbert Percy Horne (1864–1916), who was instrumental in rescuing Botticelli from neglect with a pioneering biography. The half-dozen or so rooms of paintings, sculptures, pottery, furniture and other domestic objects contain no real masterpieces, but are diverting enough if you've already done the major collections. Look out for a tiny age-bowed panel of *St Julian* by Masaccio, a *Deposition* by Gozzoli (his last documented work), Giotto's *St Stephen* (a fragment from a polyptych) and works by Filippo and Filippino Lippi, Simone Martini and Beccafumi. On the second floor there's a piece of little artistic merit but great historical interest: a copy of part of Leonardo's *Battle of Anghiari*, once frescoed on a wall of the Palazzo Vecchio.

Shops and markets

McRae

Via de' Neri 32r ☎055.238.2456. Daily 9am–7.30pm. Run by a former staff member of Seeber, this bookshop, not far from the Uffizi, has one of the best collections of English-language books in town: guides, cookery books, literature and art all covered.

Mercato delle Pulci

Piazza dei Ciompi. Summer Mon–Sat 10am–1pm & 4–7pm; winter Mon–Sat 9am–1pm & 3–7pm; also open same hours on last Sun of month. A flea market stacked with antiques and bric-a-brac. More serious antique dealers swell the ranks on the last Sunday of each month.

Mercato di Sant'Ambrogio

Piazza Ghiberti. Mon–Sat 7am–2pm. The Sant'Ambrogio market is a smaller, tattier but even more enjoyable version of the San Lorenzo food hall (see p.109). The *tavola calda* here is one of Florence's lunchtime bargains (see p.131).

Scuola del Cuio

Via San Giuseppe 5r ☎055.244.533. Mon–Sat 9.30am–6pm, Sun 10am–6pm. This academy for leather-workers sells bags, jackets, belts and other accessories at prices that compare very favourably with the shops. You won't find any startlingly original designs here, but the quality is very high and the staff are both knowledgeable and helpful.

Gelateria

Vivoli

Via Isola delle Stinche 7r. Tues–Sun 7.30am–1am; closed Aug. Operating from deceptively unprepossessing premises in a side street close to Santa Croce, this has long been rated the best ice-cream-maker in Florence – and some say in all of Italy.

Cafés and bars

Caffè Cibrèo

Via Andrea del Verrocchio 5r ☎055.234.5853. Tues–Sat 8am–1am; closed 2wks in Aug. Possibly the prettiest café in Florence, with a chi-chi clientele to match. Opened in 1989, the wood-panelled interior looks at least two hundred years older. Cakes and desserts are great, and the light meals bear the culinary stamp of the *Cibrèo* restaurant kitchens opposite (see p.129).

Caffèlatte

Via degli Alfani 39r ☎055.247.8878. Mon–Sat 8am–8pm, Sun 10am–6pm. *Caffèlatte* began life in the 1920s, when a milk and coffee supplier opened here. Nowadays, it's expanded its operation to include an organic bakery which produces delicious breads and cakes, served in the one-room café. The speciality drink, as you'd expect, is *caffè latte*, served in huge bowls.

Laid-back music and temporary exhibitions of paintings and photographs enhance the vaguely "alternative" mood.

I Visacci

Borgo degli Albizi 82r ☏055.200.1956. Mon–Sat 10.30am–2.30am, Sun 3–10pm. A bright, stylish and popular small bar, serving *crostini* and a few more substantial dishes. The *Visacci* cappuccino is lusciously good.

Wine bar

L'Antico Noè

Volta di San Piero 6r. Mon–Sat noon–3pm & 7–midnight. A long-established and utterly authentic stand-up wine bar, tucked into an uninviting little alley to the north of Santa Croce, at the end of Borgo Albizi.

Restaurants

Baldovino

Via San Giuseppe 22r ☏055.241.773. Summer daily 11am–3pm & 7pm–1am; winter closed Mon. A superb place, run by an energetic and imaginative Scottish couple. It's renowned above all for its pizzas, made in a wood-fired oven according to Neapolitan principles, but the main menu (which changes monthly) is full of excellent Tuscan and Italian dishes, with mains around €15 and up – although you pay the usual premium for the succulent *bistecca alla Fiorentina*. Portions are generous.

Benvenuto

Via della Mosca 15r ☏055.214.833. Mon–Sat 11am–3pm & 7pm–midnight. *Benvenuto* been around for years and maintains its reputation for low prices. It may not be a hugely memorable experience, but you can't go wrong here if all you want is a cheap *trattoria*-quality meal just a couple of minutes' walk from Piazza della Signoria.

Boccadama

Piazza Santa Croce 25–26r ☏055.243.640. Summer daily 8am–midnight; winter closes 3pm Mon, 11pm all other days. *Boccadama* used to function chiefly as a wine bar, offering vintages from all over the country and a good selection of snacks. Nowadays, although some people stop here just for a drink, it's essentially a restaurant – not one of Florence's very best, but certainly the top choice on Piazza Santa Croce. You'll pay about €30 a head.

Cibrèo

Via de' Macci 118r ☏055.234.1100. 12.30pm–2.30pm & 7–11.15pm; closed Sun–Mon & Aug. The *Cibrèo* restaurant – which has now spawned a café, *trattoria* and shop – is the first Florentine port-of-call for many foodies, having achieved fame well beyond the city. The recipe

▼ BALDOVINO

for success is simple: superb food with a creative take on Tuscan classics, in a tasteful dining room with friendly and professional service. You'll need to book days in advance for a table in the main part of the restaurant, but next door there's *Cibreino*, a small and somewhat spartan *trattoria* section where the food is virtually the same (though the menu is smaller), no bookings are taken and the prices are much lower: around €15 for the main course, as opposed to €40 in the restaurant.

Enoteca Pinchiorri

Via Ghibellina 87 ☎055.242.777. Tues 7.30–10pm, Thurs–Sat 12.30–2pm & 7.30–10pm; closed Aug. No one seriously disputes the *Pinchiorri*'s claim to be Florence's best restaurant, certainly not Michelin, who've given it three of their coveted rosettes. The food is as magnificent as you'd expect, given the plaudits, but the ceremony that surrounds its presentation strikes many as excessive. (Jackets are compulsory for men, for example.) Choose from 80,000 different wines, including some of the rarest and most expensive vintages on the planet. None of this comes cheap – you could easily spend in excess of €150 per person, excluding wine – but there's nowhere better for the never-to-be repeated Florentine treat.

Il Francescano

Largo Bargellini 16 ☎055.241.605. June–Sept daily noon–2.30pm & 7–11pm; Oct–May closed Tues. *Il Francescano* began life as a sibling of *Baldovino*, and though it is now independently owned it still offers good food in a friendly, clean-cut setting. The menu is simpler, smaller and a little less expensive than at *Baldovino* (mains €10 and up), but it's reliably good.

Il Pizzaiuolo

Via de' Macci 113r ☎055.241.171. 12.30–3pm & 7pm–1am; closed Sun & Aug. Many Florentines reckon the pizzas here are the best in the city. Wines and other menu items have a Neapolitan touch, as does the atmosphere, which is friendly and high-spirited. Booking's a good idea, at least in the evening. The kitchen stays open until a little after midnight.

L'Antico Noè

Volta di San Piero 6r ☎055.234.0838. Mon–Sat noon–3pm & 7–11pm. Situated next door to the *vinaio* of the same name, this tiny *trattoria* has a very insalubrious setting (you'll doubtless pass a drunk or two on your way to the door), but the food is fine and the prices astoundingly low.

La Pentola dell'Oro

Via di Mezzo 24r ☎055.241.821. Mon–Sat noon–3.30pm & 9pm–midnight. Run by Giuseppe Alessi, the owner of a fine upmarket restaurant in Fiesole, *La Pentola* has one of the more imaginative menus in Florence, mingling the innovative with the profoundly traditional (some recipes date back to the sixteenth century). The main basement restaurant isn't the cosiest of dining rooms, but the quality is difficult to match for the price. Expect to pay upwards of €35, or a little less in the more informal ground-floor section, which focuses on traditional rather than aristocratic cuisine.

Natalino

Borgo degli Albizi 17r ☎055.289.404. Tues–Sun noon–3pm & 7–11pm. Slighly pricier than your average *trattoria* but excellent food, untouristy for the location and with outside tables. The truffled courgettes with pecorino are astounding.

Osteria Caffè Italiano

Via Isola delle Stinche 11–13r ☎055.289.368. Tues–Sun 10am–1am. The high vaulted ceilings lend a medieval touch to this upmarket café-wine bar-restaurant, where the clientele tend to be à la mode Florentines. The cuisine is typically Tuscan – lots of beef, veal and wild boar – and first-rate, even the cakes; expect to pay upwards of €40 per head.

Osteria de' Benci

Via de' Benci 13r ☎055.234.4923. Restaurant open 1–2.45pm & 7.30–10.45pm; bar open 8am–midnight; closed Sun. A modern, busy and reasonably priced *osteria*, with a bar-cafè adjoining. The single dining room (augmented by outside tables in summer) is pretty and pleasant, tables have paper tablecloths and you eat off chunky ceramic plates. The moderately priced food (around €30 per person) consists of well-prepared standards plus innovative takes on Tuscan classics. Staff are young and friendly, and the atmosphere busy and informal.

Tavola Calda da Rocco

Mercato di Sant'Ambrogio. Mon–Sat noon–2.30pm. Dishing out basic and dirt-cheap lunchtime fare to the market workers, this tiny place is ideal for a bargain lunch.

▲ OSTERIA DE' BENCI

Clubs

Rex Caffè

Via Fiesolana 25r ☎055.248.0331. Mon & Wed–Sun 5pm–3am; closed June–Aug. One of the city's real night-time fixtures, this is a friendly bar-club with a varied and loyal clientele. Vast curving lights droop over the central bar, which is studded with turquoise stone and broken mirror mosaics. Big arched spaces to either side mean there's plenty of room, the cocktails are good and the snacks excellent. DJs provide the sounds at weekends.

Y.A.G. B@r

Via de' Macci 8r ☎055.246.9022. Daily 9pm–3am. This large gay/lesbian bar-club has been top of the pile for a long time, not least because of its cutting-edge playlists. No cover charge.

Live music

Jazz Club

Via Nuova de' Caccini 3 ☎055.247.9700. Mon–Sat 9pm–2am; closed July & Aug. Florence's foremost jazz venue. The €6 "membership" fee gets you down into the medieval brick-vaulted basement, where the atmosphere's informal and there's live music most nights (and an open jam-session on Tuesdays). Cocktails are good, and you can also snack on bar nibbles, *focaccia* and desserts.

Theatre and classical music

Teatro della Pergola

Via della Pergola 18 ☎055.226.4316. The beautiful little Pergola was built in 1656 and is Italy's oldest surviving theatre. It plays host to chamber concerts, small-scale operas and some of the best-known Italian theatre companies.

Teatro Verdi

Via Ghibellina 99–101 ☎055.212.320. One of the city's premier venues for classical music and mainstream theatre productions.

Central Oltrarno

Traditionally the artisanal quarter of the city, the Oltrarno – literally "beyond the Arno" – has also always contained more prosperous enclaves: many of Florence's ruling families chose to settle in this area, and nowadays some of the city's plushest shops line the streets parallel to the river's southern bank. Like the Santa Croce district, Oltrarno is an upwardly mobile zone that contains some of Florence's best bars and restaurants – though the main concentrations are around Santo Spirito and Piazza del Carmine, covered in the next chapter. Window-shopping, eating and drinking are not the area's sole pleasures, however, as the district also contains several of the city's key sights.

The first of these, the famous **Ponte Vecchio**, links the northern bank to the Oltrarno's central area, home to the **Palazzo Pitti**, a rambling palace complex whose cluster of museums includes the city's second-ranking picture gallery. Close by lies the **Giardino di Bóboli**, Italy's most visited garden. Lesser attractions include the ancient church of **Santa Felìcita**, known for one of the city's most intriguing paintings, and the extraordinary medical waxworks of **La Specola**.

The Ponte Vecchio

The direct route from the city centre to the heart of the Oltrarno crosses the Arno via the Ponte Vecchio, the "old bridge". Until 1218 the crossing here was the city's only bridge, though the version you see today dates from 1345, built to replace a wooden bridge swept away by floods twelve

▼ PONTE VECCHIO

▲ SANTA FELÌCITA

years earlier. The Ponte Vecchio has always been loaded with shops like those now propped over the water. Their earliest tenants were butchers and fishmongers, attracted to the site by the proximity of the river, which provided a convenient dumping ground for their waste. The current plethora of jewellers dates from 1593, when Ferdinando I evicted the butchers' stalls and other practitioners of what he called "vile arts". In their place he installed eight jewellers and 41 goldsmiths, also taking the opportunity to double the rents. Florence had long revered the art of the goldsmith, and several of its major artists were skilled in the craft: Ghiberti, Donatello and Cellini, for example. The third of this trio is celebrated by a bust in the centre of the bridge, the night-time meeting point for Florence's unreconstructed hippies and local lads on the make.

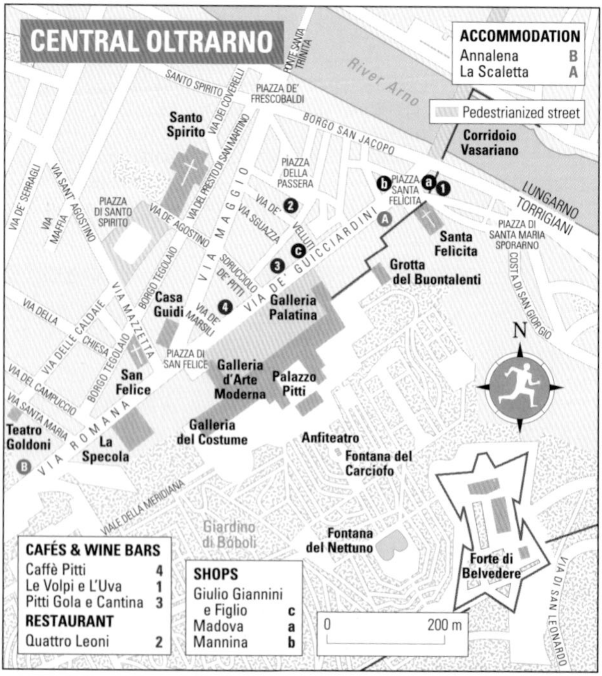

CENTRAL OLTRARNO

ACCOMMODATION
Annalena B
La Scaletta A

Pedestrianized street

CAFÉS & WINE BARS
Caffè Pitti 4
Le Volpi e L'Uva 1
Pitti Gola e Cantina 3

RESTAURANT
Quattro Leoni 2

SHOPS
Giulio Giannini e Figlio c
Madova a
Mannina b

0 200 m

Santa Felìcita

Mon–Sat 9.30am–12.30pm & 3–6.30pm, Sun 9.30am–12.30pm.

Santa Felìcita might be the oldest church in Florence, having possibly been founded in the second century by Greek or Syrian merchants, pioneers of Christianity in the city. It's known for certain that a church existed on the site by the fifth century, by which time it had been dedicated to St Felicity; new churches were built in the eleventh and fourteenth centuries, then in 1565 Vasari added an elaborate portico to accommodate the linking of the Uffizi and Palazzo Pitti; a window from the corridor looks directly into the church.

The interior demands a visit for the amazing Pontormo paintings in the **Cappella Capponi**, which lies to the right of the main door, surrounded by obstructive railings. The chapel was designed in the 1420s by Brunelleschi, but subsequently much altered – notably by Vasari, who destroyed the Pontormo fresco in the cupola when building his corridor. Under the cupola are four tondi of the Evangelists (painted with help from Pontormo's adoptive son, Bronzino), while on opposite sides of the window on the right wall are the Virgin and the angel of Pontormo's delightfully simple *Annunciation*. The low level of light admitted by this window was a determining factor in the startling colour scheme of the painter's *Deposition* (1525–28), one of the masterworks of Florentine Mannerism. Nothing in this picture is conventional: Mary is on a different scale from her attendants; the figures bearing Christ's body are androgynous beings clad in acidic sky-blue, puce green and candy-floss pink drapery; and there's no sign of the cross, the thieves, or any of the other scene-setting devices usual in paintings of this subject.

The Palazzo Pitti

Beyond Santa Felìcita, the street opens out at Piazza Pitti, forecourt of the largest palace in Florence, the Palazzo Pitti. Banker and merchant Luca Pitti commissioned the palace in the 1450s to outdo his rivals, the Medici, but in 1549 the cash-strapped Pitti were forced to sell out – to the Medici. This subsequently became the Medicis' base in Florence, growing in bulk until the seventeenth century, when it achieved its present gargantuan dimensions. Later, during Florence's brief tenure as the Italian capital between 1865 and 1871, it housed the Italian kings.

Today the Palazzo Pitti and the pavilions of the Giardino di Bóboli contain eight museums, of which the foremost is the **Galleria Palatina**, an art collection second in importance only to the Uffizi

▼ THE PALAZZO PITTI: THE MAIN STAIRCASE

(Tues–Sun 8.15am–6.50pm; €8.50, includes admission to the Galleria d'Arte Moderna & Appartamenti Reali; €11.50 ticket, valid for 3 days, covers all Pitti museums, but not available during special exhibitions). The Palatina possesses superb works by Fra' Bartolomeo, Filippo and Filippino Lippi, Caravaggio, Rosso Fiorentino and Canova, no fewer than seventeen pieces by Andrea del Sarto, and numerous paintings by **Raphael** and **Titian**.

When Raphael settled in Florence in 1505, he was besieged with commissions from patrons delighted to find an artist for whom the creative process involved so little agonizing. Among the masterpieces on show here are Raphael's portraits of Angelo Doni and his wife, Maddalena, and the wonderful *Madonna della Seggiola* (Madonna of the Chair), which was once Italy's most popular image of the Madonna – nineteenth-century copyists had to join a five-year waiting list to study the picture. According to Vasari, the model for the famous *Donna Velata* (Veiled Woman), in the Sala di Giove, was the painter's mistress, a Roman baker's daughter known to posterity as La Fornarina.

The paintings by Titian include a number of his most trenchant portraits. The lecherous and scurrilous Pietro Aretino – journalist, critic, poet and one of Titian's closest friends – was so thrilled by his portrait that he gave it to Cosimo I. Also here are likenesses of Philip II of Spain and the young Cardinal Ippolito de' Medici, also the so-called *Portrait of an Englishman*, who scrutinizes the viewer with unflinching sea-grey eyes. To his left, by way of contrast, is the same artist's sensuous and much-copied *Mary Magdalene*, the first of a series on this theme produced for the duke of Urbino.

Much of the rest of the Pitti's first floor comprises the **Appartamenti Reali**, the Pitti's state rooms (same hours & ticket as Galleria Palatina, but closed Jan); after Raphael and Titian it can be difficult to sustain a great deal of enthusiasm for such ducal elegance, notwithstanding the sumptuousness of the

▼ MUSEO DEGLI ARGENTI

The birth of opera

The Medici pageants in the gardens of the Pitti were the last word in extravagance, and the palace has a claim to be the birthplace of the most extravagant modern performing art, opera. The roots of the genre are convoluted, but its ancestry certainly owes much to the singing and dancing tableaux called *intermedii*, with which high-society Florentine weddings were padded out. Influenced by these shows, the academy known as the Camerata Fiorentina began, at the end of the sixteenth century, to blend the principles of Greek drama with a semi-musical style of declamation. The first composition recognizable as an opera is *Dafne*, written by two members of the Camerata, Jacopo Peri and Ottavio Rinucci, and performed in 1597; the earliest opera whose music has survived in its entirety is the same duo's *Euridice*, premiered in the Palazzo Pitti on the occasion of the proxy marriage of Maria de' Medici to Henry IV of France.

furnishings. On the floor above the Palatina is the **Galleria d'Arte Moderna** (same hours & ticket as Galleria Palatina), a chronological survey of primarily Tuscan art from the mid-eighteenth century to 1945. Most rewarding are the products of the *Macchiaioli*, the Italian division of the Impressionist movement; most startling, however, are the sculptures, featuring sublime kitsch such as Antonio Ciseri's *Pregnant Nun*.

The **Museo degli Argenti** (daily: Jan, Feb, Nov & Dec 8.15am–4.30pm; March 8.15am–5.30pm; April, May, Sept & Oct 8.15am–6.30pm; June–Aug 8.15am–7.30pm; closed 1st & last Mon of month; joint ticket with Museo delle Porcellane, Museo delle Porcellane, Giardino di Bóboli & Giardino Bardini €6), entered from the main palace courtyard, is a colossal museum not just of silverware but of luxury artefacts in general. The craftsmanship on show is astounding, even if the final products are likely to strike you as being in dubious taste – room after room is packed with seashell figurines, cups made from ostrich eggs, portraits in stone inlay, bizarre ivory carvings, and the like. Amid all the trinkets, look out for the death mask of Lorenzo il Magnifico.

Visitors without a specialist interest are unlikely to be riveted by the two remaining museums currently open. In the Palazzina della Meridiana, the eighteenth-century southern wing of the Pitti, the **Galleria del Costume** (same hours & ticket as Museo degli Argenti) provides the opportunity to see the dress that Eleonora di Toledo was buried in (it's the one she's wearing in Bronzino's portrait of her in the Palazzo Vecchio). The well-presented but esoteric collection of porcelain, the **Museo delle Porcellane** (same hours and ticket as Museo degli Argenti), is located at the top of the Bóboli garden, while the **Museo delle Carrozze** (Carriage Museum) has been closed for years and will almost certainly remain so for a good while yet, to the chagrin of very few.

The Giardino di Bóboli

Daily: Jan, Feb, Nov & Dec 8.15am–4.30pm; March 8.15am–5.30pm; April, May, Sept & Oct 8.15am–6.30pm; June–Aug 8.15am–7.30pm; closed 1st & last Mon of month; joint ticket with Museo delle Porcellane, Museo degli Argenti & Giardino Bardini €6. The land occupied by the formal gardens of the Palazzo Pitti, the Giardino di Bóboli, was once a quarry; the bedrock here is one of the sources of the yellow sandstone known as *pietra forte* (strong stone) that gives much of Florence its dominant hue. When the Medici acquired the house they set about transforming their back yard into an enormous garden, its every statue, view and grotto designed to elevate nature by the judicious application of art. The resulting landscape takes its name from the Bóboli family, erstwhile owners of some of the land. Opened to the public in 1766, this is the only really extensive area of accessible greenery in the centre of the city. It's no place to seek solitude, however: it attracts some five million visitors annually, more than at any other Italian garden.

Of all the garden's Mannerist embellishments, the most celebrated is the **Grotta del Buontalenti** (1583–88), to the left of the entrance, beyond Giambologna's much-reproduced statue of Cosimo I's favourite dwarf astride a giant tortoise.

▼ GIARDINO DI BÓBOLI: THE GROTTO

Embedded in the grotto's faked stalactites and encrustations are replicas of Michelangelo's *Slaves* – the originals were lodged here until 1908. Lurking in the deepest recesses of the cave, and normally viewable only from afar, is Giambologna's *Venus Emerging from her Bath*, leered at by attendant imps.

Another spectacular set piece is the fountain island called the **Isolotto**, which is the focal point of the far end of the garden; from within the Bóboli the most dramatic approach is along the central cypress avenue known as the **Viottolone**, many of whose statues are Roman originals. These lower parts of the garden are its most pleasant – and least visited – sections. You come upon them quickly if you enter the Bóboli by the Porta Romana entrance, a little-used gate at the garden's southwestern tip.

The Casa Guidi

Piazza San Felice 8. April–Nov Mon, Wed & Fri 3–6pm. Free, but donations encouraged. Within a stone's throw of the Pitti stands the home of Robert Browning and Elizabeth Barrett Browning, the Casa Guidi. It's something of a shrine to Elizabeth, who wrote much of her most popular verse here (including, naturally enough, *Casa Guidi Windows*) and died here, but it's an unatmospheric spot – virtually all the Casa Guidi's furniture went under the hammer at Sotheby's in 1913, and there's just one oil painting left to conjure the spirit of its former occupants.

La Specola

Via Romana 17. Mon, Tues, Thurs, Fri & Sun 9am–1pm, Sat 9am–5pm. €4. On the third floor of the university buildings on Via Romana there lurks what can reasonably claim to be the strangest museum in the city. Taking its name from the telescope (*specola*) on its roof, La Specola is a twin-sectioned museum of zoology. The first part is conventional enough, with ranks of shells, insects and crustaceans, followed by a mortician's ark of animals stuffed, pickled and desiccated. Beyond some rather frayed-looking sharks lie the things everyone comes to see, the **Cere Anatomiche** (Anatomical Waxworks). Wax arms, legs and organs cover the walls, arrayed around satin beds on which wax cadavers recline in progressive stages of deconstruction, each muscle fibre and nerve cluster moulded and dyed with absolute precision. Most of the six hundred models were made between 1775 and 1791 by Clemente Susini, and were intended as teaching aids, in an age when medical ethics and refrigeration techniques were not what they are today.

In a separate room towards the end you'll find the grisliest section: Gaetano Zumbo's tableaux showing Florence during the plague and the horrors of syphilis. In the centre of the room lies a dissected – and slightly putrefying – waxwork head, built on the foundation of a real skull.

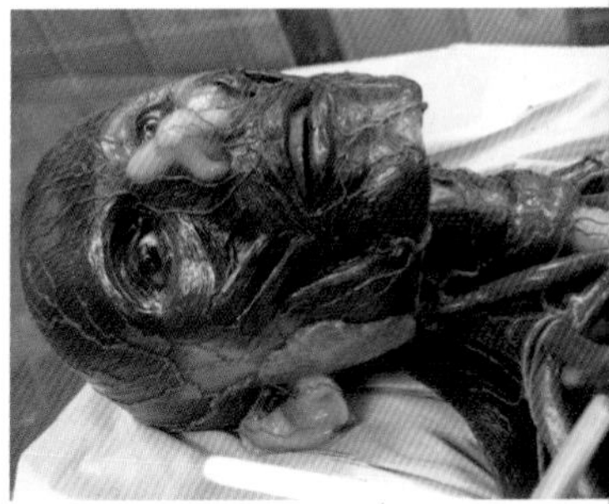

▲ WAX CADAVER AT LA SPECOLA

Shops

Giulio Giannini e Figlio

Piazza Pitti 36r ☎055.212.621. Mon–Sat 10am–7.30pm, Sun 10.30am–6.30pm. Established in 1856, this paper-making and book-binding firm has been honoured with exhibitions dedicated to its work. Once the only place in Florence to make its own marbled papers, it now offers a wide variety of diaries, address books and so forth as well.

Madova

Via Guicciardini 1r ☎055.239.6526. Mon–Sat 9.30am–7.30pm. The last word in gloves – every colour, every size, every shape. Prices range from around €35 to €90.

Mannina

Via Guicciardini 16r ☎055.282.895. Mon–Sat 9.30am–7.30pm, Sun 10.30am–1pm & 2–6pm. This famed Oltrarno shoemaker has been going for donkey's years, producing beautifully made and sensible footwear at prices that are far from extravagant.

Café

Caffè Pitti

Piazza Pitti 9 ☎055.239.9863. Daily 11am–1am; June & July closed Mon. Sit outside or in the old-style interior, which is nicely done out with wooden floors and subdued gold-yellow walls. *Panini* and other snacks are available, plus two good-value set menus at lunch. In the evenings there's live music (usually jazz or blues), with a full dinner menu until 10pm and light meals later.

Wine bars

Le Volpi e L'Uva

Piazza dei Rossi 1r ⓣ055.239.8132. Mon–Sat 10am–8pm. This discreet little place, just over the Ponte Vecchio, does good business by concentrating on the wines of small producers and providing tasty cold meats and snacks to help them down (the selection of cheeses in particular is tremendous). At any one time you can choose from at least two dozen different wines by the glass.

Pitti Gola e Cantina

Piazza Pitti 16 ⓣ055.212.704. Summer daily 11am–midnight; winter Tues–Sun 11am–9.30pm; closed 2wks in mid-Aug. A small and friendly wine bar, very handily placed for a glass of Chianti after a slog around the Pitti museums.

▼ LE VOLPI E L'UVA

▲ QUATTRO LEONI

Restaurant

Quattro Leoni

Via dei Vellutini 1r/Piazza della Passera ⓣ055.218.562. Noon–2.30pm & 7–11pm; closed Wed lunch. This is a vibrant and very successful place, occupying a three-roomed medieval interior, with tables under vast canvas umbrellas on the tiny Piazza della Passera – one of the most appealing outdoor eating venues in the city. It's popular with visiting stars, as you can tell by pictures of the likes of Dustin Hofmann and Sting on the walls; for everyone else, booking is essential. Expect to pay around €40 a head.

Theatre & classical music

Teatro Goldoni

Via Santa Maria 15 ⓣ055.210.804. This exquisite little theatre, dating from 1817, is occasionally used for chamber music and opera performances, though lately it has hosted more dance productions than anything else.

Western Oltrarno

Western Oltrarno is one of the city centre's earthier districts, though in recent years it's been steadily colonized by stylish bars, restaurants and shops that are turning it into a south-of-the-river equivalent of the lively area around Sant'Ambrogio. The piazza in front of Santo Spirito church, with its market stalls, cafés and restaurants, encapsulates the gritty yet chic character of this part of the Oltrarno, an area not hopelessly compromised by the encroachments of tourism. Other than Santo Spirito itself, there's only one major sight in this district, but it's one of the greatest sights in all of Europe – the Cappella Brancacci, in Santa Maria del Carmine.

Santo Spirito

Mon, Tues & Thurs–Sat 8.30am–noon & 4–6pm, Sun 4–6pm. Designed in 1434 as a replacement for a thirteenth-century church, Santo Spirito was one of Brunelleschi's last projects, a swansong later described by Bernini as "the most beautiful church in the world". Its floor plan is extremely sophisticated: a Latin cross with a continuous chain of 38 chapels round the outside and a line of 35 columns running without a break round the nave, transepts and chancel. The exterior wall was originally designed to follow the curves of the chapels' walls, creating a flowing, corrugated effect. As built, however, the exterior is a plain, straight wall, and even the main facade remained incomplete, disguised today by a simple plastering job. Inside the church, only the Baroque baldachin disrupts the harmony of Brunelleschi's design. (A word of warning, though – the opening hours of Santo Spirito are notoriously erratic, so it may well not be open when it should be.)

A fire in 1471 destroyed most of Santo Spirito's medieval works, including famed frescoes by Cimabue and the Gaddi family, but as a result, the altar paintings in the many chapels comprise an unusually unified collection of religious

▼ SANTO SPIRITO

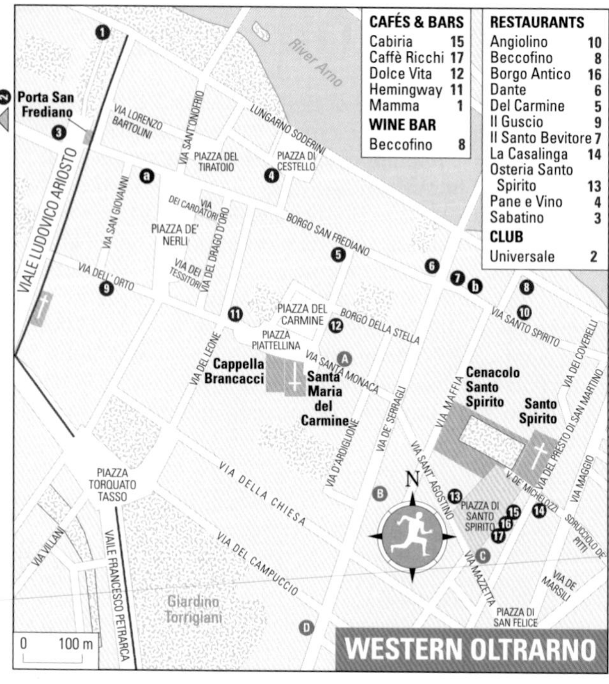

ACCOMMODATION				SHOPS	
Istituto Gould (hostel)	B	Pio X – Artigianelli (hostel)	D	Francesco da Firenze	b
Pensione Bandini	C	Residenza Santo Spirito	C	Stefano Bemer	a
		Santa Monaca (hostel)	A		

works, the majority having been commissioned in the aftermath of the fire. Most prolific among the artists is the so-called **Maestro di Santo Spirito**, but the finest single painting is Filippino Lippi's *Nerli Altarpiece* (c. 1488), an age-darkened Madonna and Child with saints, which hangs in the south transept. A door in the north aisle leads through to Giuliano da Sangallo's stunning vestibule and **sacristy** (1489–93), the latter designed in imitation of Brunelleschi's Cappella Pazzi (see p.125). Hanging above the altar is a delicate wooden crucifix attributed to Michelangelo.

A glass door at the far end of the vestibule, usually locked, gives out onto the **Chiostro dei Morti**, the only cloister in the complex that is still part of the Augustinian monastery. The 1471 fire destroyed much of the rest of the monastery, with the exception of its refectory (entered to the left of the main church, at Piazza Santo Spirito 29), which is now the home of the **Cenacolo di Santo Spirito** (Sat: April–Oct 9am–5pm; Nov–March 10.30am–1.30pm; €2.20), a one-room collection comprising an assortment of carvings, many of them Romanesque, and a huge fresco of *The Crucifixion* (1365) by Orcagna and his workshop.

Santa Maria del Carmine

Santa Maria del Carmine, a couple of blocks west of Santo Spirito in Piazza del Carmine, is a drab mess on the outside, but inside – in the frescoes of the **Cappella Brancacci** (Mon & Wed–Sat 10am–5pm, Sun 1–5pm; €4) – it provides one of Italy's supreme artistic experiences. The chapel is barricaded off from the rest of the Carmine, and visits are restricted to a maximum of thirty people at a time, for a wholly inadequate fifteen minutes. At the time of writing, tickets could only be obtained by reserving in advance on ⓣ055.276.8224 or ⓣ055.276.8558; this system is so cumbersome, however, that it surely will be replaced by something less visitor-repellent – ask the tourist office about the current situation.

The Brancacci **frescoes** were commissioned in 1424 by Felice Brancacci, a silk merchant and leading patrician figure, shortly after his return from a stint in Egypt as the Florentine ambassador. The decoration of the chapel was begun in the same year by Masolino (1383–1447); working alongside Masolino was Tommaso di Ser Giovanni di Mone Cassai – known ever since as Masaccio (1401–28). The former was aged 41, the latter just 22.

Two years into the project Masolino was recalled to Budapest, where he was official painter to the Hungarian court. Left to his own devices Masaccio began to blossom, and when Masolino returned in 1427 the teacher was soon taking lessons from the supposed pupil, whose grasp of the texture of the real world, of the principles of perspective and of the dramatic potential of the biblical texts they were illustrating far exceeded that of his precursors. In 1428 Masolino was called away to Rome, where he was followed by Masaccio a few months later. Neither would return to the chapel. Masaccio died the same year, aged just 28, but, in the words of Vasari, "all the most celebrated sculptors and painters since Masaccio's day have become excellent and illustrious by studying their art in this chapel." Work resumed between 1480 and 1485, some fifty years later, when the paintings were completed by **Filippino Lippi**.

The small scene on the left of the entrance arch is the quintessence of Masaccio's art. Plenty of artists had depicted *The Expulsion of Adam and Eve*

▼ SANTA MARIA DEL CARMINE

before, but none had captured the desolation of the sinners so graphically: Adam presses his hands to his face in bottomless despair, Eve raises her head and wails. St Peter is chief protagonist of all the remaining scenes, three of which – all by Masaccio – are especially compelling. The first of these is the **Tribute Money**, a complex narrative, with no fewer than three separate events portrayed within a single frame: the central episode shows Christ outside the gates of Capernaum being asked to pay a tribute owing to the city; to the left, St Peter fetches coins from the mouth of a fish in order to pay the tribute, Christ in the central panel having pointed to where the money will be found; and to the right Peter is shown handing over the money to the tax official. Masaccio's second great panel is **St Peter Healing the Sick**, in which the shadow of the stern and self-possessed saint (followed by St John) cures the infirm as it passes over them. The third great panel is **The Distribution of Alms and Death of Ananias**, in which St Peter instructs the people to give up their possessions to the poor. One individual, Ananias, retains some of his wealth with the knowledge of his wife, Sapphira. Rebuked by Peter, Ananias dies on the spot, closely followed by a similarly castigated Sapphira.

Filippino Lippi's work included the finishing of Masaccio's **Raising of Theophilus's Son and St Peter Enthroned**, which depicts St Peter raising the dead son of Theophilus, Prefect of Antioch. The people of Antioch, suitably impressed, built a throne from which St Peter can preach, shown to the right. The three figures to the right of the throne are thought to be portraits of Masaccio, Alberti and Brunelleschi. Lippi left other portraits in the combined scene of **St Peter before Agrippa** (or Nero) and his crucifixion: the central figure looking out in the trio to the right of the crucifixion is Botticelli, the painter's teacher, while Filippino himself can be seen at the far right.

Shops

Francesco da Firenze

Via Santo Spirito 62r ⓣ055.212.428. Mon–Sat 9am–1pm & 3.30–7.30pm; Aug closed Sat afternoon. Handmade shoes for men and women at very reasonable prices (under €200). Creations combine classical footwear with striking designs.

Stefano Bemer

Borgo San Frediano 143r ⓣ055.211.356, Mon–Sat 9am–1pm & 3.30–7.30pm. If you're in the market for made-to-measure Italian shoes of the very highest quality, there's no better place than this. Another branch, close by at Via Camaldoli 10r, is an outlet for Bemer'S [sic], the off-the-peg (but still expensive) footwear designed by Stefano and his brother Mario.

Cafés and bars

Cabiria

Piazza di Santo Spirito 4r ⓣ055.215.732. Open 8am–1.30am; closed Tues & 10 days in mid-Aug. Boho-trendy in look, feel and clientele, but still rather cosy. The main seating area is in the room to the rear, but plenty of punters (some locals and lots of foreigners) sit out on the piazza, or crowd into the bar at the front. There's a DJ most nights from around 9pm; drinks are cheaper before then.

Caffè Ricchi

Piazza di Santo Spirito 9r ☎055.215.864. Summer Mon–Sat 7am–1am; winter closes 10pm; closed last 2wks of Feb & Aug. The smartest of the cafés on this square, with a good selection of cakes, ice cream and lunchtime snacks, and superb coffee. The adjacent *Ricchi* restaurant (Mon–Sat noon–3pm & 7.30–11pm, plus 2nd Sun of month noon–3pm; ☎055.280.830) is highly recommended too – it's one of the few Florentine restaurants to place an emphasis on fish.

Dolce Vita

Piazza del Carmine ☎055.284.595. April–Oct daily 5pm–2am; Nov–March closed Mon. A smart, modern-looking and extremely popular bar that's been going for more than a decade and has stayed ahead of the game through constant updating; aluminium bar stools, sleek black-and-white photos on the walls and the chance to preen with Florence's beautiful things, who like to drop in here on their way to a club.

Hemingway

Piazza Piattellina 9r ☎055.284.781. Mon–Thurs & Sun 4.30pm–1am, Fri & Sat closes 2am; closed mid-June to mid-Sept. Self-consciously trendy, but don't let that put you off – there's nothing else like it in Florence. Choose from one of countless speciality teas, sample over twenty coffees, or knock back one of the "tea cocktails". Owners Paul de Bondt and Andrea Slitti are members of the Compagnia del Cioccolato, a chocolate appreciation society – and it shows: the handmade chocolates are sublime.

Mamma

Lungarno Santa Rosa ☎055.233.6776. April–Oct Mon–Thurs & Sun 11am–2am, Fri & Sat till 3am. Delightful venue for summer nights, occupying a small park in the shadow of the high city walls behind the Porta San Frediano. Romantic at dusk, when candles are set out, it becomes hugely busy later on – more than a thousand people have been known to come out here on fine nights. DJs two or three nights a week keep the fashionable, cocktail-drinking and almost entirely Italian crowd happy. Occasional live gigs; *antipasti* available from the bistro.

▼ MAMMA

Restaurants

Angiolino

Via Santo Spirito 36r ☎055.239.8976. April–Sept daily noon–3pm & 7–11pm; Oct–March closed Mon. Long a no-nonsense Oltrarno favourite, with a menu that's short and to the point, featuring Tuscan classics such as *bistecca*, *ribollita* and *pappa al pomodoro*. Some nights it's as good as any restaurant in its price range (around €30 per person), but quality can be erratic and service problematic.

Beccofino

Piazza degli Scarlatti 1r ☎055.290.076. Mon 7–11pm, Tues–Sat 12.30–2.30pm & 7–11pm. An upmarket venture from David Gardner, the Scottish boss of *Baldovino* (see p.129), and still one of the most stylish of the new generation of Florentine restaurants – indeed, some might find its cooking and expensively austere decor a bit too self-conscious. Prices are above average (reckon on about €50 each), but so is the quality. The similarly sophisticated bar alongside (which opens an hour earlier in the evening and closes an hour later) has a terrific selection of wines, and a menu of dishes from the restaurant's kitchen, at somewhat lower prices.

▼ IL SANTO BEVITORE

Borgo Antico

Piazza di Santo Spirito 6r ☎055.210.437. Daily noon–midnight. The spartan chic of *Borgo Antico*'s white-tile and pink-plaster decor reflects the increasingly trendy character of this once notoriously sleazy Oltrarno piazza, and there's no Oltrarno restaurant trendier than this place. It's usually very crowded and very noisy, though in summer the outside tables offer relative quiet. Choose from ten different pizzas, an inexpensive daily set-price menu or a range of Tuscan standards at reasonable prices. Salads here are good, and there's often a selection of fresh fish and seafood pastas. Servings – on the restaurant's famous huge plates – are generous to a fault.

Dante

Piazza Nazario Sauro 10r ☎055.219.219. Open till midnight; closed Wed, plus Sat in July & Aug. *Dante* is another Oltrarno institution, popular mainly for its wood-oven pizzas, though it also offers a decent menu of pasta, fish and meat dishes.

Del Carmine

Piazza del Carmine 18r ☎055.218.601. Mon–Sat noon–2.30pm & 7.30–10.30pm. Years ago this was an unsung local *trattoria*; now the tourists have taken over, but it hasn't altogether lost its soul. Uncomplicated good-value Florentine cooking, with a frequently changing menu.

Il Guscio

Via dell'Orto 49 ☎055.224.421. Tues–Sat 8–11pm; closed Aug. This rustic-style restaurant is another long-established Oltrarno favourite: high-quality Tuscan meat dishes, superb desserts and a wide-ranging wine list. You'll pay in the region of €35 each.

Il Santo Bevitore

Via Santo Spirito 64–66r ☏055.211.264. Daily 12.30–3pm & 7.30–11.30pm. The *Holy Drinker* is an airy and stylish "gastronomic enoteca" with a small but classy food menu (around €25 for a meal without drinks) to complement its enticing menu of wines.

La Casalinga

Via del Michelozzo 9r ☏055.218.624. Mon–Sat noon–2.30pm & 7–10pm; closed last 3wks of Aug. Located in a side street off Piazza di Santo Spirito, this long-established family-run *trattoria* serves up some of the best low-cost Tuscan dishes in town. No frills – paper tablecloths, so-so house wine by the flask and brisk service – but most nights it's filled with regulars and a good few outsiders.

Le Barrique

Via del Leone 40r ☏055.224.192. Tues–Sun 7.30–11pm. Formerly a wine bar, *Le Barrique* has mutated into a good mid-range restaurant, with a menu that's essentially classic Tuscan. The wine list is still extensive, and is more international than most in Florence.

Osteria Santo Spirito

Piazza di Santo Spirito 16r/Via Sant'Agostino ☏055.238.2383. Daily 12.45–2.30pm & 8pm–midnight. Run by the owners of the *Borgo Antico*, this *osteria* is part of a new wave of Florentine restaurants. Informal and modern, its walls are painted deep red and blue, and the Tuscan dishes are presented with contemporary flair. Tables are on two floors, and in summer you can eat outdoors on the piazza. Main courses from around €15.

Pane e Vino

Piazza di Cestello 3r ☏055.247.6956. Mon–Sat 8pm–midnight; closed 2wks in Aug. *Pane e Vino* began life as a bar (over by San Niccolò), so it's no surprise that the wine list is excellent and well priced. In its new home, the ambience is stylish yet relaxed and the menu small (*primi* around €10, *secondi* €15), featuring a very enticing menu degustazione (€30). Small TV screens in the dining area show the chefs beavering away in the kitchen, producing some of the best food in town – the ravioli with asparagus in a lemon cream melts in your mouth.

Sabatino

Via Pisani 2r ☏055.225.955. Mon–Sat noon–3pm & 7pm–midnight; closed Aug. Situated right by Porta San Frediano, this old-fashioned, no-frills, long-running family *trattoria* (it's been in business for half a century) is not a gourmet venue, but it's excellent value and the atmosphere is always terrific.

Club

Universale

Via Pisana 77 ☏055.221.122. Wed–Sun 8pm–3am; closed June–Sept. Located beyond the city gates, this is the most impressive nightclub venue in Florence, with a restaurant (closes midnight) and various club zones installed in a beautiful converted 1950s cinema. Self-regardingy cool, but definitely glamorous. Cover charge ranges from €10–20, and includes one drink.

Eastern Oltrarno

On the tourist map of Florence, most of eastern Oltrarno is something of a *terra incognita*: as on the opposite bank of the river, blocks of historic buildings were destroyed by mines left behind by the Nazis in 1944. Some characterful parts remain, however, notably the medieval Via dei Bardi and its continuation, Via San Niccolò. These narrow, palazzo-lined streets will take you past the eclectic Museo Bardini and the medieval church of San Niccolò, both of which can be visited as part of the walk up to San Miniato al Monte, widely regarded as one of the most beautiful Romanesque churches in Tuscany. Another target for an Oltrarno hike might be the Forte di Belvedere, a Medici fortress used occasionally for exhibitions.

The Museo Bardini

The Museo Bardini (closed for restoration at the time of writing) is like the Museo Horne just across the Arno (see p.127), in that it was built around the bequest of a private collector. But whereas Horne was a moderately well-off connoisseur, his contemporary, Stefano Bardini (1836–1922), was once the busiest art dealer in Italy. His tireless activity, at a time when Renaissance art was relatively cheap and unfashionable, laid the cornerstone of many important modern-day European and North American collections. Determined that no visitor to his native city should remain unaware of his success, he ripped down a church that stood on the site and built a vast home, studding it with fragments of old buildings. Doorways, ceiling panels and other orphaned pieces are strewn all over the place: the first-floor windows, for instance, are actually altars from a church in Pistoia. The more portable items are equally wide-ranging: musical instruments, carvings, ceramics, armour, furniture, carpets, pictures – if it was vaguely arty and had a price tag, Bardini snapped it up. His artistic pot-pourri was bequeathed to the city on his death. The museum may lack genuine masterpieces, but

▼ THE MUSEO BARDINI

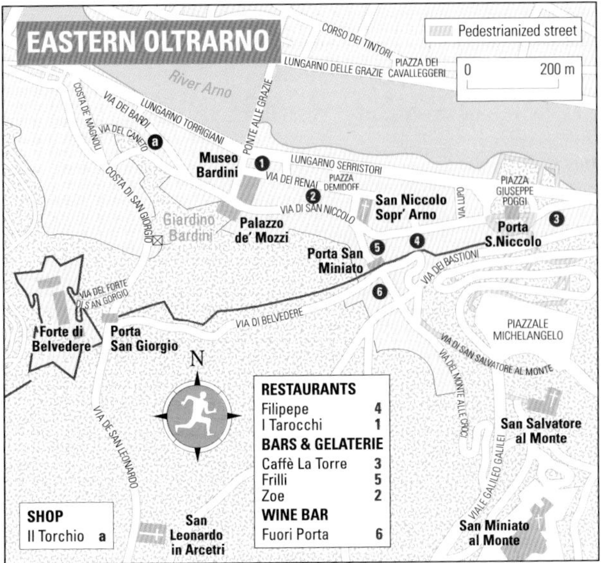

it's larger and more satisfying than the Museo Horne, as well as being crammed with a sufficiently wide variety of beautiful objects to appeal to most tastes. Displays are spread over a couple of floors and some twenty rooms, though only the more precious exhibits are fully labelled.

Giardino Bardini

Same hours and ticket as Giardino di Bóboli. €6. Close to the Bardini museum, at Via de' Bardi 1r, is an entrance to the Giardino Bardini, which was opened to the public for the first time in 2007. (If you're coming from the Bóboli gardens you can use another entrance, at the top of the garden, on Costa di San Giorgio.) The olive grove of the huge **Palazzo dei Mozzi** (the Mozzi were one of the richest families in thirteenth-century Florence), was refashioned as a semi-formal garden by Stefano Bardini after he bought the palace, and has now been restored to the appearance he gave it, with a neo-Baroque staircase and terraces dividing the fruit-growing section from the miniature woodland of the "bosco Inglese". At the summit of the garden, reached by a lovely long pergola of wisteria and hortensia, a colonnaded belvedere gives a splendid view of the city.

San Niccolò sopr'Arno

Daily 10am–noon. Beyond the Museo Bardini, Via San Niccolò swings past San Niccolò sopr'Arno. Restoration work after the 1966 flood uncovered several frescoes underneath the altars, but none is as appealing as the fifteenth-century fresco in the sacristy; known as *The Madonna of the Girdle*, it was probably painted by Baldovinetti in the late fifteenth century.

The city gates and Piazzale Michelangelo

In medieval times San Niccolò was close to the edge of the city, and two of Florence's fourteenth-century gates still stand in the vicinity: the diminutive **Porta San Miniato**, set in a portion of the walls, and the huge **Porta San Niccolò**, overlooking the Arno. From either of these gates you can begin the climb up to San Miniato: the path from Porta San Niccolò weaves up through Piazzale Michelangelo, with its replica *David* and bumper-to-bumper tour coaches; the more direct path from Porta San Miniato offers a choice between the steep Via del Monte alle Croci or the stepped Via di San Salvatore al Monte, both of which emerge a short distance uphill from Piazzale Michelangelo.

San Miniato al Monte

Daily: summer 8am–7pm; winter 8am–noon & 3–6pm. Arguably the finest Romanesque structure in Tuscany, San Miniato al Monte is also the oldest surviving church building in Florence after the Baptistery. The church's dedicatee, St Miniatus, was Florence's first home-grown martyr: around 250 he was beheaded close to the site of Piazza della Signoria, whereupon the saintly corpse was seen to carry his severed head over the river and up the hill to this spot. A chapel to Miniato is documented on the site in the eighth century, though construction of the present building began in 1013. Initially run as a Benedictine foundation, the building passed to the Cluniacs until 1373, and then to the Olivetans, a Benedictine offshoot, who reside here to this day, selling their famous liquors, honeys and tisanes from the shop next to the church.

▼ PIAZZALE MICHELANGELO

San Miniato's gorgeous marble facade alludes to the Baptistery in its geometrical patterning, and, like its model, the church was often mistaken for a structure of classical provenance during the later Middle Ages. The lower part of the facade is possibly eleventh-century, while the angular upper levels date from the twelfth century onwards, and were financed in part by the Arte di Calimala (cloth merchants' guild): their trademark, a gilded copper eagle clutching a bale of cloth, perches on the roof.

With its choir raised on a platform above the large crypt, the sublime **interior** of San Miniato is like no other in the city. The floor is adorned by an elaborately patterned pavement that's dated 1207, while the middle of the nave is dominated by the lovely tabernacle, or Cappella del Crocefisso, designed in 1448 by

Michelozzo and financed by Piero de' Medici. The tabernacle once housed the miraculous crucifix associated with St Giovanni Gualberto (see p.87); the painted panels by Agnolo Gaddi were originally arranged in the form of a cross to act as a frame for the now vanished cross.

▲ THE NAVE AT SAN MINIATO AL MONTE

Steps either side of the tabernacle lead down to the **crypt**, the oldest part of the church, where the original high altar still contains the alleged bones of St Miniatus. Above, the **choir** and **presbytery** have a magnificent Romanesque pulpit and screen dating from 1207, and a great mosaic of *Christ Pantocrator* enthroned between the Virgin and San Miniato, created in 1297, probably by the same artist who created the facade mosaic. Off the presbytery lies the **sacristy** (€1), whose walls are almost completely covered in a superlative fresco cycle by Spinello Aretino (1387), the first such complete cycle in Tuscany devoted to the life of St Benedict.

Back in the lower body of the church, off the left side of the nave, the **Cappella del Cardinale del Portogallo** constitutes one of Renaissance Florence's supreme examples of artistic collaboration. Completed in 1473, as a memorial to Cardinal James of Lusitania (who died in Florence in 1459, aged 25), the chapel was designed by Antonio di Manetto (or Manetti), a pupil and biographer of Brunelleschi, while the tomb itself was carved by Antonio and Bernardo Rossellino. This architectural and sculptural work was followed in 1466 by carefully integrated frescoes and paintings: an *Annunciation* (to the left) and the *Evangelists* and *Doctors of the Church* by Alesso Baldovinetti (lunettes and beside the arches). Antonio and Piero del Pollaiuolo produced the altarpiece depicting the cardinal's patron saint, St James, with SS Vincent and Eustace: the present picture is a copy, the original being in the Uffizi. The ceiling's tiled decoration and four glazed terracotta medallions, perhaps the finest such work in the city, were provided by Luca della Robbia.

The Forte di Belvedere and around

The Forte di Belvedere, standing on the crest of the hill above the Bóboli garden, was built by Buontalenti on the orders of Ferdinando I between 1590 and 1595, ostensibly to protect the city, but in fact to intimidate the grand duke's subjects. The panorama from here is superb, and exhibitions are often held in and around the shed-like palace in the centre of the fortress, as are occasional summer evening film screenings. The Ragione collection of twentieth-century art, formerly on show on Piazza della Signoria, may relocate here at some unspecified point in the future, or the Belvedere may become the home of a new armoury museum.

In the past it has sometimes been possible to access the fort from the Bóboli gardens, but if you want to be certain of getting in, approach the fort from the **Costa San Giorgio**, a lane which you can reach by backtracking slightly from the Museo Bardini, or pick up directly from the rear of Santa Felìcita (see map, p.134). Look out for the villa at no. 19, home to Galileo between 1610 and 1631.

San Leonardo in Arcetri

Daily 10am–noon. East from the Belvedere stretches the best-preserved section of Florence's fortified walls, paralleled by Via di Belvedere. South of the Belvedere, Via San Leonardo leads past olive groves to the rarely open church of San Leonardo in Arcetri, site of a beautiful thirteenth-century pulpit brought here from a church that's now incorporated into the Uffizi. Dante and Boccaccio are both said to have preached here.

Shop

Il Torchio

Via de' Bardi 17 ☎055.234.2862. Mon–Fri 9.30am–1.30pm & 2.30–7pm, Sat 9.30am–1pm. A marbled paper workshop using manufacturing techniques known only to the owner. Desk accessories, diaries, albums and other items in paper and leather are also available.

Gelateria

Frilli

Via San Miniato 5r. Tues–Sun 10am–8pm, but open till midnight on summer weekends. Excellent ice creams are sold at this tiny outlet, just inside the city walls – the ones made from seasonal fruit are magnificent.

Bars

Caffè La Torre

Lungarno Cellini 65r ☎055.680.643. Daily 10.30am–3am. This modern-styled bar changes its decor every year, which is one reason it has managed to remain one of the most fashionable bars in Florence. The other is its superb location, in the shadow of the tower of the Porta San Niccolò, close to the Arno, with lots of outdoor seating. Imaginative cocktails complete the picture.

Zoe

Via dei Renai 13 ☎055.243.111. Daily 9am–3pm & 6pm–3am. Just set back from the Arno, on the south side of the grassy Piazza Demidoff, *Zoe* and neighbouring *Negroni* are perennially popular for summer evening drinks. *Zoe* is a little louder and a little trendier, and it attracts lots of young Florentines right through the day – 9am–noon is breakfast time, lunch is noon–3pm, then it's "Aperitif" from 6–10pm, when the "American Bar" theme takes over. Does good snacks and simple meals but the cocktails are the main event. There's a DJ on Fridays.

Wine bar

Fuori Porta

Via del Monte alle Croci 10r ☎055.234.2483. Mon–Sat 12.30–3.30pm & 7pm–12.30am; closed 2wks in Aug. If you're climbing up to San Miniato you could take a breather at this superb and

▲ I TAROCCHI

justly famous wine bar-*osteria*. There are over four hundred wines to choose from by the bottle, and an ever-changing selection of wines by the glass, as well as a wide selection of grappas and malt whiskies. Bread, cheese, hams and salamis are available, together with a choice of pasta dishes and tasty salads.

Restaurants

Filipepe

Via San Niccolò 39r ☎055.200.1397. Daily 7.30pm–1am; closed 2wks in Aug. A well-priced and imaginative place, with a menu that's markedly different from most of the competition – it markets itself as a "Mediterranean restaurant", and offers delicious food drawn from a variety of Italian regional cuisines. The wine list is similarly wide-ranging, and the decor offbeat and attractive. You'll pay in the region of €30 per person.

I Tarocchi

Via dei Renai 12r ☎055.234.3912. Tues–Fri 12.30–2.30pm & 7pm–1am, Sat & Sun 7pm–1am only. There are a few simple dishes on the menu, but this is essentially an inexpensive pizzeria – and one of the best in the city.

The city outskirts

The peripheral attractions covered in this section – the Cascine park, Museo Stibbert and Florence's football ground – are all a stiff walk from the centre of town, or can be reached by ATAF bus.

The Cascine

Bus #1, 9, 12, 17 or 17c from the station. Florence's public park, the Cascine, begins close to the Ponte della Vittoria, a half-hour walk west of the Ponte Vecchio, and dwindles away 3km downstream, at the confluence of the Arno and the Mugnone rivers. Once a dairy farm (*cascina*), then a hunting reserve, this narrow strip of greenery mutated into a high-society venue in the eighteenth century: Florence's *beau monde* used to relax with a promenade under the trees of the Cascine. A fountain in the park bears a dedication to Shelley, who was inspired to write his *Ode to the West Wind* while strolling here on a blustery day in 1819.

Thousands of people come out here on Tuesday mornings for the colossal **market**, and on any day of the week the Cascine swarms with joggers, cyclists and roller-bladers. Parents bring their kids out here too, but it has to be said that the Cascine is a somewhat ill-kempt park, and it also has a reputation as a haunt for the city's junkies. It's emphatically not a place for a nocturnal stroll, as it has long been a hunting ground for the city's pimps.

The Museo Stibbert

Via Stibbert 26. Mon–Wed 10am–2pm, Fri–Sun 10am–6pm; guided tour €5. Bus #4 from the station. About 1500m north of San Marco stands the Museo Stibbert. This rambling, murky mansion was the home of the half-Scottish half-Italian Frederick Stibbert, who in his twenties made a name for himself in Garibaldi's

▼ THE CASCINE

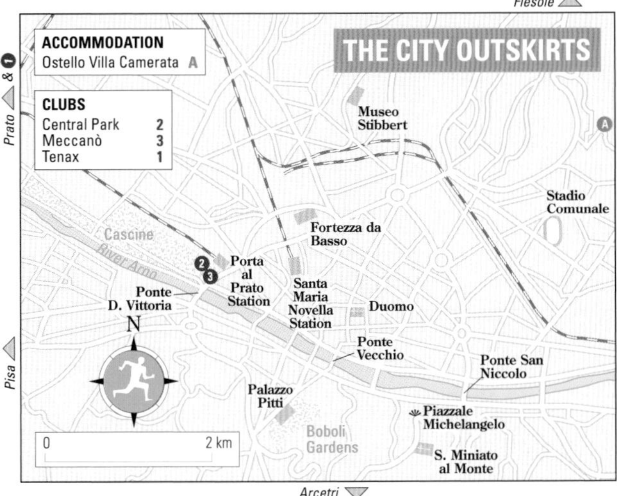

army. Later he inherited a fourteenth-century house from his mother, then bought the neighbouring mansion and joined the two together, thus creating a place big enough to accommodate the fruits of his compulsive collecting. The 64 rooms contain over fifty thousand items, ranging from snuffboxes to paintings by Carlo Crivelli and a possible Botticelli.

Militaria were Frederick's chief enthusiasm, and the Stibbert **armour** collection is reckoned one of the world's best. It includes Roman, Etruscan and Japanese examples (the highlight of the whole museum), as well as a fifteenth-century condottiere's outfit and the armour worn by the great Medici soldier Giovanni delle Bande Nere, retrieved from his grave in San Lorenzo in 1857. The big production number comes in the great hall, between the two houses, where a platoon of mannequins is clad in full sixteenth-century gear.

Campo di Marte

Bus #17 from the train station.

As befits this monument-stuffed city, Florence's football team play in a stadium that's listed as a building of cultural significance, the **Stadio Comunale** (or Stadio Artemio Franchi) at Campo di Marte. It was designed by Pier Luigi Nervi in 1930, and was the first major sports venue to exploit the shape-making potential of reinforced concrete – its spiral ramps, cantilevered roof and slim central tower still make quite an impact.

Market

Cascine market

Every Tuesday. The biggest of all Florence's markets happens Tuesday morning at the Cascine park, near the banks of the Arno, where hundreds of stallholders set up an alfresco budget-class department store. Clothes (some secondhand) and shoes are the best bargains.

▲ MUSEO STIBBERT: THE ARMOURY

Clubs

Central Park

Via Fosso Macinante 2, Parco delle Cascine ☎055.353.505. Summer Tues–Sat 11pm–4am; winter Fri & Sat 11pm–4am only. One of the city's biggest and most commercial clubs, with adventurous, wide-ranging and up-to-the-minute music from DJs who know what they're doing and have access to a superb sound system. A card system operates for drinks – you pay when you leave, which can entail a long wait at the check-out tills. It's unsafe to wander around the park in the dead of night, especially for women. Admission free.

Meccanò

Viale degli Olmi 1/Piazzale delle Cascine ☎055.331.371. Summer Tues–Sat 11pm–4am; winter Mon–Sat 11pm–4am only; closed Nov & 2wks in Aug. People flock here for a night out from across half of Tuscany. The place is labyrinthine, with a trio of lounge and bar areas, and a huge and invariably packed dance floor playing mostly house. In summer, when the action spills out of doors, you can cool off in the gardens bordering the Cascine. The €10–20 admission includes your first drink.

Tenax

Via Pratese 46 ☎055.282.340. Thurs–Sat 10.30pm–4am; closed mid-May to mid-Sept. Florence's big-hitting club, pulling in the odd big-name DJ. Given its location in the northwest of town, near the airport (take a taxi), you'll escape the hordes of *internazionalisti* in the more central clubs. With two large floors, it's a major venue for concerts as well. Admission varies from around €10 to around €20.

Football

Stadio Artemio Franchi

Following bankruptcy in 2002, Florence's football team – Fiorentina (Ⓦwww.acffiorentina.it) – was kicked out of Serie A and demoted to Serie C2B – in effect, the bottom of the heap. Most of its star players then jumped ship, but the club fought its way back up the leagues, returning to Serie A for the 2004/2005 season. The *Viola* (after their violet shirts) are now once again a securely top-flight outfit. Match tickets cost from around €20 and can be bought at the ground itself or from numerous outlets in the city – they're listed on the club website.

▲ FIORENTINA FOOTBALL SHIRTS

Fiesole

The hill-town of Fiesole, which spreads over a cluster of hills above the Mugnone and Arno valleys some 8km northeast of Florence, is conventionally described as a pleasant retreat from the crowds and heat of summertime Florence. Unfortunately, its tranquillity has been so well advertised that in high season it's now hardly less busy than Florence itself; that said, Fiesole offers a grandstand view of the city, has something of the feel of a country village, and bears many traces of its long history.

First settled in the Bronze Age, later by the Etruscans and then absorbed by the Romans, it rivalled its neighbour until the early twelfth century, when the Florentines overran the town. From that time it became a satellite, favoured as a semi-rural second home for wealthier citizens such as the ubiquitous Medici.

The #7 ATAF **bus** runs every twenty minutes from Santa Maria Novella train station to Fiesole's central Piazza Mino da Fiesole, stopping very close to the Duomo on Borgo San Lorenzo on the way. The journey takes around twenty minutes, and costs the standard city fare of €1 each way.

The Duomo

Daily 7.30am–noon & 3–6pm; winter 5pm. When the Florentines wrecked Fiesole in 1125, the only major building they spared was the Duomo, on the edge

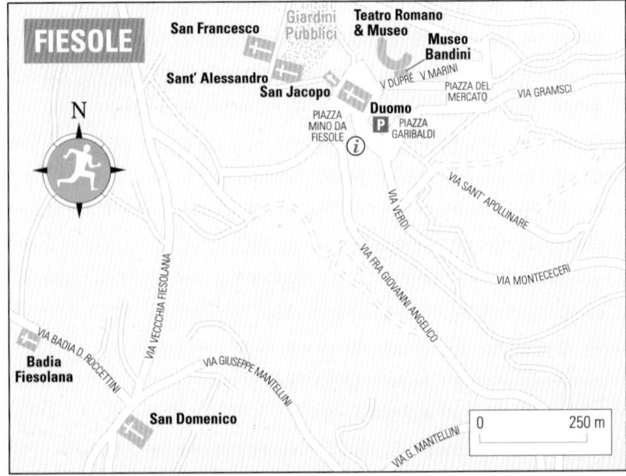

▲ SANT'ALESSANDRO

of Piazza Mino. Subsequently, nineteenth-century restorers managed to ruin the exterior, which is now notable only for its lofty campanile. The most interesting part of the bare interior is the raised choir: the altarpiece is a polyptych, painted in the 1440s by Bicci di Lorenzo, and the Cappella Salutati, to the right, contains two fine pieces carved around the same time by Mino da Fiesole – an altar frontal of *The Madonna and Saints* and the tomb of Bishop Salutati. Fiesole's patron saint, St Romulus, is buried underneath the choir in the ancient crypt.

The Museo Bandini

Via Dupré 1. March & Oct daily 9.30am–6pm; April–Sept daily 9.30am–7pm; Nov–Feb Mon & Thurs–Sun 11am–5pm. €7. The Museo Bandini possesses a workaday collection of glazed terracotta in the style of the della Robbias, the odd piece of Byzantine ivory work and a few thirteenth- and fourteenth-century Tuscan pictures, none of them outstanding.

Teatro Romano

Same hours and ticket as Museo Bandini. Built in the first century BC, the three-thousand-seat Teatro Romano was excavated towards the end of the nineteenth century and is in such good repair that it's used for performances during the Estate Fiesolana festival (see p.182). Most of the exhibits in the site's small museum were excavated in this area, and encompass pieces from the Bronze Age to the Roman occupation.

Sant'Alessandro, San Jacopo and San Francesco

Fiesole's other major churches, Sant'Alessandro and San Francesco, are reached from the piazza by the steep Via San Francesco, which runs past the tiny Oratorio di San Jacopo (Sat & Sun 10am–7pm; same ticket as museum) and a terrace that gives a knockout view of Florence. Sant'Alessandro (open for occasional exhibitions only) was founded in the sixth century on the site of Etruscan and Roman temples; repairs have rendered the outside a

▲ BADÌA FIESOLANA

whitewashed nonentity, but the beautiful *marmorino cipollino* (onion marble) columns of the basilical interior make it the most atmospheric building in Fiesole.

Restoration has not improved the Gothic San Francesco (daily 9am–noon & 3–6/7pm) which occupies the site of the acropolis – the interior is a twentieth-century renovation, but the tiny cloisters are genuine. The church itself contains an *Immaculate Conception* by Piero di Cosimo (second altar on right) and a triptych by Bicci di Lorenzo. Within the church is a small museum featuring material gathered mainly by missions to the Far East, much of it from China. From the front of San Francesco a gate opens into a wooded public park, the most pleasant descent back to Piazza Mino.

San Domenico and the Badìa Fiesolana

The most enjoyable excursion from Fiesole is a wander down the narrow Via Vecchia Fiesolana, which passes the Villa Medici – built for Cosimo il Vecchio by Michelozzo – on its way to the hamlet of San Domenico. Fra' Angelico was once prior of the Dominican monastery at this village, and the **church** (daily: summer 7.30am–12.30pm & 4.30–6.30pm; winter 8.30am–noon & 4–6pm) retains a *Madonna and Angels* by him, in the first chapel on the left; the chapterhouse also has a Fra' Angelico fresco of *The Crucifixion* (ring at no. 4).

Five minutes' walk northwest from San Domenico stands the Badìa Fiesolana (Mon–Fri 9am–5.30pm, Sat 9am–12.30pm), Fiesole's **cathedral** from the ninth century to the eleventh. Cosimo il Vecchio had the church altered in the 1460s, a project which left the magnificent Romanesque facade embedded in the rough stone frontage while the interior was transformed into a superb Renaissance building.

Accommodation

Hotels

Accommodation in Florence can be a problem: hotels are plentiful but prices are high and demand is inexhaustible. The tourist invasion has very few slack spots: "**low season**" is defined by most hotels as meaning mid-July to the end of August (the weeks during which nearly all Italians head for the beaches or the mountains), and from mid-November to mid-March, except for the Christmas and New Year period. Between **March and October** you'll need to book your room well in advance or reconcile yourself to staying some way from the centre.

The tourist office no longer offers assistance in finding somewhere to stay. There's a private fee-charging hotel-search office at the train station, but you'd be better advised to make sure you have somewhere sorted out before you arrive. If none of our recommended places has a vacancy, search the listings on the official tourism website: Ⓦwww.firenzeturismo.it. Never respond to the touts who hang around the train station: their hotels are likely to be expensive, or remote, or unlicensed private houses.

All our recommended hotels, *affitacamere*, *residenze* and hostels are marked on the relevant chapter maps, in addition to the maps in this chapter.

Piazza del Duomo

Aldini Via dei Calzaiuoli 13 Ⓣ055.214.752, Ⓦwww.hotelaldini.it. The rooms are somewhat functional but this two-star could hardly be more centrally placed. All fourteen rooms (doubles around €140 in high season; singles €90) have private bathrooms.

Benivieni Via delle Oche 5 Ⓣ055.238.2133, Ⓦwww.hotelbenivieni.it. This small, friendly and family-run three-star is situated between the Duomo and Piazza della Signoria, tucked away on a quiet backstreet. Fifteen smallish rooms are ranged around two floors of a former synagogue; the rooms on the upper floor are brighter but all are simple, modern and in perfect condition. As they should be: the place only opened in 2001. Doubles at around €220.

Brunelleschi Piazza Santa Elisabetta 3 Ⓣ055.27.370, Ⓦwww.hotelbrunelleschi.it. Designed by architect Italo Gamberini, this four-star hotel is built around a Byzantine chapel and fifth-century tower. A small in-house museum displays Roman and other fragments found during building work. Decor is simple and stylish, with the original brick and stone offset by lots of wood; the 96 rooms and suites are spacious – the best, on the fourth floor, have views of the Duomo and Campanile. The rack rate for a

Renting an apartment

The high cost of hotel rooms in Florence makes self-catering an attractive option – for the price of a week in a cramped double room in a three-star hotel you could book yourself a two-bedroomed apartment right in the centre of the city. Many package holiday companies have a few apartments in their brochures, but a trawl of the Internet will throw up dozens of places at more reasonable prices. One of the best places to look is Ⓦwww.holiday-rentals.com, a site which puts you in touch directly with the owners and features some forty properties in Florence, from as little as €400pw in low season.

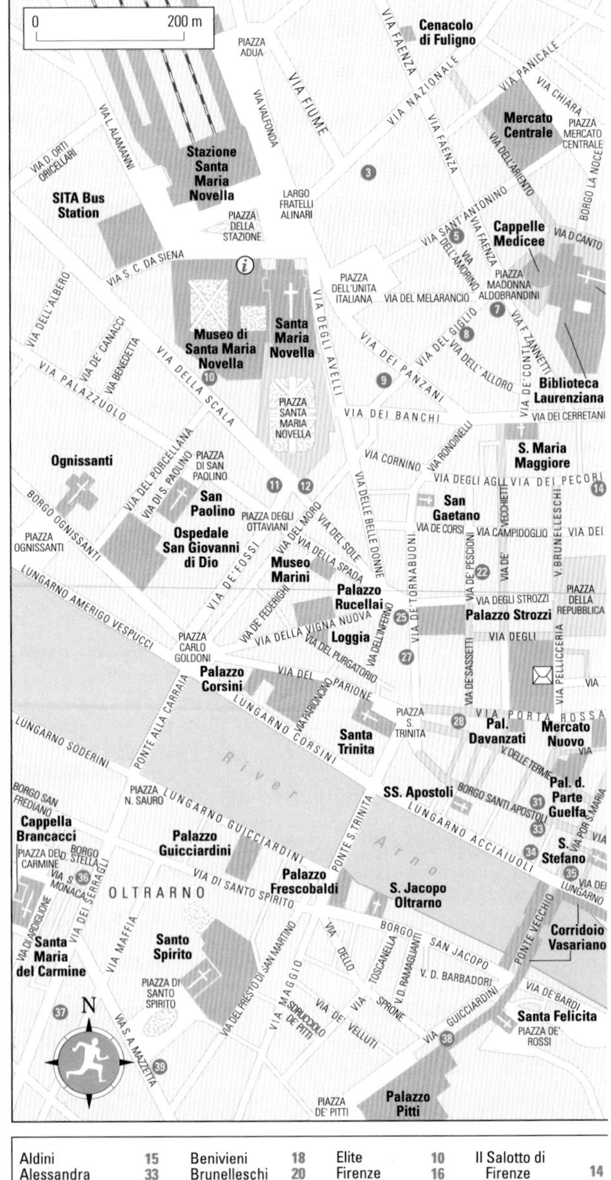

Aldini	15	Benivieni	18	Elite	10	Il Salotto di Firenze	14
Alessandra	33	Brunelleschi	20	Firenze	16	Instituto Gould	37
B&B in Piazza della Signoria	30	Casci	4	Gallery Hotel Art	34	J.K. Place	12
Bavaria	23	Concordia	5	Helvetia & Bristol	22	La Scaletta	38
Beacci Tornabuoni	27	Costantini	15	Hermitage	35	Le Stanze di Santa Croce	32
Belletini	7	Dali	17				
		Dei Mori	26				

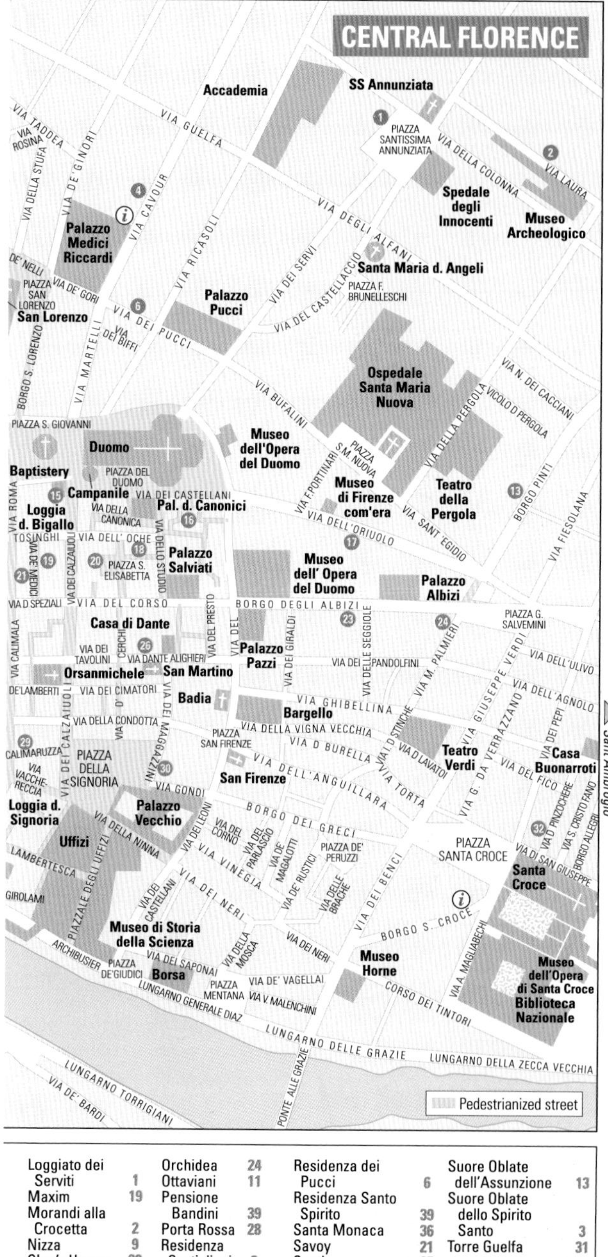

Loggiato dei Serviti 1
Maxim 19
Morandi alla Crocetta 2
Nizza 9
Olga's House 29
Orchidea 24
Ottaviani 11
Pensione Bandini 39
Porta Rossa 28
Residenza Castiglioni 8
Residenza dei Pucci 6
Residenza Santo Spirito 39
Santa Monaca 36
Savoy 21
Scoti 25
Suore Oblate dell'Assunzione 13
Suore Oblate dello Spirito Santo 3
Torre Guelfa 31

double is around €380, but there are often special deals to be had.

Costantini **Via dei Calzaiuoli 13 ⓣ055.213.995, ⓦwww.hotelcostantini.it.** This fourteen-room two-star shares a great location with the *Aldini*, at the top of the city's main pedestrian street. Offers en-suite doubles for less than €150 in summer.

Dali **Via dell' Oriuolo 17 ⓣ055.234.0706, ⓦwww.hoteldali.com.** One of the least expensive one-star options close to the centre, with doubles from €60. The nine rooms, five with bath (€80), are plain and rather basic, but the location – on the top floor of a palazzo built in 1492 – helps, as does the view from the back rooms of the giant magnolia in the garden below. The friendly young owners speak good English.

Firenze **Piazza dei Donati 4 ⓣ055.214.203, ⓕ055.212.370.** Clean and central no-frills two-star hotel. It has 57 rooms, so there's a good chance of finding space here. Most rooms are doubles costing around €100–120; all have private bathrooms. Rooms on upper floors enjoy a touch more daylight.

The Bargello and around

Bavaria **Borgo degli Albizi 26 ⓣ055.234.0313, ⓦwww.hotelbavariafirenze.it.** A simple and decent one-star near the city centre with just nine rooms, including some palatial chambers on the upper floor, and several inexpensive rooms with shared bathroom. The hotel occupies part of a sixteenth-century palazzo built for a follower of Eleonora di Toledo. Be sure to book, especially in summer, when it's popular with student tour groups. Doubles from as little as €70 in high season, rising to €120 in summer.

Via dei Calzaiuoli and west

Alessandra **Borgo Santi Apostoli 17 ⓣ055.283.438, ⓦwww.hotelalessandra.com.** A very good two-star, with 27 rooms (nearly all with bathroom, at around €170 in summer) occupying a sixteenth-century palazzo and furnished in a mixture of antique and modern styles. Used by the fashion-show crowd, so booking is essential in September.

Beacci Tornabuoni **Via de' Tornabuoni 3 ⓣ055.212.645, ⓦwww.hotelbeacci.com.** With 28 rooms occupying the top two floors of a fifteenth-century palazzo, this is a beguilingly antiques-stuffed anachronism of a three-star hotel, perfectly placed on Florence's poshest shopping street. A few more rooms are available in the adjoining *Residenza Tornabuoni* and *Relais Tornabuoni*. Doubles cost up to €350 in high season, but around half that amount in low season.

Gallery Hotel Art **Vicolo dell'Oro 5 ⓣ055.272.6400, ⓦwww.lungarnohotels.com.** This immensely stylish four-star is unlike any other hotel in central Florence. A member of the Design Hotels group, it has a sleek, minimalist and hyper-modern look – lots of dark wood and neutral colours – and tasteful contemporary art displayed in the reception and all 74 rooms and suites. There is a small but smart bar, and an attractive lounge with art-filled bookshelves and comfortable sofas. The location is perfect, in a small, quiet square ten-seconds' walk from the Ponte Vecchio. Doubles usually from around €350 in high season, but special promotions can bring the price down by as much as €100.

Helvetia & Bristol **Via dei Pescioni 2 ⓣ055.266.51, ⓦwww.royaldemeure.com.** In business since 1894 and favoured by such luminaries as Pirandello, Stravinsky and Gary Cooper. Following a refit in the 1990s, this is now undoubtedly Florence's finest small-scale five-star hotel. The public spaces and 67 bedrooms and suites (each unique) are faultlessly designed and fitted, mixing antique furnishings and modern facilities – such as Jacuzzis in many bathrooms – to create a style that evokes the *belle époque* without being suffocatingly nostalgic or twee. If you're going to treat yourself, this is a leading contender. Double rooms start at around €250, rising to €1000.

Hermitage **Vicolo Marzio 1/Piazza del Pesce ⓣ055.287.216, ⓦwww.hermitagehotel.com.** Pre-booking is essential to secure one of the 28 rooms in this superbly located three-star hotel right next to the Ponte Vecchio, with unbeatable views from some rooms as well as from the flower-filled roof garden. The service is friendly, and rooms are cosy, decorated with the odd antique flourish; bathrooms are small but nicely done. Double-glazing has eliminated the noise problems once suffered by the front rooms, and you'll need to book many months in advance to secure one of these. Rooms from the former *Archibusieri* hotel, now incorporated into the *Hermitage*, are slightly less appealing. Doubles cost around €250 in high season, €120 in low.

Maxim **Entrances at Via dei Calzaiuoli 11 (lift) and Via de' Medici 4 (stairs) ⓣ055.217.474, ⓦwww .hotelmaximfirenze.it.** Few two-star hotels offer a better location than this friendly 26-room place just a minute from the Duomo. The clean double rooms are good value at around €150, and all have en-suite bathrooms; the quietest look onto a central courtyard.

Porta Rossa **Via Porta Rossa 19 ⓣ055.287.551, ⓦwww.hotelportarossa .com.** Florence has smarter three-star hotels, but none as venerable as the 78-room *Porta Rossa*, which has been a hotel since the fourteenth century and hosted, among others, Byron and Stendhal. You come here for character and nineteenth-century ambience, rather than luxurious modern touches. There are two fabulous tower rooms, available at almost twice the standard room price of around €200.

Savoy **Piazza della Repubblica 7 ⓣ055.27.351, ⓦwww.hotelsavoy.it.** The *Savoy* had become something of a doddery old dowager before being taken in hand by the Rocco Forte group. Now it's once again one of the city's very best hotels, having been refurbished in discreetly luxurious modern style, with plenty of bare wood, stone-coloured fabrics and peat-coloured marble. And the location could not be more central. Costs vary according to the time of year and whether there are special offers, but you can expect to pay around €500 for a double in summer, though the best rooms cost twice that.

Scoti **Via de' Tornabuoni 7 ⓣ055.292.128, ⓦwww.hotelscoti.com.** The one-star *Scoti* is the best budget option on this notoriously expensive street, with doubles available for around €120 in high season, €90 in low. It has just 11 rooms, all of them simple but smartly maintained.

Torre Guelfa **Borgo Santi Apostoli 8 ⓣ055.239.6338, ⓦwww .hoteltorreguelfa.com.** A dozen tastefully furnished rooms are crammed into three floors of this ancient tower (the tallest private building in the city), the pick of them having a tiny roof garden. Very charismatic (if slightly shabby in places), very popular, and quite pricy too – around €260 for the best room in high season, though a room on the first floor costs some €100 less.

Santa Maria Novella district

Elite **Via della Scala 12 ⓣ055.215.395, ⓕ055.213.832.** A ten-room two-star run by one of the most pleasant managers in town. All the double rooms have private bathrooms and are available for less than €100.

J.K. Place **Piazza Santa Maria Novella 7 ⓣ055.264.5181, ⓦwww.jkplace.com.** This twenty-room four-star is maybe the most appealing of Florence's designer hotels, and occupies a fine eighteenth-century building on Piazza Santa Maria Novella. *J.K. Place*'s big idea is to create a homely rather than hotel-like atmosphere, with a hostess rather than a receptionist, a bar from which you help yourself and a communal breakfast table where you can chat with fellow guests. The rooms all bear designer Michele Bönan's exotic-elegant stamp. Doubles from around €300 in low season, rising to €900 for a deluxe suite in high season.

Nizza **Via del Giglio 5 ⓣ055.239.6897, ⓦwww.hotelnizza.com.** A smart 18-room family-run two star, with helpful staff and very central location. All rooms are en suite, and are better furnished and decorated than many in this price range. Doubles €65–130.

Ottaviani **Piazza degli Ottaviani 1 ⓣ055.239.6223, ⓕ055.293.355.** The best of this one-star's twenty rooms (seven with private bathrooms) overlook Piazza Santa Maria Novella; others aren't so good, but the price (around €50–80) and location are unbeatable.

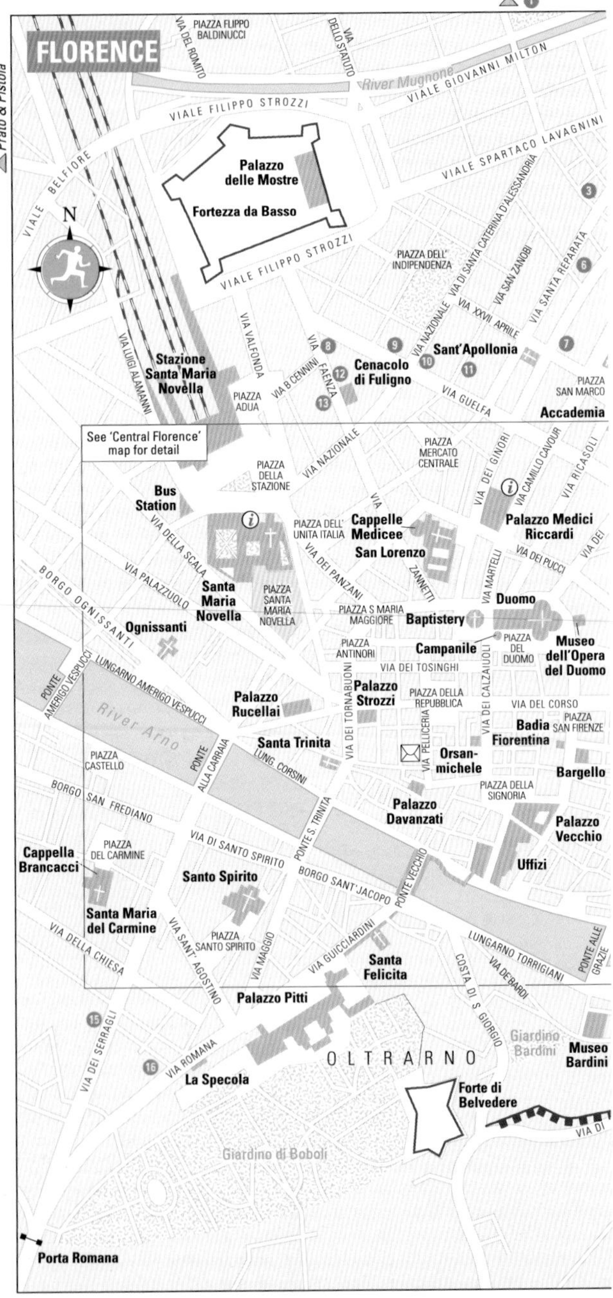
FLORENCE
Prato & Pistoia
Palazzo delle Mostre
Fortezza da Basso
Stazione Santa Maria Novella
Cenacolo di Fuligno
Sant'Apollonia
Accademia
See 'Central Florence' map for detail
Bus Station
Cappelle Medicee
San Lorenzo
Palazzo Medici Riccardi
Santa Maria Novella
Ognissanti
Duomo
Baptistery
Campanile
Museo dell'Opera del Duomo
Palazzo Strozzi
Palazzo Rucellai
Santa Trinita
Badia Fiorentina
Orsanmichele
Bargello
Palazzo Davanzati
Palazzo Vecchio
Uffizi
Cappella Brancacci
Santo Spirito
Santa Maria del Carmine
Santa Felicita
Palazzo Pitti
OLTRARNO
Giardino Bardini
Museo Bardini
La Specola
Forte di Belvedere
Giardino di Boboli
Porta Romana
River Arno
River Mugnone

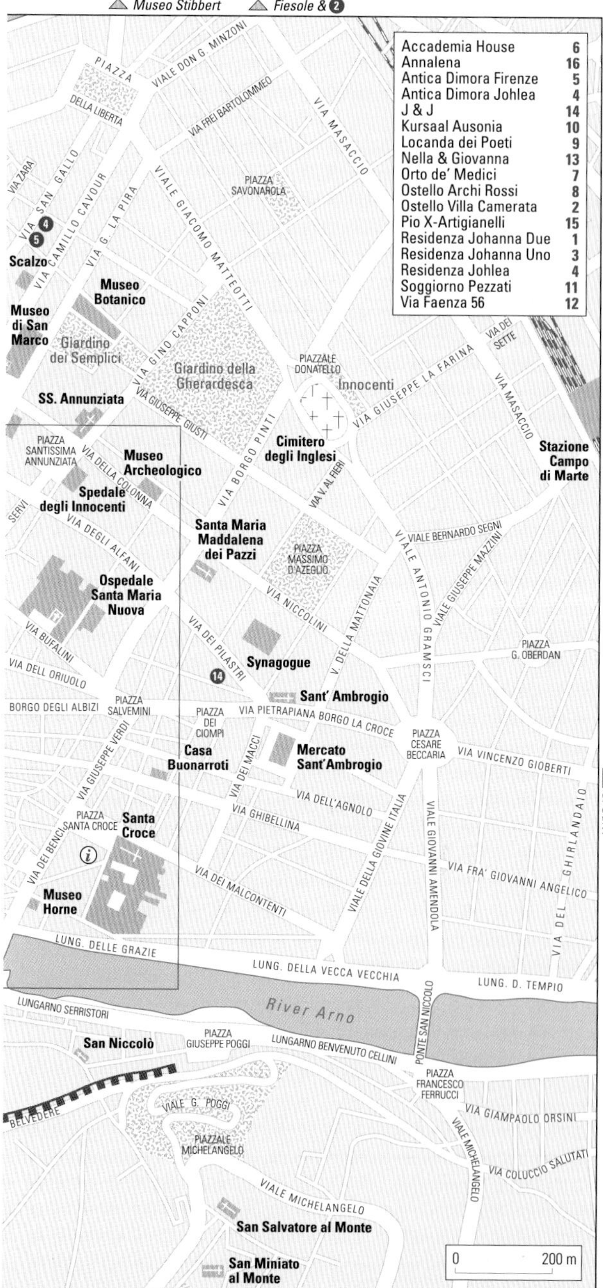
Museo Stibbert
Fiesole & 2
Accademia House 6
Annalena 16
Antica Dimora Firenze 5
Antica Dimora Johlea 4
J & J 14
Kursaal Ausonia 10
Locanda dei Poeti 9
Nella & Giovanna 13
Orto de' Medici 7
Ostello Archi Rossi 8
Ostello Villa Camerata 2
Pio X-Artigianelli 15
Residenza Johanna Due 1
Residenza Johanna Uno 3
Residenza Johlea 4
Soggiorno Pezzati 11
Via Faenza 56 12
Stadio Comunale
S. Salvi
Scalzo
Museo Botanico
Museo di San Marco
Giardino dei Semplici
Giardino della Gherardesca
Innocenti
SS. Annunziata
Cimitero degli Inglesi
Stazione Campo di Marte
Museo Archeologico
Spedale degli Innocenti
Santa Maria Maddalena dei Pazzi
Ospedale Santa Maria Nuova
Synagogue
Sant' Ambrogio
Casa Buonarroti
Mercato Sant'Ambrogio
Santa Croce
Museo Horne
River Arno
San Niccolò
San Salvatore al Monte
San Miniato al Monte
Piazza della Libertà
Viale Don G. Minzoni
Via Frei Bartolommeo
Via Masaccio
Piazza Savonarola
Via Zara
Via San Gallo
Via Camillo Cavour
Via G. La Pira
Viale Giacomo Matteotti
Via Gino Capponi
Via Giuseppe Giusti
Piazzale Donatello
Via Giuseppe La Farina
Via dei Sette
Piazza Santissima Annunziata
Via della Colonna
Via Borgo Pinti
Via V. al Fieri
Servi
Via degli Alfani
Viale Bernardo Segni
Viale Antonio Gramsci
Viale Giuseppe Mazzini
Piazza Massimo D'Azeglio
Via Niccolini
Via della Mattonaia
Via Bufalini
Via dei Pilastri
Piazza G. Oberdan
Via dell Oriuolo
Borgo degli Albizi
Piazza Salvemini
Piazza dei Ciompi
Via Pietrapiana
Borgo La Croce
Piazza Cesare Beccaria
Via Vincenzo Gioberti
Via Giuseppe Verdi
Via dei Macci
Via dell'Agnolo
Via Ghibellina
Viale della Giovine Italia
Viale Giovanni Amendola
Via del Ghirlandaio
Piazza Santa Croce
Via dei Benci
Via Fra' Giovanni Angelico
Via dei Malcontenti
Lung. delle Grazie
Lung. della Vecca Vecchia
Lung. D. Tempio
Lungarno Serristori
Piazza Giuseppe Poggi
Lungarno Benvenuto Cellini
Ponte San Niccolo
Piazza Francesco Ferrucci
Via Giampaolo Orsini
Belvedere
Viale G. Poggi
Piazzale Michelangelo
Viale Michelangelo
Via Coluccio Salutati
0 200 m

The San Lorenzo district

Bellettini **Via dei Conti 7 ⓣ055.213.561, ⓦwww.hotelbellettini.com.** The warm welcome of owner Signora Gina counts for much in this 27-room two-star, close to San Lorenzo; so, too, do her copious breakfasts. All rooms have private bathrooms and air-conditioning, around half have TVs; the price is around €150.

Casci **Via Cavour 13 ⓣ055.211.686, ⓦwww.hotelcasci.com.** It would be hard to find a better two-star in central Florence than this 26-room hotel. Only two (soundproofed) rooms face the busy street: the rest are quiet, clean and well fitted-out, and well-priced at €175 for a double in high season (falling to €100 out of season). The welcome is warm and the owners are unfailingly helpful and courteous. The big buffet breakfast in the reception area is a major plus, as is free Internet access.

Concordia **Via dell'Amorino 14 ⓣ055.213.233, ⓦwww.albergoconcordia.it**. An extremely convenient hotel, located at the back of San Lorenzo church. Recently upgraded to two-star status, it has sixteen rooms, all with private bathrooms, for €120 a night.

Kursaal Ausonia **Via Nazionale 24 ⓣ055.496.324, ⓦwww.kursonia.com.** Welcoming and very recently refurbished three-star near the station, formed in 2007 by the merger of two formerly separate hotels. The "superior" doubles cost around €150; the price of a "standard" room can go as low as €70.

Nella & Giovanna **Via Faenza 69 ⓣ055.265.4346, ⓦwww.hotelnella.net**. Small, tidy and cheap, much like the *Giovanna* at the same address (ⓣ & ⓕ055.238.1353). Both have just seven rooms each, for around €80, but whereas only four of *Giovanna*'s rooms have private bathrooms, every room at the *Nella* has.

Via Faenza 56 Several budget hotels are crammed into this address near the station. Best of the one-stars is the *Merlini* (ⓣ055.212.848, ⓦwww.hotelmerlini.it), with ten rooms, most of which have a private bathroom; prices are from €60 for a double without bathroom in low season to twice that for a double with bathroom in summer. It's on the third floor, along with the seven-room *Paola* (ⓣ055.213.682, ⓦwww.albergopaola.com), while on the first floor there's the slightly less scruffy seven-room *Armonia* (ⓣ055.211.146); both have rooms (with shared bathroom, mostly) for €70–80 a night in summer. On the first floor you'll also find the two-star *Azzi* (ⓣ055.213.806, ⓦwww.hotelazzi.com), which has garden views from most of its rooms, and charges €70–130 per double.

The San Marco and Annunziata districts

Loggiato dei Serviti **Piazza Santissima Annunziata 3 ⓣ055.289.592, ⓦwww.loggiatodeiservitihotel.it.** This elegant, extremely tasteful and well-priced three-star hotel is situated on one of Florence's most celebrated squares. Its 33 rooms have been stylishly incorporated into a structure built in the sixteenth century (in imitation of the Brunelleschi hospital across the square) to accommodate the Servite priests who worked there and provide lodgings for itinerant Servites. Their relative plainness reflects something of the building's history, but all are decorated with fine fabrics and antiques, and look out either onto the piazza or peaceful gardens to the rear: top-floor rooms have glimpses of the Duomo. The five rooms in the nearby annexe, at Via dei Servi 49, are similarly styled, but the building doesn't have the same charisma. Doubles in high season cost around €230, but there are often special offers at around half that price.

Morandi alla Crocetta **Via Laura 50 ⓣ055.234.4747, ⓦwww.hotelmorandi.it.** An intimate three-star gem, whose small size and friendly expat welcome – owner Katherine Doyle has lived in Florence since she was 12 – ensure a home-from-home atmosphere. Rooms are tastefully decorated with antiques and old prints, and vivid carpets laid on parquet floors. Two rooms have balconies opening onto a modest garden: the best room – with fresco fragments and medieval nooks and crannies – was converted from the site's former convent chapel. Doubles in high season cost around

€240, but in Nov, Dec, Jan and Feb there are special offers at around €150.

Orto de' Medici Via San Gallo 30 ⓣ055.483.427, ⓦwww.ortodeimedici.it. A 31-room frescoed and antique-furnished three-star, occupying a quiet palazzo in the university area. Via San Gallo is not the most attractive street in Florence, but the hotel has been very recently and impressively refurbished. Rooms cost up to €300.

Santa Croce & Sant'Ambrogio districts

J & J Via di Mezzo 20 ⓣ055.263.12, ⓦwww.cavalierehotels.com/firenze. The bland exterior of this former fifteenth-century convent, located very close to Piazza Sant'Ambrogio, conceals a romantic eighteen-room four-star hotel. Some rooms are vast split-level affairs, and all have charm (except the gloomy room 1) and are furnished with modern fittings, attractive fabrics and a few antiques. Common areas are decked in flowers and retain frescoes and vaulted ceilings from the original building. In summer breakfast is served in the convent's lovely old cloister. In high season you'll pay around €500 for the best rooms, but the website is worth checking for special offers.

Orchidea Borgo degli Albizi 11 ⓣ055.248.0346, ⓦwww.hotelorchideaflorence.it. A lovely twelfth-century building, with half a dozen big if basic one-star rooms, two with private bathroom. Doubles are a bargain at €50–80.

Central Oltrarno

Annalena Via Romana 34 ⓣ055.222.402, ⓦwww.hotelannalena.it. Situated a short way beyond Palazzo Pitti, this twenty-room three-star occupies part of a building once owned by the Medici, which passed to a young Florentine noblewoman (Annalena) who retired from the world after a disastrous love affair and bequeathed the building to the Dominicans. The best rooms open onto a gallery with garden views, and a sprinkling of antiques lend a hint of old-world charm. Doubles cost a very reasonable €100–180, depending on the season.

La Scaletta Via Guicciardini 13 ⓣ055.283.028, ⓦwww.lascaletta.com. An eleven-room two-star hotel in similar vein to the *Bandini* (see below), but slightly better turned-out; from the rooftop terrace you look across the Bóboli gardens in one direction and the city in the other. Doubles €100–200.

Western Oltrarno

Pensione Bandini Piazza Santo Spirito 9 ⓣ055.215.308, ⓔpensionebandini@tiscali.it. Some of the thirteen rooms in this one-star *pensione* are vast and have marble fireplaces, but other rooms are grim – so make sure you inspect before paying. Location is a plus, unless street noise bothers you: the hotel is on Piazza Santo Spirito, one of the city's more happening squares, and the hotel's loggia, which runs round two sides of the building, gives you a grandstand view. Prices are from around €100 without bath, or €120 en suite.

Affitacamere and residenze

To be classified as a hotel in Florence, a building has to have a minimum of seven bedrooms. Places with fewer rooms operate under the title *affitacamere* ("rooms for rent") or *residenze d'epoca* (if occupying a historic building) – though, confusingly, a *residenze d'epoca* might have as many as a dozens rooms. Some *affitacamere* are nothing more than a couple of rooms in a private house (and, though calling themselves "bed and breakfast", may not actually offer breakfast), but several – and most *residenze d'epoca* – are in effect small hotels in all but name, and some of the city's *residenze d'epoca* are among the most charismatic accommodation you can find in Florence. What follows is our pick of the small-scale places to stay; for full listings of accredited *affitacamere*, *residenze* and all other types of accommodation, go to Ⓦwww.firenzeturismo.it. One thing to bear in mind: like the budget hotels, *affitacamere* are often on the upper floors of large buildings, and usually can be reached only be stairs.

Piazza del Duomo

Il Salotto di Firenze Via Roma 6 ⓣ055.218.347, Ⓦwww.ilsalottodifirenze.it. Six well-appointed rooms, four of them doubles (three overlooking Piazza del Duomo). Not a good choice if you're a light sleeper, but the standard of accommodation is high and the location absolutely central. €90–250.

Piazza della Signoria

Bed & Breakfast in Piazza della Signoria Via dei Magazzini 2 ⓣ055.239 9546, Ⓦwww.inpiazzadellasignoria.com. This luxurious *residenza d'epoca* has ten spacious bedrooms, several of them giving a view of the piazza. The style is antique, but tastefully restrained, and the management is very friendly. Doubles €200–260.

Olga's House Via Calimaruzza 4 ⓣ330.883.421, Ⓦwww.olgashouse.com. *Olga's House* is in effect a four-room micro-hotel. The modern decor is a refreshing change from the usual bygone style, and the owners are extremely pleasant. Some might find the 80-step staircase a bit of a slog, though. €80–160.

The Bargello and around

Dei Mori Via Dante Alighieri 12 ⓣ055.211.438, Ⓦwww.deimori.it. *Dei Mori* was one of the first B&Bs to open in Florence, and is still one of the best. Five rooms, all with bathroom, for €90–150.

San Lorenzo district

Locanda dei Poeti Via Guelfa 74 ⓣ055.488.701, Ⓦwww.locandadeipoeti.com. Run by an actor and his partner, this small B&B has a poetry theme, as you might have guessed. Various parts of the building are dedicated to different poets, and poems are written on some of the walls. The wackiness doesn't extend to the four individually styled bedrooms, however. €90–160.

Residenza Castiglioni Via del Giglio 8 ⓣ055.239.6013, Ⓦwww.residenzacastiglioni.com. There are six big and handsome rooms in this fabulous eighteenth-century house, in which several walls and ceilings are frescoed. €90–200.

Residenza dei Pucci Via dei Pucci 9 ⓣ055.264.314, Ⓦwww.residenzadeipucci.com. Located very close to the Duomo, the *Residenze dei Pucci* occupies a fine nineteenth-century town house, and offers six beautifully furnished and decorated rooms, each of them different from all the others. €80–250.

Soggiorno Pezzati Via San Zanobi 22 ⓣ055.291.660, Ⓦwww.soggiornopezzati.it. The rooms here are plain and not large, but the price is very good, at €70–90 for a double.

San Marco and Annunziata districts

Accademia House Via San Gallo 61 ⓣ055.484.879, Ⓦwww.accademiahouse.com. This B&B has three rooms ("modern", "antique" and "classic"), in a beautifully restored sixteenth-century building. €60–110.

Residenza Johanna Uno Via Bonifacio Lupi 14 ⓣ055.481.896, ⓦwww.johanna.it. Genteel place that feels very much a "residence" rather than a hotel, hidden away in an unmarked apartment building in a very quiet, leafy corner of the city, five minutes' walk north of San Marco; ring the bell on the brass plaque by the wrought-iron gates. Rooms are cosy and well kept, there are books and magazines, and the two *signore* who run the place are as friendly and helpful as you could hope for. The very similar *Residenza Johanna Due* (ⓣ055.473.377) is located a bit further from the main sights, at Via Cinque Giornate 12, to the north of the Fortezza da Basso. *Johanna Uno* costs in the region of €100–150 a night; *Due* is a little cheaper.

Residenza Johlea Via San Gallo 76 ⓣ055.463.3292, ⓦwww.johanna.it. Another venture from the people who created the nearby *Residenza Johanna* (see above), offering the same low-cost, high-comfort package, with the same level of hospitality. At neighbouring Via San Gallo 80 you'll find the *Antica Dimora Johlea* (ⓣ055.461.185), which is a somewhat plusher version of the *Residenza*, with deluxe doubles for around €150–200, and a nice roof terrace. The same team run the similarly upmarket *Antica Dimora Firenze* at Via San Gallo 72 (ⓣ055.462.7296; ⓦwww.anticadimorafirenze.it), which has six very comfortable rooms (some with four-poster beds) for €100–160.

Santa Croce & Sant'Ambrogio districts

Le Stanze di Santa Croce Via delle Pinzochere 6 ⓣ347.259.3010, ⓦwww.viapinzochere6.it. This excellent B&B has four comfortable and brightly decorated rooms (though one of them has skylights rather than windows), and very hospitable owners. Doubles for around €160.

Western Oltrarno

Residenza Santo Spirito Piazza Santo Spirito 9 ⓣ055.265.8376, ⓦwww.residenzasspirito.com. This very well-presented B&B has two vast double rooms (both with fantastic frescoed ceilings, and both overlooking the piazza) and a two-roomed suite. The doubles cost around €140 in high season, the suite about €100 more.

Hostels

Florence has only a handful of hostels and the best of these is some distance from the centre. To help matters a little, there are a number of places run by religious bodies.

Istituto Gould Via dei Serragli 49 (Western Oltrarno) ⓣ055.212.576, ⓔgould.reception@dada.it. Occupies part of a former seventeenth-century palazzo (the doorbell is easily missed). Its 88 beds (in 33 rooms, most with bathroom) are extremely popular, so it's wise to book in advance, especially during the academic year. Street-front rooms can be noisy (rear rooms are better) but the old courtyard, terracotta floors and stone staircases provide atmosphere throughout. Open for check-in Mon–Fri 8.45am–1pm & 3–7.30pm, Sat 9am–1.30pm & 2–6pm, but closed Sun. From €17–34 per person per night, depending on how many beds to a room.

Ostello Archi Rossi Via Faenza 94r (San Lorenzo district) ⓣ055.290.804, ⓦwww.hostelarchirossi.com. A five-minute walk from the train station, this newish and privately owned hostel is spotlessly clean but decorated with guests' wall-paintings and graffiti. It's popular – the 96 places fill up quickly. Breakfast and evening meals are available at extra cost; spacious dining room with satellite TV and films shown on request in the evening. Beds from around €20–35 per night, depending on size of room (1–12 beds) and whether or not there's an internal bathroom; all prices include breakfast and 30min Internet time. No credit cards. Curfew at 2am.

Ostello Villa Camerata Viale Augusto Righi 2–4 (city outskirts) ⓣ055.601.451, ⓦwww.ostellionline.org. An HI hostel tucked away in a beautiful park to the northeast of the city. This is one of Europe's most attractive hostels, a sixteenth-century house with frescoed ceilings, fronted by lemon trees in terracotta pots. Doors open at 2pm; if you'll arrive later, call ahead to make sure there's space. There are 322 dorm places, and a few family rooms. Breakfast and sheets are included, but there are no kitchen facilities; optional supper costs about €8. Films in English are shown every night. Dorm beds €18; two/three-bed rooms €30/23 per person in high season. Take bus #17b from the train station (takes about 30min).

Pio X – Artigianelli Via dei Serragli 106 (Western Oltrarno) ⓣ055.225.044, ⓦwww.hostelpiox.it. One of the cheapest options in town, often booked up by school groups. Don't be put off by the huge picture of Pope Pius X at the top of the steps; the management is friendly and the atmosphere relaxed. Get there by 9am, as the 64 beds are quickly taken. Rooms have 3–6 beds and cost €17 per person, or €19 with en-suite bathrooms. Open all day throughout the year; 12.30am curfew; no reservations by phone.

Santa Monaca Via Santa Monaca 6 (Western Oltrarno) ⓣ055.268.338, ⓦwww.ostello.it. Privately owned hostel in Oltrarno, close to Santa Maria del Carmine. Has 115 beds, arranged in single-sex dorms (the smallest have 4 beds), with kitchen facilities and Internet access, and a useful noticeboard with information on lifts and onward travel. It's a fifteen-minute walk from the station, or take bus #11, #36 or #37 to the second stop after the bridge. Credit cards accepted. Open for check-in 6am–2am. Beds €15–19. Curfew 2am.

Suore Oblate dell'Assunzione Via Borgo Pinti 15 (Santa Croce and Sant'Ambrogio districts) ⓣ055.248.0582, ⓕ055.234.6291. Not far from the Duomo, this convent-run hostel is open to both men and women, as long as rooms are not required by the nuns or their visitors. There's no breakfast. Singles €38, doubles €37 per person, both with private bathrooms. Triples and quads also available. No credit cards. 11.30pm curfew.

Suore Oblate dello Spirito Santo Via Nazionale 8 (San Lorenzo district) ⓣ055.239.8202, ⓕ055.239.8129. Also run by nuns, this clean and pleasant hostel, a few steps from the station, is open to women, families and married couples only, and is closed to the public during school terms. Doubles, triples and quads all have private bathroom. Breakfast included, and there's a minimum stay of two nights. Doubles and triples cost €27 per person.

Essentials

Arrival

Your point of arrival is most likely to be Santa Maria Novella train station, which is located within a few minutes' walk of the heart of the historic centre: rail and bus connections from the three airports that serve the city all terminate at the station, as do international trains and buses from all over Italy.

By air

Most scheduled and charter flights fly to **Pisa's** Galileo Galilei airport (Ⓣ050.849.300, Ⓦwww.pisa-airport.com), 95km west of Florence and 3km from the centre of Pisa. *Terravision* shuttle **buses** are scheduled to synchronise with incoming European budget airline flights and leave from in front of the terminal; they take seventy minutes to reach Florence's Santa Maria Novella station, and tickets (€8 single) are sold at the stand right in front of you as you come out into the airport concourse. **Trains** from the airport station are cheaper (€6) if often slower (70–100min in total, depending on connections at Pisa Centrale); there are only seven direct trains daily (6.40am–10.20pm), but every thirty minutes a shuttle train runs from the airport to Pisa Centrale (6min), where you can change to one of the hourly services to Florence (journey time 1hr). Train tickets can be bought from the office at the opposite end of the concourse from the station. Remember to validate your ticket in the platform machines before boarding the train. If you're arriving very late, you'll have to take the five-minute bus, train or taxi ride to Pisa Centrale, from where trains to Florence start running from around 4am. Returning from Florence to Pisa Aeroporto, shuttle buses run from 5.50am to 7.10pm, from the station. After that, there is a direct train at around 8.30pm, but after that you'll have to take the train to Pisa Centrale and catch a connecting bus, train or taxi.

A few airlines use Florence's small **Perètola** (Amerigo Vespucci) airport (Ⓣ055.306.1300, Ⓦwww.aeroporto.firenze.it), 5km northwest of the city centre. The SITA and ATAF bus companies operate a joint service from Perètola called Volainbus (Ⓦwww.ataf.net), which provides half-hourly shuttles into the city from immediately outside the arrivals area. The first bus into the city is 6am (last 11.30pm), the first out to the airport at 5.30am (last 11pm). Tickets (€4.50) can be bought on board or from machines at the airport, and the journey takes about thirty minutes. Most buses arrive and depart from the main SITA bus terminal on Via di Santa Caterina da Siena, off Piazza della Stazione a few steps west of Santa Maria Novella train station; after 9pm, however, the buses depart from outside *Bar Cristallo* in Largo Alinari, off the eastern side of Piazza della Stazione. A **taxi** from Perètola into central Florence should cost about €15, and take around twenty minutes.

A few airlines use **Bologna** (Ⓦwww.bologna-airport.it) – about the same distance from Florence as Pisa – as a gateway airport for Florence. Aerobus shuttles depart every twenty minutes (7.30am–11.45pm) from outside the airport's Terminal A to Bologna's main train station (about 25min), from where regular trains run to Florence's Santa Maria Novella station in about an hour. Note, however, that Ryanair services to Bologna in fact fly to Forlì airport, which is more than 60km southeast of Bologna, and very inconvenient for Florence.

By train

Florence's central station, Santa Maria Novella ("Firenze SMN" on timetables), is located just north of the church and square of Santa Maria Novella, a couple of blocks west of the Duomo. In the station are an accommodation service, left-luggage facilities and a 24-hour pharmacy. While in and around the station, you should keep a close eye on your bags at all times: it's a prime hunting ground for thieves and pickpockets. Also avoid the concourse's various taxi and hotel touts, however friendly they may appear.

Information

The main **tourist office** (Mon–Sat 8.30am–6.30pm, Sun 8.30am–1.30pm; ⓣ 055.290.832 or 055.290.833, ⓦ www.firenze.turismo.toscana.it) is at Via Camillo Cavour 1r, five-minutes' walk north of the Duomo. A quieter office, run by the town council, is located just off Piazza Santa Croce at Borgo Santa Croce 29r (Mon–Sat 9am–7pm, Sun 9am–2pm; ⓣ 055.234.0444). There's also an office right outside the train station, to the right of the church on the far side of the large Piazza della Stazione (Mon–Sat 8.30am–7pm, Sun 8.30am–2pm; ⓣ 055.212.245).

All three provide an adequate map and various leaflets, including a sheet with updated opening hours and entrance charges, and the office at Via Cavour also handles information on the whole of Florence province. (But note that none of these offices will book accommodation.) Another excellent source of information is *Firenze Spettacolo*, a monthly, mostly bilingual listings magazine available from bookshops and larger newsstands. Also useful is *The Florentine* (ⓦ www.theflorentine.net) a bi-weekly English-language paper, available at the tourist office, most bookshops and various other spots (the website lists all of the places it can be picked up).

City transport

Within the historic centre, walking is generally the most efficient way of getting around, and the imposition of the **zona a traffico limitato** (ZTL) – which limits traffic in the centre to residents' cars, delivery vehicles and public transport – has somewhat reduced the once unbearable pollution and noise. That said, there are spots in the city where it's hard to believe that any restrictions are in place, and the ZTL has increased the average speed of the traffic, so you should be especially careful before stepping off the narrow pavements.

Florence on the Internet

Agenzia per il Turismo di Firenze ⓦ www.firenze.turismo.toscana.it. An official tourist office site (there are several), with an English-language option. Useful for information on forthcoming exhibitions and hotel listings.

Firenze.net ⓦ www.firenze.net. Smart, stylish website, packed with city info and links.

Firenze Spettacolo ⓦ www.firenzespettacolo.it. The online edition of Florence's listings magazine.

Polo Museale ⓦ www.polomuseale.firenze.it. For information on Florence's museums.

Your Way to Florence ⓦ www.arca.net/florence.htm. A comprehensive English-language site, with news plus information on transport, accommodation and opening hours.

Florentine addresses

Note that there is a **double address** system in Florence, one for businesses and one for all other properties – that, at least, is the theory behind it, though in fact the distinction is far from rigorous. Business addresses are followed by the letter r (for *rosso*) and are marked on the building with a red number on a white plate, sometimes with an r after the numeral, but not always. The two series are independent of each other, which means that no. 20, for example, may be a long way from no. 20r.

Buses

If you want to cross town in a hurry, or visit some of the peripheral sights, your best option is to use one of the frequent and speedy orange **ATAF buses**.

Tickets are valid for unlimited usage within seventy minutes (€1.20), 24 hours (€5) or 72 hours (€12). A Biglietto Multiplo gives four seventy-minute tickets for €4.50. You can buy tickets from the main ATAF information office in the bays to the east of Santa Maria Novella train station (daily 7am–8pm; Ⓦwww.ataf.net), from any shops and stalls displaying the ATAF sign, and from automatic machines all over Florence; tickets cannot be bought on buses. Once you're on board, you must stamp your ticket in the machine to begin its period of validity. There's a hefty on-the-spot **fine** for any passenger without a validated ticket.

Most of the routes that are useful to tourists stop by the station, notably #7 (for Fiesole), and #12/13 (to/from Piazzale Michelangelo and San Miniato). In addition to these, small **electric buses** run along four very convenient central city routes. Bus #A runs from the station right through the historic centre, passing close by the Duomo and Signoria, then heading east just north of Santa Croce; #B follows the north bank of the Arno; while #C descends from Piazza San Marco, heading south past Santa Croce and across the Ponte delle Grazie on its way to Via Bardi. These three buses follow similar routes on their return journeys. Bus #D leaves the station and crosses the river at Ponte Vespucci; from here it becomes a handy Oltrarno bus, running right along the south bank of the river and, on the return journey, jinking up past Palazzo Pitti, Santo Spirito and the Carmine church on its way back to the Ponte Vespucci.

Taxis

Taxis are white with yellow trim. It's difficult to flag down a cab on the street but there are plenty of central ranks: key locations include the station, Piazza della Repubblica, Piazza del Duomo, Piazza Santa Maria Novella, Piazza San Marco, Piazza Santa Croce and Piazza Santa Trìnita. You can also call a "radio taxi" on Ⓣ055.4242, Ⓣ055.4798 or Ⓣ055.4390. If you do, you'll be given the car's code name – usually a town, city or country – and its number, both of which are emblazoned on the cab. Italians tend not to order cabs far in advance; simply call up a few minutes beforehand.

All rides are metered; expect to pay €5–8 for a short hop within the centre. Supplements on the metered fare are payable between 10pm and 6am, all day on Sunday and public holidays, for journeys outside the city limits (to Fiesole, for example) and for each piece of luggage placed in the boot. When the cab sets off there will already be a small sum on the meter – ranging from just under €3 during the day to twice that at night. There's a surcharge of a couple of euros for calling out a radio taxi.

Museum admission

All of Florence's state-run museums belong to an association called Firenze Musei (Ⓦwww.firenzemusei.it), which sets aside a daily quota of tickets that can be reserved in advance. The Uffizi, the Accademia and the Bargello belong to this group, as do the Palazzo Pitti museums, the Bóboli gardens, the Medici chapels in San Lorenzo, the archeological museum and the San Marco museum. You can **reserve tickets** (for a €3 booking fee) by phoning ⓣ055.294.883 (Mon–Fri 8.30am–6.30pm, Sat 8.30am–12.30pm), or at the Firenze Musei booth at Orsanmichele (Mon–Sat 10am–5.30pm), or at the museums themselves. If you use the phone line, an English-speaking operator will allocate you a ticket for a specific hour, to be collected at the museum, again at a specific time, shortly before entry. That's the theory, but in reality the line tends to be engaged for long periods at a stretch, so perseverance is nearly always required. Generally, the Orsanmichele booth is the easiest option. Pre-booking is strongly recommended at any time of year for the Uffizi and the Accademia, whose allocation of reservable tickets is often sold out many days ahead.

Note that on-the-door admission to all state-run museums is free for EU citizens under 18 and over 65, on presentation of a passport; 18–25s get a fifty percent discount, as do teachers, on proof of identity. Nearly all of Florence's major museums are routinely **closed on Monday**, though some are open for a couple of Mondays each month. In the majority of cases, museum ticket offices close thirty minutes before the museum itself. At the Palazzo Vecchio and Museo Stibbert, however, it's one hour before, while at the Uffizi, Bargello, Museo dell'Opera del Duomo, the dome of the Duomo, the Campanile and Pitti museums it's 45 minutes.

Directory

Banks and exchange Florence's main bank branches are on or around Piazza della Repubblica, but exchange booths (*cambio*) and ATM cash-card machines (*bancomat*) for Visa and Mastercard advances can be found across the city. Banks generally open Mon–Fri 8.20am–3.35pm (some close for an hour in the middle of the day), though some are open longer hours. A useful Travelex branch is near the north side of the Ponte Vecchio, at Lungarno Acciaiuoli 6r (Mon–Sat 9am–6pm, Sunday 9.30am–5pm; ⓣ055.289.781); American Express is at Via Dante Alighieri 22r (Mon–Fri 9am–5.30pm, Sat 9am–12.30pm; ⓣ055.50.981).

Bus information City buses are run by ATAF ⓣ800.424.500, ⓦwww.ataf.net.

Consulates UK, Lungarno Corsini 2 ⓣ055.284.133, ⓔconsular.florence@fco.gov.uk; US, Lungarno Amerigo Vespucci 38 ⓣ055.266.951.

Doctors The Studio Medico Associato is a private service used to dealing with foreigners; they have doctors on call 24 hours a day on ⓣ055.475.411, or you can visit their clinic at Via Lorenzo il Magnifico 59 (Mon–Fri 11am–noon & 5–6pm, Sat 11am–noon). Note that you'll need insurance cover to recoup the cost of a consultation, which will be at least €65. Florence's central hospital is on Piazza Santa Maria Nuova.

Emergencies Police ⓣ112 or ⓣ113; fire ⓣ115; car breakdown ⓣ116; first aid ⓣ118. If your passport is lost or stolen, report it to the police and contact your consulate.

Flight information Aeroporto Galileo Galilei, Pisa ⓣ050.849.300, ⓦwww.pisa-airport.com; information also from the check-in desk at Santa Maria Novella train station, platform 5 (daily 7am–8pm). Aeroporto Florence-Perètola (Amerigo Vespucci), Via del Termine 11 ⓣ055.306.1300, ⓦwww.aeroporto.firenze.it – for recorded information on international flights call ⓣ055.306.1702, on domestic flights ⓣ055.306.1700.

Internet access Internet Train (ⓦwww.internettrain.it) has more than a dozen outlets in Florence, including Via de' Benci 36r (off Piazza Santa Croce), Via Guelfa 54/56r (north of Mercato Centrale), and Piazza Stazione 1. New Internet cafés are opening all the time, with the main concentrations being around the train station, San Lorenzo and the university/San Marco area. The tourist office has a full list.

Left luggage Santa Maria Novella station by platform 16 (daily 6am–midnight); €3.80 per piece for 5hr, then €0.60 for every extra hour up to 12hr, and €0.20 for every extra hour after that.

Lost property Lost property handed into the city or railway police ends up at Via Circondaria 19, in the northwest of the city, beyond the Fortezza da Basso (Mon–Sat 9am–noon; Ⓣ055.328.3943; take bus #23 to Viale Corsica). There's also a lost property office at Santa Maria Novella station, on platform 16 next to left luggage (daily 7am–noon; Ⓣ055.235.2190).

Pharmacies The Farmacia Comunale, on the train station concourse, is open 24hr, as is Al Insegna del Moro, Piazza San Giovanni 20r, on the north side of the Baptistery, and Farmacia Molteni, Via dei Calzaiuoli 7r. Normal opening hours for pharmacies are Mon–Sat 8.30am–1pm & 4–8pm. All pharmacies display a late-night roster in their window; otherwise ring Ⓣ182 for information.

Police Emergency Ⓣ112 or 113. The Questura, where you should report a lost passport or a theft, is at Via Zara 2, north of San Marco (daily 8.30am–8pm; Ⓣ055.49.771). If you do report a theft or other crime, you will have to fill out a form (*una denuncia*); this may be time-consuming, but it's essential if you want to make a claim on your travel insurance on returning home.

Post office The main central post office is near Piazza della Repubblica at Via Pellicceria 3 (Mon–Fri 8.15am–7pm, Sat 8.15am–12.30pm); the poste restante section is through the door immediately on the left as you enter. If you're having mail sent to you poste restante, make sure it's marked for Via Pellicceria, otherwise it will go to Florence's biggest post office, at Via Pietrapiana 53–55 (Mon–Fri 8.15am–7pm, Sat 8.15am–12.30pm). If all you want are stamps (*francobolli*), then it's easier to buy them at one of the city's innumerable tabacchi, which are marked by a sign outside with a white "T" on a blue background.

Telephones Nearly all of Florence's public call-boxes accept coins, but you get more time for your euros if you use a phone card, which can be bought from any tabacchi and any shop displaying the Telecom Italia sticker. You're never far from a pay phone – every sizeable piazza has at least one.

Train information Ⓣ89.20.21 (within Italy), Ⓦwww.trenitalia.it.

Festivals

The Florentine calendar is punctuated by several long-established festive events and by the Maggio Musicale, Italy's oldest and most prestigious music festival. The major celebrations are listed below, in chronological order.

Scoppio del Carro

For **Easter Sunday's Scoppio del Carro** (Explosion of the Cart) a cartload of fireworks is hauled by six white oxen from the Porta a Prato to the Duomo; there, during the midday Mass, the whole lot is set off by a "dove" that whizzes down a wire from the high altar. The origins of this incendiary descent of the Holy Spirit lie with one Pazzino de' Pazzi, leader of the Florentine contingent on the First Crusade. On getting back to Florence he was entrusted with the care of the flame of Holy Saturday, an honorary office which he turned into something more festive by rigging up a ceremonial wagon to transport the flame round the city. His descendants continued to manage the festival until the Pazzi conspiracy of 1478, which of course lost them the office. Since then, the city authorities have taken care of business.

Festa del Grillo

On the **first Sunday after Ascension Day (forty days after Easter), the Festa del Grillo** (Festival of the Cricket) is held in the Cascine park. In amongst the stalls and the picnickers you'll find people selling tiny wooden cages containing crickets, which are then released onto the grass – a ritual that may hark back to the days when farmers had to scour their land for locusts, or to the tradition of men placing a cricket on the door of their lovers to serenade them.

Maggio Musicale Fiorentino

Confusingly, the **Maggio Musicale** isn't restricted to May (*Maggio*), but lasts for a couple of months from late April or early May. The festival has its own orchestra, chorus and ballet company, plus guest appearances from foreign ensembles. Events are staged at the Teatro Comunale (or its Teatro Piccolo), the Teatro della Pergola, the Palazzo dei Congressi, the Teatro Verdi and occasionally in the Bóboli gardens. Information and tickets can be obtained from the Teatro Comunale, Corso Italia 16. ⓦwww.maggiofiorentino.com.

Estate Fiesolana

Slightly less exclusive than the Maggio Musicale, concentrating more on chamber and symphonic music, the **Estate Fiesolana** is held in Fiesole every summer, usually from **June to late August**. Films and theatre are also featured, and most events are held in the open-air Teatro Romano. ⓦwww.estatefiesolana.it.

St John's Day and the Calcio Storico

The saint's day of **John the Baptist**, Florence's patron, is **June 24** – the occasion for a massive fireworks display up on Piazzale Michelangelo, and for the first game of the Calcio Storico. Played in sixteenth-century costume, this uniquely Florentine mayhem is a three-match series played on the 24th and two subsequent dates in late June or early July (they change from year to year), with fixtures nearly always being held in Piazza Santa Croce. Each of the four historic quarters fields a team of 27 players, Santa Croce playing in blue, San Giovanni in green, Santa Maria Novella in red and Santo Spirito in impractical white. The prize for the winning side is a vast quantity of steak, equivalent to the white calf which traditionally was awarded to the victors.

Festa delle Rificolone

The **Festa delle Rificolone** (Festival of the Lanterns) takes place on the Virgin's birthday, **September 7**, with a procession of children to Piazza Santissima Annunziata. Each child carries a coloured paper lantern with a candle inside it – a throwback to the days when people from the surrounding countryside would troop by lantern light into the city for the Feast of the Virgin. The procession is followed by a parade of floats and street parties.

Festa dell'Unità

October's Festa dell'Unità is part of a nationwide celebration run by the Italian Communists. Florence's is the biggest event after Bologna's, with loads of political stalls and restaurant-marquees. The box office will have details of venues, while news about the *Feste* and other political events in Florence can be found in *Anteprima*, a local supplement published with Friday's edition of the Communist daily *L'Unità*.

Chronology

Chronology

Eighth century BC ▸ The Etruscans are settled throughout the area now known as Tuscany, with their principal settlements in Roselle, Vetulonia, Populonia, Volterra, Chiusi, Cortona, Arezzo and – most northerly of all – Fiesole.

59 BC ▸ The Roman colony of Florentia is established by Julius Caesar as a settlement for army veterans. By now the Romans have either subsumed or exterminated most Etruscan towns.

Second and third centuries AD ▸ Rapid expansion of Florentia as a river port.

Fourth century ▸ Christianity is spreading throughout Italy. The church of San Lorenzo and the martyr's shrine at San Miniato are both established in Florentia.

552 ▸ Florence falls to the hordes of the Gothic king Totila. Less than twenty years later the Lombards storm in, subjugating the city to the duchy whose capital was in Pavia.

End of the eighth century ▸ Charlemagne's Franks have taken control of much of Italy, with the administration being overseen by imperial margraves, based in Lucca. These proxy rulers develop into some of the most powerful figures in the Holy Roman Empire and are instrumental in spreading Christianity even further.

978 ▸ Willa, widow of the margrave Uberto, establishes the Badìa in Florence, the first monastic foundation in the centre of the city.

1027 ▸ The position of margrave passes to the Canossa family, who take the title of the Counts of Tuscia, as Tuscany was then called. The most influential figure produced by this dynasty is Matilda, daughter of the first Canossa margrave.

1115 ▸ The year she dies, Matilda grants Florence the status of an independent city. The new commune of Florence is essentially governed by a council of one hundred men, the great majority drawn from the rising merchant class. In 1125 the city's increasing dominance of the region was confirmed when it crushed the rival city of Fiesole. Fifty years later, as the population booms with the rise of the textile industry, new walls are built around what is now one of the largest cities in Europe.

The thirteenth century ▸ Throughout Tuscany, conflict develops between the Ghibelline faction and the Guelphs – the former, broadly speaking, are pro-empire, with the Guelphs defined chiefly by their loyalty to the papacy. When Charles of Anjou conquers Naples in 1266, association with the anti-imperial French becomes another component of Guelphism, and a loose Guelph alliance soon stretches from Paris to Naples, substantially funded by the bankers of Tuscany. Florence and Lucca are generally Guelph strongholds, while Pisa, Arezzo, Prato, Pistoia and Siena tend to side with the empire.

1207 ▸ Florence's governing council is replaced by the *podestà*, an executive official who is traditionally a non-Florentine. Around this time the first *arti* (guilds) are formed to promote the interests of the traders and bankers.

1248 ▸ Florence's Ghibellines enlist the help of Emperor Frederick II to oust the Guelphs, but within two years they have been displaced by the Guelph-backed regime of the Primo Popolo, a quasi-democratic government drawn from the mercantile class.

1280 ▸ Power passes to the Secondo Popolo, a regime run by the Arti Maggiori (Great Guilds). The fulcrum of power in Florence shifts definitively towards its bankers, merchants and manufacturers.

1293 ▸ The Secondo Popolo excludes the nobility from government and invests power in the Signoria, a council drawn from the Arti Maggiori.

1348 ▸ The Black Death destroys as many as half the city's population. However, the plague is equally devastating throughout the region, and does nothing to reverse the economic and political supremacy of the city.

1406 ▸ Florence takes control of Pisa and thus gains a long-coveted seaport. Despite the survival of Sienese independence into the sixteenth century, the history of Tuscany increasingly becomes the history of Florence.

1431–1434 ▸ Cosimo de'Medici is imprisoned by the city authorities, having provoked the big families of the Signoria with his support for the members of the disenfranchised lesser guilds. In 1434, after a session of the Parlamento – a general council called in times of emergency – he is invited to return. Having secured the military support of the Sforza family of Milan, Cosimo (Cosimo il Vecchio) becomes the pre-eminent figure in the city's political life for more than three decades. Florence's reputation as the most innovative cultural centre in Europe is strengthened by his patronage of Donatello, Michelozzo and a host of other artists.

1439 ▸ Council of Florence is convened, to try to reconcile the Catholic and Eastern churches. The consequent influx of Greek scholars adds momentum to the study of classical philosophy and literature.

1478 ▸ The Pazzi family conspire with Pope Sixtus IV to murder Lorenzo il Magnifico (Cosimo's grandson, and the de facto ruler of Florence) and his brother Giuliano; the plot fails, and only increases the esteem in which Lorenzo is held.

1494 ▸ Lorenzo's son Piero is obliged to flee Florence following his surrender to the invading French army of Charles VIII. This invasion is the commencement of a bloody half-century dominated by the so-called Wars of Italy.

1498 ▸ Having in effect ruled the city in the absence of the Medici, the Dominican friar Girolamo Savonarola is executed as a heretic.

1512 ▸ Following Florence's defeat by the Spanish and papal armies, the Medici return, in the person of the vicious Giuliano, Duke of Nemours.

1527 ▸ Holy Roman Emperor Charles V's army pillages Rome. The humiliation of Pope Clement VII (a Medici) spurs the people of Florence to eject his deeply unpopular relatives.

1530 ▸ After a siege by the combined papal and imperial forces, Florence is obliged to receive Alessandro, who was proclaimed Duke of Florence, the first Medici to bear the title of ruler.

1537 ▸ Alessandro is assassinated and power passes to another Cosimo (not a direct heir but rather a descendant of Cosimo il Vecchio's brother), thanks to support from the emperor Charles V, whose daughter was married to Alessandro.

1557 ▸ Cosimo buys the territory of Siena from the Habsburgs, giving Florence control of all of Tuscany with the solitary exception of Lucca. Two years later Florentine hegemony in Tuscany was confirmed in the Treaty of Cateau-Cambrésis, the final act in the Wars of Italy.

1570 ▸ Cosimo takes the title Cosimo I, Grand Duke of Tuscany. In European terms Tuscany is a second-rank power, but it's one of the strongest states in Italy. It is Cosimo who builds the Uffizi, extends and overhauls the Palazzo Vecchio, installs the Medici in the Palazzo Pitti, has the Ponte Santa Trìnita constructed across the Arno and commissions much of the public sculpture around the Piazza della Signoria. His descendants remain in power until 1737.

1630s ▸ The market for Florence's woollen goods collapses, and the city's banks go into a terminal slump.

1737 ▸ Under the terms of a treaty signed by Anna Maria de' Medici (the sister of Gian Gastone de'Medici, the last male Medici) Florence passes to the House of Lorraine, cousins of the Austrian Habsburgs.

1799 ▸ Napoleon dislodges the Austrians from Italy, but after his fall from power the Lorraine dynasty is brought back, remaining in residence until the last of the line, Leopold II, consents to his own deposition in 1859.

1865 ▸ Florence becomes the capital of the new Kingdom of Italy, a position it holds until 1870, when Rome takes over. The city's subsequent decline is accelerated by the economic disruption that follows World War I.

1943 ▸ After the Allied landing at Monte Cassino, Tuscany is a battlefield between the Nazis and the partisans. Substantial parts of Florence are wrecked by the retreating German army, who bomb all the bridges except the Ponte Vecchio and blow up much of the medieval city near the banks of the Arno.

To the present ▸ After World War II the province of Florence establishes itself as the third largest industrial centre in Italy. Textiles, metalwork, glass, ceramics, pharmaceuticals and chemical production remain major industries in the province, while in Florence itself many long-established crafts continue to thrive, notably jewellery and gold-working, the manufacture of handmade paper, perfumery, and leatherwork. But tourism is the mainstay of the Florentine economy, with the city attracting upwards of eight million tourists a year.

Language

Basics

What follows is a run-down of essential words and phrases. For more detail, get *Italian: Rough Guide Dictionary Phrasebook*, which has a huge but accessible vocabulary in dictionary format, a grammar section, a detailed menu reader and useful scenarios. These scenarios can also be downloaded free as audio files from ®www.roughguides.com. Before going to Florence, you'd do well to master at least a little Italian, a task made more enjoyable by the fact that your halting efforts will often be rewarded by smiles and genuine surprise that an English-speaker should make an attempt to learn Italian.

Pronunciation

Italian **pronunciation** is simple to grasp, since every word is spoken exactly as it's written, and usually enunciated with exaggerated, open-mouthed clarity. The only difficulties you're likely to encounter are the few **consonants** that are different from English:

c before e or i is pronounced as in **ch**urch, while ch before the same vowels is hard, as in cat.
sci or sce are pronounced as in **sh**eet and **sh**elter respectively.
g is soft before **e** and **i**, as in **g**eranium; hard when followed by **h**, as in **g**arlic.
gn has the "ni" sound of our "o**ni**on".
gl in Italian is softened to something like "li" in English, as in stal**li**on.
h is not aspirated, as in **h**onour.

When **speaking** to strangers, the third person is the polite form (ie Lei instead of Tu for "you"); using the second person is a mark of disrespect or stupidity. Also remember that Italians don't use "please" and "thank you" half as much as we do: it's all implied in the tone, though if you're in any doubt, err on the polite side.

The great majority of Italian words are **stressed** on the penultimate syllable; an **accent** (´ or `) usually denotes the exceptions (as in *città* or *caffè*), although these accents are sometimes omitted, especially when it comes to proper names (eg St Jerome in Italian is Girolamo, pronounced Giròlamo but always spelt without the stress accent). Note that the ending **-ia** or **-ie** counts as two syllables, hence *trattoria* is stressed on the **i**. Thanks largely to Dante, Florence's dialect became the basis for modern Italian, so the only local linguistic problems you'll come across relate to pronunciation. Most obviously, Florentines tend to use a throaty "h" sound where standard Italian has a hard "c", so, *una cosa* (a thing) becomes "una hosa".

Words and phrases

Basic words and phrases

Buongiorno	Good morning
Buonasera	Good afternoon/ evening
Buonanotte	Good night
Arrivederci	Goodbye
Si	Yes
No	No
Per favore	Please
Grázie (molte/ mille grazie)	Thank you (very much)
Prego	You're welcome
Va bene	Alright/that's OK
Come stai/sta?	How are you? (informal/formal)
Bene	I'm fine
Parla inglese?	Do you speak English?
Non ho capito	I don't understand
Non lo so	I don't know
Mi scusi	Excuse me
Permesso	Excuse me (in a crowd)
Mi dispiace	I'm sorry
Sono inglese	I'm English
scozzese	Scottish
americano	American
irlandese	Irish
gallese	Welsh
Oggi	Today
Domani	Tomorrow
Dopodomani tomorrow	Day after
Ieri	Yesterday
Adesso	Now
Più tardi	Later
Aspetta!	Wait a minute!
Di mattina	In the morning
Nel pomeriggio	In the afternoon
Di sera	In the evening
Qui/Là	Here/there
Buono/Cattivo	Good/bad
Grande/Piccolo	Big/small
Economico/Caro	Cheap/expensive
Ingresso libero	Free entrance
Caldo/Freddo	Hot/cold
Vicino/Lontano	Near/far
Libero/Occupato	Vacant/occupied
Gabinetto/Bagno	WC/Bathroom
Con/Senza	With/without
Più/Meno	More/less
Basta	Enough, no more
Signor ...	Mr ...
Signora ...	Mrs ...
Signorina ...	Miss ... (il Signor, la Signora, la Signorina when speaking about someone else)

Numbers

uno	1
due	2
tre	3
quattro	4
cinque	5
sei	6
sette	7
otto	8
nove	9
dieci	10
undici	11
dodici	12
tredici	13
quattordici	14
quindici	15
sedici	16
diciassette	17
diciotto	18
diciannove	19
venti	20
ventuno	21
ventidue	22
trenta	30
quaranta	40
cinquanta	50
sessanta	60
settanta	70
ottanta	80
novanta	90
cento	100
centuno	101
centodieci	110
duecento	200
cinquecento	500
mille	1000
cinquemila	5000
diecimila	10,000
cinquantamila	50,000

Some signs

Entrata/Uscita	Entrance/exit
Aperto/Chiuso	Open/closed
Arrivi/Partenze	Arrivals/departures

Chiuso per restauro	Closed for restoration
Chiuso per ferie	Closed for holidays
Tirare/Spingere	Pull/push
Non toccare	Do not touch
Pericolo	Danger
Attenzione	Beware
Pronto soccorso	First aid
Suonare il campanello	Ring the bell
Vietato fumare	No smoking

Transport

Autostazione	Bus station
Stazione ferroviaria	Train station
Un biglietto a ...	A ticket to ...
Solo andata/ andata e ritorno	One-way/return
A che ora parte?	What time does it leave?
Da dove parte?	Where does it leave from?

Accommodation

Albergo	Hotel
Ha una cámera	Do you have a room ...
per una/due/ tre person(a/e)	for one/two/ three people
per una/due /tre notte/i	for one/two/ three nights
per una/due settiman(a/e)	for one/two weeks
con un letto matrimoniale	with a double bed
con una doccia/ un bagno	with a shower/bath
Quanto costa?	How much is it?
È compresa la prima colazione?	Is breakfast included?
Ha qualcosa che costa di meno?	Do you have anything cheaper?
Posso vedere la camera?	Can I see the room?
La prendo	I'll take it
Vorrei prenotare una camera	I'd like to book a room
Ho una prenotazione	I have a booking
Ostello per la gioventù	Youth hostel

Questions and directions

Dove? (Dov'è/Dove sono)	Where? (where is/are ...?)
Quando?	When?
Cosa? (Cos'è?)	What? (what is it?)
Quanto/Quanti?	How much/many?
Perché?	Why?
È/C'è (È/C'è ... ?)	It is/there is (is it/is there ... ?)
Che ore sono?	What time is it?
Per arrivare a . . ?	How do I get to ... ?
A che ora apre?	What time does it open?
A che ora chiude?	What time does it close?
Quanto costa? (Quanto costano?)	How much does it cost ? (...do they cost?)
Come si chiama in italiano?	What's it called in Italian?

In the restaurant

Una tavola	A table
Vorrei prenotare una tavola per due alle quattro	I'd like to book a table for two people at eight o'clock
Abbiamo bisogno di un coltello	We need a knife
una forchetta	a fork
un cucchiaio	a spoon
un bicchiere	a glass
Che cosa mi consiglia lei?	What do you recommend?
Cameriere/a!	Waiter/waitress!
il conto	Bill/check
È incluso il servizio?	Is service included
Sono vegetariano/a	I'm a vegetarian

Menu reader

Basics and snacks

Aceto	Vinegar
Aglio	Garlic
Biscotti	Biscuits
Burro	Butter
Caramelle	Sweets
Cioccolato	Chocolate
Focaccia	Oven-baked bread-based snack
Formaggio	Cheese
Frittata	Omelette
Gelato	Ice cream
Grissini	Bread sticks
Marmellata	Jam
Olio	Oil
Olive	Olives
Pane	Bread
Pane integrale	Wholemeal bread
Panino	Bread roll
Patatine	Crisps
Patatine fritte	Chips
Pepe	Pepper
Pizzetta	Small cheese-and-tomato pizza
Riso	Rice
Sale	Salt
Tramezzini	Sandwich
Uova	Eggs
Yogurt	Yoghurt
Zucchero	Sugar
Zuppa	Soup

Starters (Antipasti)

Antipasto misto	Mixed cold meats and cheese (and a selection of other things in this list)
Caponata	Mixed aubergine, olives, tomatoes and celery
Caprese	Tomato and mozzarella salad
Crostini di milza	Minced spleen on pieces of toast
Donzele/donzelline	Fried dough balls
Fettuna/bruschetta	Garlic toast with olive oil
Finocchiona	Pork sausage flavoured with fennel
Insalata di mare	Seafood salad
Insalata di riso	Rice salad
Melanzane in parmigiana	Fried aubergine in tomato and parmesan cheese
Mortadella	Salami-type cured meat
Pancetta	Bacon
Peperonata	Grilled green, red or yellow peppers stewed in olive oil
Pinzimonio	Raw seasonal vegetable in olive oil, with salt and pepper
Pomodori ripieni	Stuffed tomatoes
Prosciutto	Ham
Prosciutto di cinghiale	Cured wild boar ham
Salame	Salami
Salame toscano	Pork sausage with pepper and cubes of fat
Salsicce	Pork or wild boar sausage

The first course (Il primo)

Soups

Acquacotta	Onion soup served with toast and poached egg
Brodo	Clear broth
Cacciucco	Fish stew with tomatoes, bread and red wine
Carabaccia	Onion soup
Garmugia	Soup made with fava beans, peas, artichokes, asparagus and bacon
Minestra di farro	Wheat and bean soup

Minestrina	Any light soup
Minestrone	Thick vegetable soup
Minestrone alla fiorentina	Haricot bean soup with red cabbage, tomatoes, onions and herbs
Panzanella	Summer salad of tomatoes, basil, cucumber, onion and bread
Pappa al pomodoro	Tomato soup thickened with bread
Pasta e fagioli	Pasta soup with beans
Pastina in brodo	Pasta pieces in clear broth
Ribollita	Winter vegetable soup, based on beans and thickened with bread
Stracciatella	Broth with egg
Zuppa di fagioli	Bean soup

Pasta and gnocchi

Cannelloni	Large tubes of pasta, stuffed
Farfalle	Literally "bow"-shaped pasta; the word also means "butterflies"
Fettuccine	Narrow pasta ribbons
Gnocchi	Small potato and dough dumplings
Gnocchi di ricotta	Dumplings filled with ricotta and spinach
Lasagne	Lasagne
Maccheroni	Tubular spaghetti
Pappardelle	Wide, short noodles, often served with hare sauce (con lepre)
Pasta al forno	Pasta baked with minced meat, eggs, tomato and cheese
Pasta alla carrettiera	Pasta with tomato, garlic, pepper, parsley and chilli
Penne	Smaller version of rigatoni
Penne strasciate	Quill-shaped pasta in meat sauce
Ravioli	Small packets of stuffed pasta
Rigatoni	Large, grooved tubular pasta
Risotto	Cooked rice dish, with sauce
Spaghetti	Spaghetti
Spaghettini	Thin spaghetti
Tagliatelle	Pasta ribbons; another word for fettucine
Tortellini	Small rings of pasta, stuffed with meat or cheese
Vermicelli	Very thin spaghetti (literally "little worms")

Pasta sauces

Aglio e olio	Tossed in garlic and olive oil
(e peperoncino)	(and hot chillies)
Arrabbiata	Spicy tomato sauce
Bolognese	Meat sauce
Burro e salvia	Butter and sage
Carbonara	Cream, ham and beaten egg
Frutta di mare	Seafood
Funghi	Mushroom
Matriciana	Cubed pork and tomato sauce
Panna	Cream
Parmigiano	Parmesan cheese
Pesto	Ground basil, pine nut, garlic and pecorino sauce
Pomodoro	Tomato sauce
Ragù	Meat sauce
Vongole	Clam and tomato sauce

The second course (Il secondo)

Meat (carne)

Agnello	Lamb
Arista	Roast pork loin with garlic and rosemary
Bistecca	Steak
Bistecca alla fiorentina	Thick grilled T-bone steak
Cibreo	Chicken liver and egg stew
Coniglio	Rabbit
Costolette	Chops
Cotolette	Cutlets
Fegatini	Chicken livers
Fegato	Liver
Involtini	Steak slices, rolled and stuffed
Lingua	Tongue
Lombatina	Veal chop
Maiale	Pork
Manzo	Beef
Ossobuco	Shin of veal
Peposo	Peppered beef stew
Pollo	Chicken
Pollo alla diavola/ al mattone	Chicken flattened with a brick, grilled with herbs
Polpette	Meatballs (or minced balls of anything)
Rognoni	Kidneys
Salsiccia	Sausage
Saltimbocca	Veal with ham
Scottiglia	Stew of veal, game and poultry, cooked with white wine and tomatoes
Spezzatino	Stew
Spiedini di maiale	Skewered spiced cubes of pork loin and liver, with bread and bay leaves
Tacchino	Turkey
Trippa	Tripe
Trippa alla fiorentina	Tripe in tomato sauce, served with parmesan
Vitello	Veal

Fish (pesce) and shellfish (crostacei)

Acciughe	Anchovies
Anguilla	Eel
Aragosta	Lobster
Baccalà alla livornese	Salt cod with garlic, tomatoes and parsley
Bronzino/Branzino	Sea bass
Calamari	Squid
Caparossoli	Shrimps
Cape sante	Scallops
Coda di rospo	Monkfish
Cozze	Mussels
Dentice	Dentex (like sea bass)
Gamberetti	Shrimps
Gamberi	Prawns
Granchio	Crab
Orata	Bream
Ostriche	Oysters
Pescespada	Swordfish
Polpo	Octopus
Rombo	Turbot
San Pietro	John Dory
Sarde	Sardines
Schie	Shrimps
Seppie	Cuttlefish
Sogliola	Sole
Tonno	Tuna
Tonno con fagioli	Tuna with white beans and raw onion
Triglie	Red mullet
Trota	Trout
Vongole	Clams

Vegetables (contorni) and salad (insalata)

Asparagi	Asparagus
Asparagi alla fiorentina	Asparagus with butter, fried egg and cheese
Basílico	Basil
Bróccoli	Broccoli
Cápperi	Capers
Carciofi	Artichokes
Carciofini	Artichoke hearts
Carotte	Carrots
Cavolfiori	Cauliflower

Cavolo	Cabbage
Ceci	Chickpeas
Cetriolo	Cucumber
Cipolla	Onion
Fagioli	Beans
Fagioli all'uccelletto	White beans cooked with tomatoes, garlic and sage
Fagiolini	Green beans
Finocchio	Fennel
Frittata di carciofi	Fried artichoke flan
Funghi	Mushrooms
Insalata verde/ insalata mista	Green salad/ mixed salad
Melanzana	Aubergine/eggplant
Patate	Potatoes
Peperoni	Peppers
Piselli	Peas
Pomodori	Tomatoes
Radicchio	Chicory
Spinaci	Spinach
Zucca	Pumpkin
Zucchini	Courgettes

Desserts (dolci)

Amaretti	Macaroons
Brigidini	Anise wafer biscuits
Buccellato	Anise raisin cake
Cantucci/ cantuccini	Small almond biscuits, served with Vinsanto wine
Cassata	Ice-cream cake with candied fruit
Castagnaccio	Unleavened chestnut-flour cake containing raisins, walnuts and rosemary
Cenci	Fried dough dusted with powdered sugar
Frittelle di riso	Rice fritters
Gelato	Ice cream
Macedonia	Fruit salad
Meringa	Frozen meringue with whipped cream and chocolate
Necci	Chestnut-flour crêpes
Panforte	Hard fruit, nut and spice cake
Ricciarelli	Marzipan almond biscuits
Schiacciata alla fiorentina	Orange-flavoured cake covered with powdered sugar, eaten at carnival time
Schiacciata con l'uva	Grape- and sugar-covered bread dessert
Torta	Cake, tart
Zabaglione	Dessert made with eggs, sugar and Marsala wine
Zuccotto	Sponge cake filled with chocolate and whipped cream
Zuppa Inglese	Trifle

Cheese (formaggi)

Caciocavallo	A type of dried, mature mozzarella cheese
Fontina	Northern Italian cheese used in cooking
Gorgonzola	Soft blue-veined cheese
Mozzarella	Bland soft white cheese used on pizzas
Parmigiano	Parmesan
Pecorino	Strong-tasting hard sheep's cheese
Provolone	Hard strong cheese
Ricotta	Soft white cheese made from ewe's milk, used in sweet or savoury dishes

Fruit and nuts (frutta and noce)

Ananas	Pineapple	Mele	Apples
Arance	Oranges	Melone	Melon
Banane	Bananas	Pere	Pears
Ciliegie	Cherries	Pesche	Peaches
Fichi	Figs	Pignoli	Pine nuts
Frágole	Strawberries	Pistacchio	Pistachio nut
Limone	Lemon	Uve	Grapes
Mándorle	Almonds		

Cooking terms

Affumicato	Smoked	Brasato	Cooked in wine
Al dente	Firm, not overcooked	Cotto	Cooked (not raw)
Al ferro	Grilled without oil	Crudo	Raw
Al forno	Baked	Fritto	Fried
Al Marsala	Cooked with Marsala wine	In úmido	Stewed
Al vapore	Steamed	Lesso	Boiled
Alla brace	Barbecued	Milanese	Fried in egg and breadcrumbs
Alla griglia	Grilled	Pizzaiola	Cooked with tomato sauce
Allo spiedo	On the spit	Ripieno	Stuffed
Arrosto	Roasted	Sangue	Rare
Ben cotto	Well done	Surgelato	Frozen
Bollito	Boiled		

Drinks

Acqua minerale	Mineral water	Spumante	Sparkling wine
Alla spina	Draught (beer)	Succo	Concentrated fruit juice with sugar
Aranciata	Orangeade	Tè	Tea
Bicchiere	Glass	Tonico	Tonic water
Birra	Beer	Vino	Wine
Bottiglia	Bottle	Rosso	Red
Caffè	Coffee	Bianco	White
Cioccolata calda	Hot chocolate	Rosato	Rosé
Ghiaccio	Ice	Secco	Dry
Granita	Iced coffee or fruit drink	Dolce	Sweet
Latte	Milk	Litro	Litre
Limonata	Lemonade	Mezzo	Half
Selz	Soda water	Quarto	Quarter
Spremuta	Fresh fruit juice	Salute!	Cheers!

small print & Index

A Rough Guide to Rough Guides

In 1981, Mark Ellingham, a recent graduate in English from Bristol University, was travelling in Greece on a tiny budget and couldn't find the right guidebook. With a group of friends he wrote his own guide, combining a contemporary, journalistic style with a practical approach to travellers' needs. That first Rough Guide was a student scheme that became a publishing phenomenon. Today, Rough Guides include recommendations from shoestring to luxury and cover hundreds of destinations around the globe, including almost every country in the Americas and Europe, more than half of Africa and most of Asia and Australasia. Millions of readers relish Rough Guides' wit and inquisitiveness as much as their enthusiastic, critical approach and value-for-money ethos. The guides' ever-growing team of authors and photographers is spread all over the world.

In the early 1990s, Rough Guides branched out of travel, with the publication of Rough Guides to World Music, Classical Music and the Internet. All three have become benchmark titles in their fields, spearheading the publication of a range of more than 350 titles under the Rough Guide name, including phrasebooks, waterproof maps, music guides from Opera to Heavy Metal, reference works as diverse as Conspiracy Theories and Shakespeare, and popular culture books from iPods to Poker. Rough Guides also produce a series of more than 120 World Music CDs in partnership with World Music Network.

Visit www.roughguides.com to see our latest publications.

Rough Guide travel images are available for commercial licensing at www.roughguidespictures.com

Publishing information

This second edition published March 2008 by Rough Guides Ltd, 80 Strand, London WC2R 0RL.
345 Hudson St, 4th Floor, New York, NY 10014, USA.

Distributed by the Penguin Group
Penguin Books Ltd, 80 Strand, London WC2R 0RL
Penguin Group (USA), 375 Hudson Street, NY 10014, USA
14 Local Shopping Centre, Panchsheel Park, New Delhi 110017, India
Penguin Group (Australia), 250 Camberwell Road, Camberwell, Victoria 3124, Australia
Penguin Group (Canada), 10 Alcorn Avenue, Toronto, ON M4V 1E4, Canada
Penguin Group (NZ), 67 Apollo Drive, Mairangi Bay, Auckland 1310, New Zealand
Typeset in Bembo and Helvetica to an original design by Henry Iles.
Cover concept by Peter Dyer.

Printed and bound in China.

208 includes index

A catalogue record for this book is available from the British Library

ISBN 978-1-85828-925-0

1 3 5 7 9 8 6 4 2

Help us update

We've gone to a lot of effort to ensure that the second edition of Florence DIRECTIONS is accurate and up-to-date. However, things change – places get "discovered", opening hours are notoriously fickle, restaurants and rooms raise prices or lower standards. If you feel we've got it wrong or left something out, we'd like to know, and if you can remember the address, the price, the phone number, so much the better.

Please send your comments with the subject line "Florence DIRECTIONS Update" to Ⓔmail@roughguides.com. We'll credit all contributions and send a copy of the next edition (or any other Rough Guide if you prefer) for the very best emails.

Have your questions answered and tell others about your trip at Ⓦcommunity.roughguides.com

Rough Guide credits

Text editor: Karoline Densley
Layout: Pradeep Thapliyal
Photography: James McConnachie, Michelle Grant
Cartography: Jaiprakash Mishra
Picture editor: Jj Luck
Proofreader: Anna Leggett
Production: Rebecca Short
Cover design: Chloë Roberts

The author

Jonathan Buckley writes the *Rough Guide to Venice and the Veneto, Directions: Venice* and is the co-author of the Rough Guides to Tuscany & Umbria and Florence & Siena, and he has published five novels: *The Biography of Thomas Lang, Xerxes, Ghost MacIndoe, Invisible* and *So He Takes the Dog.*

Photo credits

All images © Rough Guides except the following:

Front cover picture: The Duomo © 4cornersimages
Back cover picture: Ponte Vecchio
© Mark Thomas/Axiom

p.10 Birth of Venus by Sandro Botticelli
© Summerfield Press/Corbis
p.14 Crucifixion (Christ on the Cross and the Virgin), Perugino © Photo Scala, Florence
p.15 Funeral of Saint Francis, Domenico Ghirlandaio © Photo Scala, Florence – courtesy of the Ministero Beni s Att. Culturali.
p.15 Birth of the Virgin, Andrea del Sarto
© Photo Scala, Florence
p.15 Expulsion from Paradise, Masaccio
© Photo Scala, Florence/Fondo Edifici di Culto – Min. dell'Interno
p.15 The Last Supper, Andrea del Castagno
© Photo Scala, Florence.
p.22 Cappella del Cardinale del Portogallo
© Serge Domingie/Alinari
p.24 Three reading desks with manuscripts, Biblioteca Laurenziana (Laurentian Library) © Photo Scala, Florence – courtesy of the Ministero Beni s Att. Culturali.
p.25 Tomb of Giuliano, Duke of Nemours (Night, front view), Michelangelo, Medici Chapels, Florence © Photo Scala, Florence – courtesy of the Ministero Beni e Att. Culturali
p.25 Prisoner known as Atlas, Michelangelo, Accademia © Photo Scala, Florence – courtesy of the Ministero Beni e Att. Culturali
p.42 Portrait of Lorenzo the Magnificent, Agnolo Bronzino, Galleria degli Uffizi © Photo Scala, Florence – courtesy of the Ministero Beni e Att. Culturali.
p.43 Portrait of Alessandro de' Medici, Giorgio Vasari, Galleria degli Uffizi © Photo Scala, Florence – courtesy of the Ministero Beni e Att. Culturali.
p.68 Primavera (tempera on panel), Sandro Botticelli © Galleria degli Uffizi, Florence, Italy/The Bridgeman Art Library
p.69 The Battle of San Romano in 1432 (tempera on panel), Paolo Uccello © Galleria degli Uffizi, Florence, Italy/Alinari/The Bridgeman Art Library
p.72 Madonna with the Long Neck, Parmigianino (Francesco Mazzola), Galleria degli Uffizi
© Bridgeman Art Library
p.105 View of the stairs from the right hand corner, Michelangelo and Bartolomeo Ammannati, Biblioteca Laurenziana (Laurentian Library) © Photo Scala, Florence – courtesy of the Ministero Beni Att. Culturali
p.107 Procession of the Magi, Benozzo Gozzoli, Palazzo Medici-Riccardi © Photo Scala, Florence – courtesy of the Ministero Beni Att. Culturali.
p.116 Annunciation, Fra Angelico, Museo di San Marco © Photo Scala – courtesy of the Ministero Beni s Att. Culturali.
p.156 14th and 15th century Armour at Stibbert Museum © Massimo Listri/Corbis

Index

Maps are marked in colour

INDEX